M000288912

In Memoriam

Jules and Thérèse André

A YEAR AT THE EDGE
OF THE JUNGLE

A Year at the Edge of the Jungle

A Congo Memoir: 1963-1964

by
Frederic Hunter

Cune

A Year at the Edge of the Jungle:
A Congo Memoir: 1963—1964
© 2016 Frederic Hunter
Cune Press, Seattle, 2016
First Edition
2 4 6 8 9 7 5 3

Hardback   ISBN 9781614571254 $34.95
Paperback ISBN 9781614571308 $19.95
eBook   ISBN 9782624571315 $ 9.99
Kindle   ISBN 9781614571322 $ 9.99

Library of Congress Cataloging-in-Publication Data

Hunter, Frederic.
A year at the edge of the jungle : a Congo memoir : 1963-1964 / by Frederic Hunter.
    pages cm
Includes bibliographical references and index.
ISBN 978-1-61457-125-4 (hardback : alk. paper) -- ISBN 978-1-61457-130-8 (pbk. : alk.
paper) -- ISBN 978-1-61457-131-5 (ebook)
1. Hunter, Frederic--Travel--Congo (Democratic Republic) 2. United States Information
Service. 3. Congo (Democratic Republic)--Description and travel. 4. Congo (Democratic
Republic)--History--Civil War, 1960-1965. I. Title.

DT647H86 2015
916.7510431--dc23

2015012813

Cune   www.cunepress.com
               www.cunepress.info

TABLE OF CONTENTS

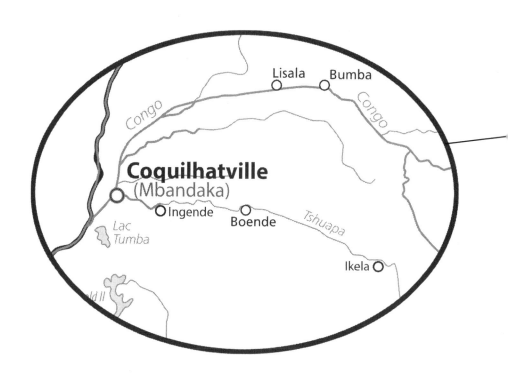

Republic of the Congo, 1963-1964

ONE

THE FIRST LETTER BEGINS:

Léopoldville, 1 August 1963

Hi,

As you see, I've arrived in Léo. Spent last night in the small hotel room of a young Foreign Service Officer headed for Stanleyville and should have a room of my own in a day or two.

Léopoldville proved to be two cities. The first was a small well-maintained European one sited on Stanley Pool, a lake in the middle of the mighty Congo River. It had outlying European suburbs of well-appointed homes. The second city was African: large and full of jumble and noise. At the huge African market within easy walking distance of the city center the scents and the color, the yakking and the palavering of African commerce reverberated in the warm equatorial air.

Needless to say, US Embassy people, of whom I was briefly one, worked in the European city and lived in suburban homes of a size they had rarely previously known, attended by servants. They were constantly adjusting to the realities of Africa and to the political turbulence of the capital city of a country that had acceded to independence three years earlier without any real preparation for it.

Plenty of adjustments lay ahead for me for I had just been transferred from Brussels, Belgium, Old Europe. There I'd completed a splendid ten-month break-in tour—I had also managed to fall in love —as a United States Information Service Officer of the USIS Foreign Service. The posting ahead of me did not sound all that different from what I had been doing in Belgium. There would, however, be no falling in love.

I had arrived in Léo in the southwestern Congo expecting to fly almost immediately to take up a post in Elisabethville, the country's second largest city. It lay far away in the southeast. It was capital of the wealthy and highly industrialized Katanga copper-mining region rife with hopes of seceding from that part of the country that seemed unable to govern itself.

My first letter continues:

My assignment has been changed. I am not going to Elisabethville. I am to go instead, in a month or two, to Coquilhatville at the confluence of the Congo and the Equator. I'm to open an American Cultural Center. I'll be the "American presence," the only American there—at least the only official American. I imagine the loneliness will be well nigh overwhelming; it may nearly drive me crazy.

Frank members of the staff whisper that Coq is a hellhole. To be the American presence in hell is apparently a terrific opportunity. People keep telling me that it will look swell on my record, as if a record were a life.

PAO Steve Baldanza, the USIS mission chief in the Congo, maybe fifty, took me to the ambassador's staff meeting this morning. He has served in tough posts (Ethiopia, Afghanistan, now Léo) and feels little sympathy for officers reluctant to tackle difficult assignments. We had coffee together at a sidewalk café on the way back to the office. He admired a Congolese woman, very shapely, who passed on the street, and said, "They get better looking every day." Perhaps to suggest that the bush will have its compensations. He also warned me to do nothing, nothing!, for CIA. I'm only to do USIS work in Coquilhatville.

Baldanza feels that USIS has little role to play in Europe, thus the resultant lack of drive and high morale there. It does have a role to play here, I suppose. Congolese clearly need information about the world. By now I've seen enough to suspect that opening a cultural center might really attract one to Africa, despite the rigors. As Robt E Lee said: "If war weren't so terrible, we would all love it too much." That may prove true here.

My first visit to Coquilhatville occurred about two weeks later. I went there with a man I'll call Hank Clifford, the USIS Branch Post Coordinator in the Congo.

Léopoldville, 15 August 1963

Hi,

When we flew in to Coquilhatville, I had a feeling of recognition. The vegetation looked African: lush, dense, richly green.

In the center of Coq nobody seems in much of a hurry. There are a lot of Africans sitting around on the porches of the post office and the two general stores. Much of the town is run-down. Everything needs a coat of paint. The paved streets are dotted with potholes, filled with orange mud after rain. (Paving ends just beyond our center.) There is one gas station, one restaurant, one hotel, one butcher shop, a museum (Institut Culturel Mongo*), a boat dock. And a* Centre Culturel Américain.

Out beyond the center are the cités indigènes *as the* ex-colons *call them. The natives live there in places effectively cut off from the town itself.*

Coq has lost much of its European population; it's down to "une cinquantaine de ménages" *(fifty households) said Mme André, the wife of the electrician. Those who remain may love the country (as she professed to do), but many of them are also stuck. They have large investments that they cannot face leaving behind. If they do, years of work will go for naught.*

Hank Clifford introduced me to Monsieur and Madame André not because they were the most influential people in town. (I never did figure out who among the *ex-colons* might truly be called influential.) But because they were the couple in Coq most willing to work with American officials whose business in the town provoked a great deal of suspicion among what was left of the once sizable Belgian community. André was perhaps thirty-five; Madame a year or two younger, both slight and of no more than medium height. He had an eagerness to talk. She had dark eyes, often flashing with irony, and a ready smile, an attractive woman in so unlikely a place. Among the *ex-colons*, he was notable for having remained in Coquilhatville during all the upheavals of the immediate post-independence period. Madame and the four children had taken refuge in Namur, their hometown in Belgium. They had returned to their Coquilhatville moorings less than a year before.

The Andrés lived in a two-story house facing the *place*, the town square, in the center of Coq. As the town's electrician—in fact, I suspect, the only electrician in the entire Equateur—André kept Coq's electricity and water running. At a time when the society was disintegrating, being a competent electrician gave a man an important role in the community. Adjacent to the house stood his office and a salesroom; behind them lay a work yard where African assistants repaired air-conditioners and electrical appliances.

Some weeks earlier when Clifford visited Coq to find a building that would serve as the *Centre Culturel Américain*, he discussed with the Andrés the possibility of using their home/office as the center building. But he had leased instead an empty house, much in need of upgrading.

The Andrés would prove crucial to my survival in Coquilhatville. The letter reporting on that first visit continues:

The distribution system throughout the Congo has fallen apart. One passes almost empty stores; some have lovely displays in the windows but nothing to sell. The butcher shop was empty the three days we were there. Yesterday morning huge crowds were pushing around the entrance of a store. Hank asked what the commotion was about. "They have merchandise," we were told. When we passed the store several hours later, only a few people sat on the steps watching the world. "They had *merchandise," Hank and I said to each other.*

It's a staggering job to halt the momentum of disintegration and reverse it.

The Congo doesn't possess the trained manpower to handle technical jobs. Yesterday as I walked around, a Congolese on a bicycle asked me when I had arrived, where I had come from. He turned out to be the chef de sûreté *and wanted to see my passport. He looked at it as if he had seen few passports, carefully examined the visa allowing me into Burundi, then he returned it. Hearing my accent, he asked if I were English, then was I Protestant. When I said I was, he smiled broadly and said, "Moi aussi."*

Coq lacks community spirit; even the Europeans seem not to mix much among themselves. The woman in the restaurant did not know the woman who ran the hotel; her home was only one hundred yards from the restaurant. Maître Herman, the lawyer from whom Hank rented the small house that is to serve as the center, described Coq as très sympathique. *But before independence it was considered* enfer *(hell); washed-up civil servants were sent there. Maybe the backwash of humanity just enjoys itself.*

About these letters. Perhaps I should explain that I grew up at a time when people telephoned long distance only in times of emergency. People who just wanted to keep in touch wrote letters. I started to write regular letters at boarding school in St. Louis, Missouri. As I remember it, stamped and sealed envelopes, presumably containing letters, had to be submitted for mailing by the Home Department before we could have Sunday lunch.

So in high school I wrote letters to my family in Los Angeles. I wrote more of them, but with less regularity, from Principia College in Illinois. More from Alaska where I did my US Army service. More from New York where my twin brother and I shared an apartment and I worked in the Wall Street area as a public relations writer for Western Electric Co., the manufacturing arm of the then Bell Telephone System.

Only a few from San Francisco where I wrote for the Pacific Telephone Magazine and studied for the Foreign Service exam.

The flow of them picked up again when I was in Washington doing an interminable ten months' training for USIS. And it continued from Brussels, my first Foreign Service post. The letters grew fewer when I was having an active social life, when I could vent, joke and exchange ideas with friends and a girlfriend.

Ever since my army days in Alaska my family had received what we called "carbonated letters." (My brother sent them, too, from Korea where he served.) I would write a letter, keep the original and mail carbon copies to my parents and brother in Los Angeles and my sister with her husband and two small kids in Texas. Often the envelopes also carried separate messages to various family members, especially to my brother.

When I got to the Congo and knew no one, I once more needed an outlet for my thoughts, insights, complaints. Moreover, Africa was so strange in those days, a place so outside the consciousness of most Americans, that I felt I should be disciplined about keeping an up-to-date log of what happened.

Léopoldville, 21 August 1963 Wednesday

Hi,

Tomorrow the diplomatic pouch goes out carrying mail and I want to get a small hello off to you tonight.

I'm getting more of a feel for things, but my awarenesses are developing slowly. After three weeks here, I am just starting to understand the tiniest bit about these people and the way they live. Just as an African has no frame of reference for an appreciation of the subtleties of American living so have I none for those of the Congo.

Yesterday I attended a press conference held by the Vice-Prime Minister, a Mr. Kasongo, a member of the Mouvement National Congolais-Lumumba. *One of the stronger political parties, MNC-L has had no effective leadership since Lumumba's assassination. Prime Minister Adoula put Kasongo, a moderate, in his govt to appease the MNC-L and give its moderate wing some power. But the young people of the MNC-L led by a fellow named Gbenye have tried to throw Kasongo out of the party. All very complicated.*

As soon as Kasongo began to read a prepared statement, a young man stood and shouted, "Non, messieurs, non! Don't listen to him! He doesn't represent the party!" Kasongo kept reading. Then more people started jeering him. Soon about half the meeting got up and ambled militantly out— if one can do that. Kasongo seemed inured to the whole procedure and kept on reading.

After a while the demonstrators returned to hand out leaflets and hurl more abuse at the speaker. While Kasongo kept reading, a woman came forward. She turned toward the assembled people and with her back toward Kasongo bent from the waist forward and raised the backs of her skirts, baring her big, black behind. Two more women came forward and did the same thing.

Then the first one, now about halfway back in the crowd, lifted first her back skirts, then pulled up her front ones. Kasongo looked bored. Many of the newsmen were giggling, mostly Africans. Great fun. I picked out a window I was going to jump through if things got violent.

I went to this press conference with Al Ball, newly arrived to begin the Junior Officer Training I received in Brussels. He suggested that we walk to work in convoy. Soon after their arrival a couple of thieves gained access to his apartment and surprised Al and wife Grace naked in bed. They wanted Al's clothing.

People have been expecting some sort of eruption here, by the way. The Youlou government across the river in Brazzaville has fallen. Shots were reportedly heard in Léo, but I know no one who heard them. Ferry service has been erratic. An embassy wife who foolishly crossed yesterday (without passport or ID) is now being held over there. (How to jeopardize your husband's career!) Anyway people expect that sparks blown across the river will set off some fire here.

More soon.

These letters spent long years in filing cabinets, both the originals I brought back from the Congo and the carbons I sent my parents. Very occasionally I would glance at them, usually with chagrin at the person I was as a young man, pouring the tender thoughts of my young heart onto literally reams of paper.

Then my mother, in her nineties, sent me family memorabilia. Among the material was a three-ring binder. It was labelled "F's Letters 1963-1965." Looking through that binder I discovered a collection of materials that I did not have among my own letters. They were a couple of dozen legal-size sheets of decades-old copying paper, the color of *cafe-au-lait* with bluish printing on them. They were an account I had written very hastily of the most dangerous events I experienced in the Congo.

Among them was the text of a telex message I had sent during a pelting rainstorm from the post office in Coquilhatville. It read:

FOR 250 LÉOPOLDVILLE AMERICAN EMBASSY
URGENT URGENT URGENT
EUROPEAN POPULATION READY TO EVACUATE TOWN NOW
MORALE OF MILITARY LOW WRANGLING AMONG OFFICERS
APPARENTLY NO DEFENSE CAPABILITY
CAN YOU SEND C-130 AIRCRAFT TO EVACUATE 300 PERSONS
TODAY
RESPOND VIA UN RADIO
HUNTER

Somehow in all the moving around that accompanied that dangerous time my own copies of the materials, the originals, got lost.

Reading the copies, I was struck by the fact that some of the bluish printing had faded. Small portions of it were all but illegible. It seemed probable that the fading would continue, that exposing the ancient copying paper to light might speed that process. So I copied the notes into a computer. At some points I had to use a magnifying glass to read the print. In one or two cases I could not make it out. But I succeeded in rescuing most of it.

As I transcribed the materials, several aspects of them struck me. One was the conscientiousness the young man who I was decades earlier had committed to the project of keeping a record of events. I was amused now and then to bump into an instruction in mid-page that read: "Try it this way:" Such an instruction would be followed by a second (sometimes even a third or fourth) rendering of the previous paragraph. Here a USIS Foreign Service Officer writing as fast as he could was combined with something rather like a conscious literary artist insisting that it be done better.

I was also jolted by the immediacy of what I read.

That immediacy made me mull a notion I'd had off and on for years: that portions of the letters and notes should be put into publishable form. They recorded one man's eyewitness glimpse of history on the move.

And they told several stories. One dealt with a young man's quest for identity while facing unusual challenges. Another told of an older man's fear in confronting danger and of a decision that tainted his reputation. A third story watched a brave young couple face the prospect of losing all they'd tried to build in a once peaceful part of the world. Taken together the stories showed people caught up in historical processes they could not control.

But the notion of working on the project provoked a host of questions: Why another Africa project? Hadn't I gotten it out of my system yet? I recognized by now that I had come of age in Africa. My Congo experiences of isolation and challenge, loneliness and danger gave me a chance to grow up in a way I might never have had if my life had taken a more traditional course.

In the years since leaving the Congo and resigning from USIS, I had played with Africa projects. I had completed a degree in African Studies at UCLA. I had lived in Nairobi for four years while serving as *The Christian Science Monitor*'s Africa correspondent. During twenty-plus years of working as a screenwriter I had produced pitches, treatments and screenplays about the continent. Wasn't that enough?

If I had "come of age" in Africa—that melodramatic phrase!—I realized I felt a kind of mission about it, even decades later. For many Americans Africa was a "dark continent," full of dark things: disease and danger; genocide in Rwanda; greed and venality in Congo/Zaire; apartheid in South Africa; starvation in Somalia; civil wars, AIDS and ebola epidemics in more places than one wanted to name.

As for Africa itself, I felt I had something to say about it. To me it was a continent of splendor and beauty that filled the soul, of dancing and laughter, color and joyful people, of excitement and fascination. It was a place where one could still get in touch with primal beginnings, with natural landscapes, wild animals and human customs and modes of social organization very different from our own. It was a place where one could still connect with elements and qualities now mostly lost in the busy-ness, comfort, and gadgetry of American life.

And if one wanted to look into history, it was a place that allowed one to confront some dark aspects of Western culture that victimized Africans: the ravages of the slave trade; the racism that facilitated guilt-free plundering of a continent; the greed and exploitation that underlay colonialism; the exploitation and self-interestedness of American policy over the last half of the 20th century.

I felt that embracing Africa was a means of discovering more about who we were and why. Doing a little of that had been part of my coming of age in the Congo, an aspect of the journalism I had done there. The notes and letters would show how I had grappled with some of those questions fifty years earlier, how little I understood, how confused I had been.

One morning at 4:00 AM I found myself pacing in my office in Santa Barbara, goaded by questions about writing a memoir. The letters and notes could show how my maturation had occurred. Somehow that memoir seemed worth doing. What follows is the result. These are not all the letters; there are too many. Those included here have been edited for brevity and clarity; some have been slightly re-written. The account that came to me from my mother as fading blue print on brittle copy paper remains largely as originally written.

Two

WHEN I WAS TRANSFERRED TO THE CONGO in the summer of 1963, it had then been an independent nation only three years. Ill-prepared for nationhood, its birth pangs had proved catastrophic. The Congolese people had been given false promises about what independence would bring. In a matter of days they realized the promises were empty. They also realized that colonial restraints were gone.

Within a week of the Congo's acceding to independence from Belgium inter-tribal fighting occurred in Léopoldville and Luluabourg. Houses were burned, residents killed. In Coquilhatville the higher wages promised did not materialize. As a result, workers struck; Congolese troops killed nine of them. The Congolese army mutinied against its Belgian officers. Chaos ensued. Panic swept the country. Former colonials fled in terror. Belgian troops entered the country to restore order. Secession threatened in Katanga. Congolese President Joseph Kasavubu and Prime Minister Patrice Lumumba requested United Nations assistance. Fearing that the Belgians and their Western allies were trying to reimpose colonialism, Lumumba made overtures to the Communist Bloc for troops. The United States and other Western nations reacted strongly. The Congo threatened to become an East-West battleground. United Nations troops entered the country. UN aid technicians followed.

In the summer of 1963 the aid technicians were still on the ground. The disorders of its early days had passed, but the country was still in a state of semi-collapse. The country's population had little education. It had its own political institutions, but no experience in dealing with institutions inherited from colonial rulers.

One may wonder why the American Embassy should want to establish a cultural center in a place like Coquilhatville. God knows Coq's *ex-colons* did. Named for a Belgian explorer, the town, now called Mbandaka, was a river port, the main town of the Equateur, the Congo's remotest and least developed region.

The Cold War was raging. Perhaps that was reason enough. Moreover, the Congo was rich in natural resources that the West wanted to control. It was also strategically placed at the very heart of Africa. Obsessive policy-makers wanted to prevent the Congo from becoming an arena for East-West rivalry. They considered keeping the country allied to Western interests absolutely essential.

Although the assassinated Patrice Lumumba had been replaced as Prime Minister by the compliant Cyrille Adoula, some Congolese leaders still flirted with the notion of securing aid from the Communist Bloc. For that reason, American policy-makers determined that there should be an American presence in every part of the country. An embassy was operating in the capital Léopoldville (now Kinshasa). Consulates had opened in three ex-colonial province capitals: Elisabethville (now Lubumbashi), Stanleyville (now Kisangani), and Bukavu. In the two remaining ex-provincial capitals USIS cultural centers would be set up. The center in Coquilhatville would be established first. Luluabourg would follow.

Pesthole. Hellhole. Coq had a bad reputation. It was deemed an inhospitable backwater, a sleepy toe-hold of civilization in the midst of a vast jungle. The Equateur saw the worst atrocities committed against Africans by the lieutenants of the rapacious Léopold II, king of the Belgians, who held the Congo as a personal fief until his shocked subjects wrested control from him. Moreover, the first disturbances after independence occurred there. Despite this unappealing history, American policymakers were determined to establish a cultural center there. If it had no other function, it could serve as a listening post.

It was unusual for a very junior officer like me to open a post. That happened because experienced officers refused to serve in the Congo. The officer assigned to open the Coquilhatville center flatly refused to go there; he would not take his wife to that "pisshole." I was unmarried, a junior officer. My superiors could simply instruct me to go do the job.

Before going to Coquilhatville I was sent to direct the work of the American Cultural Center in Bukavu on the country's eastern frontier. The man assigned as its incoming BPAO (Branch Public Affairs Officer) resigned rather than work in the Congo. So I went to serve temporarily in this lovely town overlooking Lake Kivu on the backbone of Africa. After about two months USIA in Washington deemed it a matter of urgency that a body be put into Coq. USIA had reported to Congress that an officer was in place there. It did not want to be caught misleading Congress. So a body must be sent there. My body. To hell with Bukavu.

To fill out my preparation for Coq, I routed my return trip to Léo through Stanleyville. I would visit the Cultural Center there to see yet another in operation.

Stanleyville, 22 October 1963

Hi,

You see from the dateline that I'm in Stan. I arrived yesterday noon. Flew over the escarpment down past the tangle of jungle drained by the Congo, an endless carpet of trees occasionally cut by a brown trail of water.

Stan's cut out of the jungle in much the same way Coq is, but Stan sits on the north side of the river and has spilled a fifth of itself onto the southwest bank. Ferries ply across the river, and in the evenings a mist sits hovering over the opposite bank. It's as flat here as the Kansas prairie, only you see dense green jungle instead of wheat, and the jungle does give a certain irregularity to the line of the horizon. It's been overcast for the better part of the time I've been here and the result is a pleasant coolness.

Truth to tell, I'm pleased this stop was possible. It's given me hope about what Coq may be like, and I'm feeling less sense of desolation in the prospect of facing it.

Part of the reason is Stan itself. Whereas the jungle seemed in control in Coq, here civilization has the upper hand. According to Dean Claussen, the BPAO here, with whom I'm staying, this control has been regained only in the last year. But it's evident now. Many of the buildings in the town center sport recent coats of paint. In comparison to the other Congo towns I've been in, Stan seems to sparkle.

The paint is the result of a return of Europeans. But even the local government has undertaken to paint white the tree trunks of the center up to a height of about three feet. This white paint says: "Order." Raw nature is being groomed. So for the moment Stan comes closest to that mental image the movies give of a town in the midst of a steamy jungle, but with everything in order. I suppose that is a colonial order—white socks on trees are certainly not an African idea—but I find it reassuring.

The Claussens gave a small cocktail party last night for Congolese elites. Since I'm staying with them and am de la maison *I helped out a bit. The guests—government ministers, editors—arrived exactly on time. In fact, we saw them standing outside the apartment building waiting for the designated hour. But they did not leave at the designated hour. They stayed on and on, enjoying Uncle Sam's drinks.*

Eventually the Claussens and I hatched a little plan. I circulated among the guests, shaking their hands and saying in farewell that it had been a pleasure to meet them. The idea, of course, was that it was time for them to leave. Then, departing, I went to the room where I'm staying, expecting to be called momentarily after the other guests left. Only they didn't leave. They stayed on. Then suddenly at once they all left. When Dean asked why the sudden exodus, guests pointed out that the nearby cinema was starting. They stayed snacking and drinking till the movie began.

As my departure for Coq drew nearer, I felt some trepidation about the prospect of going there alone, an uneasiness that grew the more I heard about the place. Still at this time of my life my strongest desire was to see the world, to taste it.

Like other young Americans, I was attracted to the idea that America had a destiny in the world. The success of the Marshall Plan in Europe demonstrated that Americans could use their wealth and generosity to help others achieve better standards of living, better lives. I thought it might be possible for us to play a similar role in the emerging world.

I'm sure I had a very imprecise notion of how this could happen. Obviously it was one kind of undertaking to help Europeans achieve better standards of living for everyone understood that these standards were Western ones. But we were in Africa. The people here needed to achieve better African lives. What did that mean?

What did it mean in our own country? I wanted racial integration to succeed. But did this mean I wanted African-Americans merely to become black-skinned white people? I'm sure I wanted what was best for them. But how could I know what that involved? I had known almost no black Americans.

In the Army in Alaska I'd had a friend who was black. We hung around the same offices. He was a motor pool driver while I was a headquarters clerk. I realize now that he must have been gay. I had no awareness of that then. He'd been in the fashion business and, unusual at twenty-two, he talked of dressing nude models for runway appearances without any reference to their bodies. He was one of the few men I could talk easily with about things like art, culture, the business of fashion.

A member of my USIS Junior Officer Training course was also black. When I went to Yvonne's home one afternoon, I realized she belonged to the most affluent African-American community in Washington, DC. A bunch of us "sat in" with her one noon at a coffee shop near where we trained. The proprietor refused to serve us, but made no objection to our staying. That brief moment of homage to young people in Nashville braver than we were made me aware of how little I knew about people in my own society, how little connected I was to them.

And now I wanted to help Africans.

In the summer of 1963 most Americans had little concrete idea of what this meant. With more naiveté than arrogance (although there was arrogance aplenty), most Westerners—missionaries and colonialists, capitalists and do-gooders—assumed that helping people in underdeveloped countries involved moving them toward becoming Westerners. The assumption seemed to proclaim: "How happy you will be when you are more like us!" I hope that I did not regard America's role, its destiny, as a matter of transforming others into clones of ourselves. But there must have been some of that. Americans of that era were self-satisfied, well-meaning and very naive. The cynicism that now pervades national life was then hardly a part of it.

I feel certain I went to Africa hoping that I could make some small contribution to helping the rising tide of Third World expectations become reality. The people of the Congo obviously needed help. Of course, I realized that USIS was an arm of American foreign policy. Still. I assumed it would prove possible to serve American interests and African ones at the same time. I expected that the information work I would do for USIS would help Congolese by giving them knowledge of the world beyond what they knew from their own experience.

As for my background. My father was a Los Angeles architect trained at the University of Pennsylvania. He was the youngest of four children born to a prosperous farmer and his wife who left tiny Buffalo, Illinois, outside Springfield, to settle in California. They went first to Redlands (where, according to family lore, the grandfather I never knew owned that community's first automobile), then to Los Angeles and Santa Monica.

My mother oversaw the multitude of errands that kept our lives running smoothly. Liking figures more than cooking or housework, she helped my father with the financial aspects of his architectural practice.

Her father Fred Houston was an entrepreneur who developed vacuum cleaning equipment in Rockford, Illinois, before selling his company to American Standard and moving to Evanston to work for that company in Chicago. My maternal grandmother was a college graduate at a time when relatively few women received college educations. Before marrying she established the Home Economics department at the University of Iowa in Ames. The Houstons married late. Mary was thirty-six, Fred thirty-eight.

Fred Houston retired at age fifty-five, assuming he would enter a new field of business. He and Mary went to California for a visit. They stayed to make their home in Los Angeles. Fred played golf three days a week. My mother who attended a boarding school for girls in western Massachusetts was advised not to go to college there. Because the family had become westerners, she attended Pomona College.

Fred Houston was plagued with annual colds. Mary suggested that he seek healing through Christian Science. The colds were healed and the Houstons became Christian Scientists. My father adopted Christian Science after marrying my mother.

My twin brother, younger sister and I had imparted to us solidly middle-class values. During the Depression before we were born my father worked as an architectural draftsman, first for $12 a week, then for nothing, grateful to be fulfilling the draftsman-years requirement for his architectural license.

In those days there were only crude automatic washers and no dryers, no microwave ovens, dishwashers or frozen foods, and my mother did not work outside the home. In fact, she had help from a farm girl who had fled Kansas. If we were socially conservative and conventionally middle-class, being Christian Scientists meant that we were also a little different, adventurous philosophically.

We were also interested in the world beyond California. My mother had studied for a year in Paris. The demands of my father's architectural practice precluded our taking family vacations. Nonetheless, my mother dreamed of our all going to Europe together and worked for several years on plans for a family trip. She persuaded my Dad to take on a partner to make the trip possible.

And so the crowning event of our family life was three months together in Europe in 1957 after my brother and I got home from our military service. Aspirations toward the Foreign Service probably stemmed from that trip.

Does listing all this make the Hunters sound upper middle class? Were we? I did not think so. My Dad was a professional. We were comfortable, not wealthy. What family resources there were went into education. A Christian Science background involves learning to say no to many things. I had a deep-seated sense that saying no made me different from others, something of an outsider.

Returning to Léo from Stanleyville, I found myself in the midst of intra-embassy bickering. The consul in Bukavu wanted me to remain to run the cultural center there. He thought it inexplicable for USIS to establish a Coquilhatville branch post when it couldn't staff what it had already opened in Bukavu. This interference infuriated Steve Baldanza. He had orders from Washington to get me into Coquilhatville. Steve was certain that I had conspired with the consul to have me stay in the much more attractive and pleasant Bukavu. I hadn't, but I found myself on Steve's bad list, especially after I had the temerity to suggest that a year alone in Coq ought to be sufficient. Steve became irate at that. He was a yeller and he yelled at me. I was unsure how to react. People assured me that he yelled at his wife. Was knowing that supposed to help?

Poor Steve Baldanza. He had a terrible time staffing his posts. Officers resigned rather than serve in the Congo. Middle level officers refused to confront Coq. That meant he had to send a guy just off training to do the job.

Steve was also aware that he was sending me off to Coq virtually naked. I would have no regular communication with Léo. I would not be afforded the protections of a diplomatic post. If I got sick or in some kind of trouble, I was on my own. There had been talk of Hank Clifford's accompanying me to help set up the center. But there was nothing yet to set up. The center's equipment was making its slow way into the embassy and up the Congo River.

"Do you want to take a gun?" I was asked. A gun? Really? Certainly not! A gun was sure to increase my danger.

Probably because of being on the bad list, I regarded the USIS office in Léo as a psychic war zone, a place of much wasted effort and the frustrations of too many people trying to do too much work in too little space. I decided that knowing I would get no moral support, no attaboys, freed me from wanting them (but, of course, I was never free of that). I looked forward to being my own boss in Coq, even if I felt apprehensions about going there.

The day before I left, my "nakedness" became apparent for USIS Léo had to deal with a crisis.

Léopoldville, 5 November 1963

Hi,

Here's the last from Léo for a while. I leave tomorrow morning at 7:30 for Coq. The Embassy's Lebanese "meeter and greeter" will get me at the hotel at 6:15 and take me to the airport.

Things have been hectic here as usual, but I, fortunately, have been merely an observer of the crises. News came over the weekend that Dean Claussen was taken seriously ill in Stanleyville. (Gee, I was only there two weeks ago.) It was said to be pleurisy complicated by pneumonia. Telegrams began arriving IMMEDIATE and have been coming in today FLASH, the highest of the State Dept's categories. Dean has been too ill to move—at least by Congo facilities.

As the situation grew more critical (an exploratory operation threw the diagnosis into question), the embassy's full concentration was focused on the problem. It does give one a sense of confidence to see what can be done once the decision has been made to do it (US Govt can act FAST when it chooses) and to see the philosophy governing such cases.

Ambassador has been spending a great deal of time arranging Dean's evacuation. Wiesbaden (there's a US hospital there) was notified to stand by to receive Dean. FLASH telegrams there and to Wheelus Air Base in Libya (which services our APO, by the way) fixed Dean's medical needs and got things rolling. (Could an operation be performed in Stanleyville? What medicines were needed? Could Stanleyville airport accommodate a US Air Force jet?) The embassy nurse flew up this morning with a doctor from Louvanium University outside Léo. A medical team flew down from Wheelus some time this afternoon with all supplies and has now brought Dean to Léopoldville. They should have landed within the last half hour, in fact. Here Dean can get the emergency medical care he will need (probably an operation) and later he can be evacuated to a US Govt hospital in Germany.

Naturally, this problem has made all others shrink by comparison. I said a short goodbye to Steve Baldanza this afternoon. Dean's illness has served as a sharp reminder of the real isolation we BPAOs live with. Stan is the Congo's third city and has been proved not really equipped to handle this sort of problem, at least not medically. Fortunately, there was a consulate and the full capability of consular communications. By comparison to Stan, Coq has nothing. Steve told me to "get on a plane and come down here" if I felt sick. Steve said he would work on getting the length of tour shortened in some of these posts.

And off I went to Coquilhatville.

THREE

ONE OF THE FIRST LETTERS I wrote from my new home was to Penny, my American friend in Brussels.

Coquilhatville, 15 November 1963

My Dear Penny,

This is the morning of my tenth day in Coq. It's 10:00 AM and I have just returned from a first visit to Coquilhatville's barber. The atmosphere is heavy with equatorial humidity, the air stirs sluggishly, and the sky is covered for as far as one can see with a thick blanket of clouds.

Outside the Sédec store, the Delhaize of the Congo, there is a crowd of about 200 Congolese. They are pressed up to the door, as they have been pressed up to it for the past three mornings. As far as I can tell, the door has never been opened. Whispers tell me that Sédec has sugar; can this really account for these crowds on three consecutive days?

At Coq a river called the Ruki enters the Congo, and the confluence is studded with islands. The river drifts by outside my window, at least one of its channels does, and in the middle of this channel is a follow-the-leader line of water hyacinth clumps. An occasional pirogue passes (a pirogue is a long, hardwood, dugout canoe), being poled along at the river's edge by an African using a paddle that looks like a spear.

Late this afternoon when the sun is setting across the river, these pirogues will lodge themselves against the bank, their tenders will strip, and standing calf-deep in the river, they will take their baths. They will stand facing the road behind the hotel, soap and scrub themselves, and watch the world go by. Then they will duck down again into the Congo, the muddy water will absorb the soap with hardly a trace, and the man will then sit on the edge of his pirogue and examine his arms and legs and torso very carefully, rather like an animal searching for fleas.

Women walk by on the road, dressed sometimes in three different mammy-cloth wrap-arounds, all of bright colors and different patterns, probably carrying a child slung across the smalls of their backs, perhaps toting a package on their heads, perhaps breast-feeding an infant as they walk.

Young boys may be shinnying up the slender trunks of coconut palms to hack off the dozen or so coconuts not yet fully ripe, nestled just beneath where the palm fronds shoot out. (There is such a competition here for fruit that can be taken or poached that it is always harvested before it's ripened and thus lower in nutritional value.) The boys will crack open the coconuts by hurling them onto the pavement. Once cracked they will tear off the shell with their teeth. Husks litter the roadside.

The hotel has no restaurant, but does have a bar, patronized almost entirely by Congolese and all afternoon African music will pulsate from the bar, shattering the air all around the hotel. There is no music yet, and I don't know what is wrong. Usually it has started by now.

The barber was, by the way, an old, light-skinned Congolese (a kind of shiny, dark-nicotine-stain colored skin) who looked as if he'd been fathered by a Portuguese. Besides being barber, he is also the local jeweler (or at least watch-repairman) and he is evidently both deaf and mute. He whined excitedly and unintelligibly when I set the chair so that I looked into the light; he wanted it so that the light would be on my hair. (We did it his way.) When I walked in, I made a scissors sign with my fingers so he would know I wasn't there for watch repair and wrote "courte" on a piece of paper on which he wrote seventy when he had finished. That's about twnety cents.

His barbershop-watch workshop was a narrow room with a hip-high partition separating the "atelier" from the part in which he lived (an un-made bed, an armoire, a clothesline with a towel hanging from it) and an opening in the wall (it looked as if someone had used a battering ram to make the opening) behind which I could make out a bathtub in cave-like darkness. But he did a good job with the coupe, which was all I wanted; shagginess adds to the discomfort of the heat.

Coq's one restaurant is located at the very opposite end of town from the hotel. Coq's small, but terribly spread out. I trudge down there twice a day for same-tasting food (no breakfasts, closed Sundays) and it's quite a long walk in the noonday sun. (Two of the three waiters have asked me for jobs at the cultural center, and I guess the third guy doesn't know yet what I'm doing here.) The Christmas menu is already posted in the menu book with a kind of edge-of-the-wilderness pride that depresses me.

For the moment I have little to do. My supplies have not yet arrived from Léopoldville. I make daily visits to the shipping firm without result. No transportation is a nuisance, and the Europeans kid me about being "toujours à pied."

I wish you had been here last night. I had dinner with five Belgians *and it was like being back in Belgium. It was such fun. A recorder played tapes of the same music we heard all last year: Richard Anthony's "J'entends siffler le train," the French version of "Twist Again Like We Did Last Summer," Gilbert Bécaud's "Et Maintenant" and Petula Clark's "Cœur Blessé."*

Well, Penny, it is noon and I must trudge off now to lunch, stop to collect whatever mail there may be, and trudge back to work this afternoon on the play.

How are things with you?

Some background is in order here.

In Belgium I fell in love with an American girl from Illinois, spending her first year out of Oberlin College studying French at the Université Libre de Bruxelles on a Fulbright scholarship. Once we got to know one another, we were together constantly. She met my parents when they visited in the spring. When I drove her to Paris in June, we dallied along the way: picnicked in flower-filled fields, visited the invasion beaches in Normandy (on Omaha Beach she swam in a bathing suit; I ran in in my boxers), stayed at inns in Brittany. We talked about getting married. She might join me in Elisabethville, she said. It was a Belgian city; she knew how to navigate those. She would get a job there and if we were sure it was right, we would get married.

When she returned to Illinois, however, she re-entered the real context of her life. And changed her mind.

After some weeks, I broke this news to my parents and brother. I concluded the letter by saying, "Please don't worry."

"Please don't worry." My poor parents! What a letter to get from a son going into a remote and crisis-torn country! Just when they thought they could transfer my emotional care and nurturing to a young woman, she decided to make the safe choice and embrace a predictable life. But it was the Congo, after all. Who could blame her?

My mother urged me not to count myself out of the game, especially if I thought Penny and I truly loved one another. She advised me to write her "again and again, pelt her with letters." So I wrote her now and then.

When I arrived in Coq, lugging two suitcases, gear for the center and a standard model typewriter (through which I could connect with the outside world), the airport was deserted. So was the parking lot behind the terminal. I seemed to have been the only passenger bound for Coq. Soon I was alone on the tarmac. I knew from the earlier visit that the airport lay seven miles from the river, from "downtown Coq" and the post office near where the forlorn house that would become the center was located.

I did not quite know what to do. There was nothing like a taxi in Coq, nothing like an airport bus. In the Congo one did not leave luggage untended. Even if a place seemed deserted, the luggage was still likely to disappear.

USIS Léo had assured me that someone from the UN would fetch me. The embassy had heard that an American headed up the UN operation in Coq. It had radioed him that I was arriving. Would he be kind enough to fetch me? Probably. Probably was as much assurance as one ever received in the Congo.

Then in accordance with African time, a UN van appeared and I met Soto Tslentis, head of the UN mission in Coq. He was an ebullient, happy-go-lucky, Greek-born American, naturalized in 1956, whose upper lip sprouted a busy, very Greek mustache. He was forty-two, but looked five years younger. He was inclined to help a USIS man because he had worked, so he said, for USIS as a front-line observer during the Greek civil war. He had won his American citizenship as a result. He seemed pleased to have another American in town, a non-missionary American, for he gave me the impression that he did not quite know what to make of missionaries.

Soto drove me through the African *cités* that lay between the airport and the town center. We stopped before the house that Clifford had rented and regarded it. Clifford expected me to live there. "I wouldn't stay in that place," Soto said, "not when there's the Ancion." I knew the Ancion Hotel from the earlier visit. A splendid Equatorial hostelry in its heyday, now rather run-down (like the Congo itself), a bar but no food service, water and electricity when they were available in town.

"Let's go there," I said. I did not want to live where I was to work.

We drove across town. We entered the Ancion from the street onto an open-air reception area that gave onto a terrace overlooking the river. A receptionist in his twenties idled behind his desk; a *femme libre,* all of fourteen, sat availably in a chair in case any hotel guest wanted her services. The receptionist said that to rent a room I would have to consult Mme Ancion—and do that in person. He could not unlock the telephone.

When Mme Ancion answered her door, a one-legged man sat on her living room couch, his lower leg prosthesis resting on the cushions beside him. She told us that there was no room at the inn.

"You can stay with me," Soto said.

As we returned to the hotel, I asked, "Was that Ancion on the couch?"

"That's Gérard," Soto said. "It's a *ménage à trois* in that house. She's married to Ancion who's away at the moment. Gérard's the father of her child. When Ancion returns, he'll go away."

Soto had the largest room in the hotel, upstairs at the far end with a balcony overlooking the river. It boasted space enough for a lounge: overstuffed chairs in the Belgian style pulled up around a table on which I placed the standard model typewriter.

Soto took me to lunch with some UN people whose hospitality was easy and genuine. At the UN Headquarters, across the street from the André house, he introduced me to aid technicians. The UN Club—movies several nights a week—was in the same building. He drove me around the town, then suggested, "You want to meet Herman, don't you? He's your landlord." We drove to the home, a bit out of town, of Mâitre Herman, the attorney who owned the center building.

Herman was a solid, stolid, stocky man with greying hair, probably about forty-five. When we arrived, he measured me with an unfriendly gaze, shook my hand, and regarded me as if I smelled bad. While he was perfectly happy to take the embassy's hard currency, he seemed deeply suspicious of American activities in the Equateur.

That may have included those of Tslentis since I sensed that Soto was glad to use me as a pretext for seeing Mme. Herman, an unusual woman to find in a jungle town. Like her husband, Soto had explained, she was trained as a lawyer. In the pre-independence days she had done occasional legal work for him. Soto claimed that she was brighter, more astute, than he was.

When the Maitre led us back through the house to a terrace, I had the impression that the Hermans did not truly live in the present-day Congo. They clung to a style of living that independence had destroyed. Madame wore a tennis costume (though I had seen no tennis courts in town). She was seated—seemed to have posed herself really—on a chaise longue on a terrace overlooking the river as if she were modeling for Claude Monet. Madame made me think that *Paris Match* had come to the Equateur. She struck me as out of place in Africa, not that such a newcomer as I could accurately make such a judgment.

She called for cocktails as if Americans could be greeted in no other way. After the Maitre fetched them, she chattered in a nervous, brittle way of sports and social clubs that seemed no longer to exist, lightly flirting with Tslentis. Perhaps that was to divert our attention from the fact that her husband distrusted Americans, assuming they meant to take control of the Congo's riches the Belgians had spent eighty years developing. No doubt he assumed I was CIA.

Late in the day Soto took me swimming at the public pool (membership CF 500 per month). We lingered there to see another of his women, this one the town beauty, for whom he admitted having once had "the big eye." She was a German woman from Aachen, married to a Belgian aid technician. When she appeared, he chatted delightedly with her until darkness fell. Mosquitoes rose at that hour and I spent my first night in Coq well bitten.

Soto felt expansive because he was leaving the next day on transfer to Kitona, a military base between Léopoldville and Matadi. That my only acquaintance in town should depart so quickly distressed me. I would inherit his room, but not his contacts, his knowledge of the place, nor the *entrée* he had happily provided me to his UN circle. I would miss him.

That evening the UN Club held a farewell party for Soto. Tagging along, I met more people. I said hello to Mme André. We bantered briefly and I was delighted to bring smiles to her face. Perhaps my uncertain French did that. The party lasted well into the morning. However, I have never schmoozed easily in cocktail party situations, even in English. In French it was more than I was prepared to handle, especially as a newbie. I left early. By the end of the next day Soto— that good boy!—was gone.

I wrote my family to announce my arrival in the Equateur.

Coquilhatville, 7 November 1963

Hi,

It's my second day in Coq and my first conclusion is that this will be a bearable experience. I no longer have the dramatic, perhaps even poetic, feeling that the jungle is creeping back into the town. A positive impression is one of the beauty of Africa. One can't help being awed by the huge expanses of space here. Now that the rainy season has begun, the mistiness that was here before has gone. There is an after-rain clearness in the air and sky. It brings vividness to the colors. They are lovely, simply beautiful.

The people here seem like a good bunch as well.

The heat, the isolation and the boredom are, of course, the drawbacks. I haven't found the heat unbearable. One gets such an exaggerated idea of what sitting on the Equator would be like, as if you'd move around all day sweating like being in a Turkish bath. It's a bit stifling; you feel clothed when you're sitting in your undershorts, as I am now. And you get sweaty walking around the streets. But there is a certain amount of cloud cover and shade and, since we are now blessed with electricity in town, there's even air-conditioning.

Yesterday after getting settled I took a look at the center. It boasts the dirtiest toilet bowl you ever saw. The floors were paint-spotted, the rooms stuffy from being locked up. Edouard the sentinelle *has done some useful gardening. He's an old Congolese, one of the few I've seen graying. He's got a wife and a* boyerie *full of kids behind the center. I carried over a carton of books and some mail that had arrived at the post office. The wife was cooking bare-breasted and kids scrambling over things with little genital wrappers on. When she saw me, she screamed and ran into the* boyerie. *Edouard and two of the kids came into the building and watched me while I looked through the box and read the letters. Just stood there and watched me.*

This morning I looked around for an apartment. There seems to be nothing. We had hoped that an apartment in the Air Congo building might be available. But it will house a Congolese coming soon to assist the European manager. Talked to an old jungle type, garrulous at the sight of a new face, a white-turning-yellow mustache and beard. I liked him, but he had nothing.

Dinner tonight with some missionaries, Disciples of Christ, a fundamentalist sect based mainly in the Midwest and southwest. They are a pretty Midwestern variety of American and I doubt that I'll find much in the way of interesting companionship in their direction. We shall see.

As it turned out, I quite liked the missionaries. And no wonder! During my first weeks in Coq I was excruciatingly lonely. Day after day passed without my making meaningful connection with anyone. I waited for the center equipment to arrive. I read. I made contacts. I searched in vain for a place to live. I worked on a two-character play set in New York's Metropolitan Museum of Art. I typed letters to my family. So I was grateful there were American missionaries in town.

I soon learned that The Disciples of Christ were not fundamentalists, but a mainline Protestant denomination that began in the early 1800s. Headquarters of the DCCM (Disciples of Christ Congo Mission) was at Bolenge, ten miles or so west of Coquilhatville, but a small group of DCCM missionaries lived in Coq to conduct town business.

One of these was Ron Sallade, a heavy-set, twenty-five-year-old former ninth grade teacher from Des Moines, Iowa, doing a year-long stint as the DCCM treasurer. Ron had a small house behind the Andrés where there was always a large pot of water simmering to rid it of impurities. During the long weeks I was at the hotel, Ron brought me potable water. If I had spoken to no one in a day or two, it was a signal event to have him come by the hotel with bottles of water purified on his stove and capped with patches of aluminum foil pressed over the openings. In each bottle a small residue of river silt lay on the bottom

On Sundays when the Oasis Restaurant was closed, I often shared meals with Ron. He helped me in any number of ways while I was trying to get the center established. Two unmarried American guys in town. That eventually led to dinner invitations for us, both in Coq and at Bolenge. In my early days in town we sometimes dined with missionaries Friday evening, Saturday evening and twice Sunday.

As single guys in our twenties, we bonded. We could vent to each other. Ron explained his presence in the Congo as motivated by a desire to "help one's fellow man through love." He was not holy-holy. He considered that Coq possessed all the ingredients conducive to insanity: an extreme and unchanging climate, isolation and loneliness, frustration, lack of orderly procedures for routine business.

Sometimes he told me more than I wanted to know about his fellow missionaries: that a couple in Coq were in denial, so he said, about a schizophrenic daughter; that a missionary wife at isolated Bosobele station had surprised her husband by delivering a mixed race baby.

Ron felt that while missionary life was extremely ascetic, it was not very taxing. "An easy life," he said. "Nobody's working too hard." I myself concluded that while it might be an easy workaday life, it was not an easy emotional one. During my first weeks in Coq the three-year-old daughter of a missionary family in the bush died of convulsions.

Sometimes the letters to my family tried to give them a sense of Africa:

Coquilhatville, 12 November 1963

Hi,

During a period of wakefulness last night, I saw huge flashes of lightning throwing a gray-white light across the endless expanse of sky. The flashes showed heavy clouds far off across the river. After a while thunder began and then the rain came. It falls heavily, persistently, with an occasional rushing energy that makes it beat hard against the tin roofs, slap down noisily on the concrete roof outside my hotel window. Gusts of wind blow it in patterns, not unlike the patterns wind-gusts create in tall wheat, and the coconut palms bow against the wind and wave their fronds.

It rained this heavy kind of rain most of Sunday. It began falling at mid-morning and before it started you could watch the huge clouds forming across the river. Then the cool winds came and the river grew dark with wind pushing the floating clumps of water hyacinth in toward shore. Dogs started barking at the coming rain and birds floated around in circles in the pre-rain breezes. These storms have a certain undeniable beauty.

But it has been raining today for probably three solid hours, maybe four. (It's 7:30 now; did the rain come as early as 3:30?) It puts large stretches of land under a thin layer of water (where mosquitoes breed, probably); it washes away roads or makes them impassable. It will keep me inside today, at least until it stops. I can't go walking around town in the rain.

It's now 10:00 and still raining. A man in a blue shirt has been standing across the street under a wide roof since I got up. I can see another fellow poling a pirogue across the river. He's working hard, bending against his paddle, wearing only a wrapper, while his wife crouches in the boat with a white enamel pot held over her head.

The same letter reported my first encounter with Léon Engulu, Governor of the Cuvette Centrale province of which Coq was the capital.

> *I called Engulu's chef de protocol Mutien-Marie Bokele, who's been to the US, to arrange the interview. Called yesterday and twice this morning. The second time he suggested I come to the Mansion and sit around until Engulu could see me. That did not appeal much to me, but I went. I was sneaked in before waiting people to say hello.*
>
> *I put on a suit, the first time I've had a coat on since I arrived here. I had used the DCCM phone to arrange the interview and fortunately, Ron Sallade was running an errand in town. He drove me to the mansion. I'd have hated to appear after a sweaty walk.*
>
> *The Mansion is a large house, overlooking the confluence of the Congo and the Ruki, and seems as if it were plunked out of Pasadena, with nicely kept gardens and lawns.*
>
> *The meeting proved to be an easy, congenial saying-hello. Engulu is a young man, certainly no older than I am. He sat in the middle of a long conference table in a long conference room, looking out at the lawns and flowers. He wore a business suit and had a pad of paper before him. Engulu struck me as intelligent and poised. It's difficult to tell much about a man in a five-minute discussion, but he seemed likable. I hope that we see each other from time to time.*

Knowing I was searching for a place to live, M André walked me through a house, owned by a Belgian firm that had all but abandoned Coq. Among his business activities, André acted as agent for the company's odds and ends that had yet to be resolved. The house stood in unhappy disrepair, the result of being flooded (as was the center building) when the river rose in '60 and '61. Since the other possibilities I had seen resembled *boyeries* (that is, servant's quarters, servants being called *"boys"*), I was willing to consider this house, if repairs could be made. However, even if the embassy rented the building as my residence and paid for the repairs, the Belgian firm would demand a lease stipulating that the premises could be vacated on three months notice. I doubted that the embassy would agree to that condition.

André proved to be a voluble talker. He mentioned that after sending his wife and four children back to Namur in Belgium, he had stayed in Coq during the worst of the post-independence uncertainty. The family had returned to Coq only months before. The Andrés hoped that somehow the Congo had turned a corner, that with the disintegration lessening and the economy rebounding, it was possible once more to have a decent life in what André frequently called "*notre petit coin du pays*" (our little corner of this country).

We crept along, moving ever more slowly as he talked about the limited perspectives and the commercial mentality of Belgians. Belgium seemed so tiny after the expanse of the Equateur. André parked the car before the center. It was hardly in better repair than the house he had just shown me. We continued talking.

As he discussed problems caused by Belgium's French and Flemish language groups, I glimpsed the seeming impossibility of the family returning to what Belgians called "*le metropole.*" Before independence opportunities in the Congo had been great for young people willing to grab them while the possibilities in Belgium were limited. No wonder André hoped things had turned around.

As we said goodbye, he invited me to dinner that evening. Of course, I accepted.

Mme André's dinner party proved to be the most enjoyable evening I had spent in the Congo. She had a special talent for gathering in visitors and non-compatriots. Her guests that evening were a Belgian couple, a single Belgian (none of whom I ever saw again), the Andrés' neighbor Ron Sallade (who spoke no French) and myself. As we were chatting after dinner, the Andrés' great UN friends, the Polish doctor Janusz Michejda and his wife Barbara joined us.

Because I had spent most of the previous year in Belgium, I was accepted as almost part of the national family. There was much talk about *le métropole*. It was a home base that interested them—its decisions affected much of their lives—but for which they did not yearn. The Andrés spoke fondly of Namur from which they had both fled after the war.

The talk eventually turned to Patrice Lumumba, the independent Congo's first prime minister. As I would learn in the months ahead, this subject often came up at such gatherings. This evening the *Coquins* spoke of Lumumba's electoral campaign visit to their city. He had held a rally at the edge of the European section of town. He was said to have declared to a crowd of Congolese, "The European came here with one suitcase and now he has five trunks. When he came, he had only one shirt to hang on the clothesline, now he has ten. After independence Congolese women will no longer prepare food at the prisons; white women will do this."

I wondered how many—if any—of these recollections were accurate. For *ex-colons* this kind of talk was like picking at a scab for Lumumba symbolized the calamity—independence—that had befallen them. I listened with interest because I suspected that Lumumba's assassination (in which American policymakers were said to have had a hand) was a regrettable event, an attempt to solve a problem in a way that only created more problems.

When the Michejdas joined us, there were stories about Coq. Michejda told of a Congolese worker whom he'd had jailed for theft. Whenever the doctor encountered his work crew around town, the prisoner would greet him effusively. He even named his family's new baby "Michejda."

Another story about a cuckolded husband. The judge sent the perpetrator to jail; he also jailed the wife for adultery. So the lover and the wife lived and loved happily in jail while the innocent cuckold remained free. We all laughed, agreeing, *"C'est le Congo!"*

While we chatted, the Andrés' recorder spun tapes of the songs popular during my stay in Brussels. Letting the tunes and lyrics play through my head, I only half-listened to the stories. I reminisced about the previous year's good times, the pleasure of falling in love in Europe. But I was in the Congo now.

Mme André played a tape of Edith Piaf songs. For the first time I heard *"Milord."* Mme André sang as lustily as the Sparrow, *"Dansez, Milord! Mais vous pleurez, Milord!"* I joined her in singing bits of *"Je Ne Regrette Rien"* and wondered if somewhere down the line I would reminisce about this evening.

FOUR

DURING MY FIRST DAYS IN COQ I had virtually nothing to do and worried that I was not doing that nothing as efficiently as I should. "Ifs" haunted me.

If I were more gregarious. . . If my French were fluent. . . If I were a boozer and felt comfortable hanging out at the Oasis Bar. . . If I were adapted sufficiently to the ways of the country to apply at a girls' secondary school for a Congolese companion (as Governor Engulu was said to have done). . . If the Oasis Restaurant had a large, common table instead of tiny separate ones. . . If the mythology of the CIA and the reach of its tentacles were not so pervasive. . . If Congolese and *ex-colons* were less suspicious about why I was in town. . . If I understood better what my mission in the town actually was. . . If I knew something about Africa. . . If I could truly adjust to the pace of the somnolent town, to the rhythms of waiting, as Édouard, the *sentinelle* at the center, had obviously done, sitting staring into space for hours. . . Then it would all be easier. But none of these "ifs" applied.

I trudged from the hotel to the bakery for rolls and coffee in the morning. To the Oasis Restaurant for lunch when the sun was high and enervating and again in the evenings when the day had spent itself. I almost always sat alone, picking baked-in weevils out of my bread, drinking carbonated water because the Oasis served only *eau gazeuse*, grateful for whatever entrée was available and hoping for vegetables— and for companionship.

Returning to the hotel where bats flew low along the outside passageways, I would move through the gentle darkness, past the fires of *sentinelles* who guarded stores without goods. Invariably their dogs charged at me. No matter what ploy I chose—friendliness, indifference or anger—the dogs would sense my apprehension and unnerve me.

Every night on the walk to and from the hotel I composed mental letters to Steve Baldanza at USIS Léo, tendering my resignation.

But I did not resign.

One afternoon an African passed by the center building. Full of jokes and laughter, he wore a curly goatee, the same blackness as his skin, and a knitted visored cap of many colors. He offered for sale copies of *Le Peuple*, a two-paged mimeographed *stencillé* of local and national news that he wrote and published daily. We introduced ourselves. He called himself Essolomwa René Thy. I subscribed to his *journal*, which delighted him. I plied him with USIS magazines about America. It may have been my compliments about his cap or the money I gave him on the spot for the subscription that produced in him an ebullient, witty expansiveness.

With giggles he revealed that he had just been in Léo, seeking an alternative to UNIMO, the political party of Equateur local boy Justin Bomboko, the Congo's first foreign minister. Bomboko had once published a *journal* in Coq as Essolomwa himself was doing. Essolomwa claimed to enjoy the backing of Coq "intellectuals" and it now occurred to him, perhaps following Bomboko's example, that he might form a political party with himself as its head. In fact, he revealed, he had entered his name for one of the *conseiller* positions in upcoming elections. If elected, he would try to get his fellow *conseillers* to choose him as *bourgemestre* (mayor).

Laughingly outlining his plans, he explained that since the West Germans were already financing a political party in the Equateur, he had sought American funds for his grouping. He had also gone to the Portuguese. He showed me a telegram from a Portuguese vice-consul, a wait-and-see message that promised nothing.

As we shook hands and he moved off, laughing and calling, *"À bientôt!"* I tried to hide my bafflement. Was I to cultivate Essolomwa? Was he an opinion-maker? Did he have a following? How did I go about checking him out?

The next time Essolomwa passed by the center, delivering his *journal*, I was talking to Maitre Herman who was paying a landlord visit. Essolomwa greeted me with a sing-song *"Bonjour"* and we shook hands. Herman appraised him coolly; they nodded to one another. Essolomwa handed me the day's news and went on his way.

"What's he doing here?" Herman asked.

"He's a journalist," I replied.

Herman raised a skeptical eyebrow. "Don't encourage him," he advised. "He's a troublemaker."

"But that's why I'm here," I said. "To encourage people like him."

Again the skeptical eyebrow. "Steer clear of him."

I did not know what to make of this advice. Or of Herman. He obviously disdained both of us. But he and I were both whites, both "Europeans." Did he warn me as one European would warn another? As an experienced European would warn a younger one whose inexperience announced itself in everything he did?

"Steer clear of him," might be good advice. But Essolomwa was an editor, and I was an information man. What was I to do?

In fact, I puzzled over what a USIS information program could do in Coq. In Europe USIS courted target audiences because, while there was an enormous capacity to absorb information and a certain interest in it, USIS did not possess the means to compete for a mass audience. Here the case was just the reverse. Here there was no competition, but very little capacity to absorb information, even among "intellectuals." I supposed the trick was to identify target audiences and try to develop in them a desire for whatever info we could give them.

A couple of days later *Peuple* welcomed "M Fred" to Coquilhatville. Essolomwa had assumed, following Congolese usage, that the first name was the surname. (Obviously he and I were making mistaken, cross-cultural inferences about one another.) He also used a quote from President Kennedy, pulled from a USIS publication I had given him. (At least I knew he had looked through my offerings.) The quote espoused a free press. It was directed, I learned, at Governor Léon Engulu.

Soon Dzata Bernard, Essolomwa's right hand man, much less ostentatious and more to my liking, came to borrow a biography of Abraham Lincoln. This, it turned out, was research for an ongoing dialogue between *Peuple* and the *Présidence,* as the governor's office was called. It was a discussion in which I definitely did not want the cultural center to be involved. Dzata also sought my help in forming a Coquilhatville federation of journalists that could agitate for greater press freedom in the province. Governor Engulu acted as his own Information Minister and criticism of the regime was not countenanced.

One morning I found two different copies of *Peuple* slid under the door of the center. Glancing through them I came upon an article in each one attacking the US. The first was simply a goad. It demanded an explanation as to why *Perspectives*, a USIS publication distributed without cost, was selling in the markets for CF 10 a copy. The second article suggested that American Cultural Centers in the Congo were, in fact, spy networks. Since some of the *ex-colons* suspected this, I was chagrined that *Peuple*, however marginal its influence, was making this charge. Steer clear of him, indeed!

To counter the accusation I wrote an explanation of the American center's role in Coq, designed for all three *stencillés*. But I never distributed it, realizing that Essolomwa was baiting me for that very response.

Hank Clifford arrived for a few days to help set up the center. Thanks to the DCCM's generosity with its truck, he and I were able to fetch twenty cases of furniture and books weighing over three tons. We hauled them from the Otraco dock and spent two days erecting shelving, setting up tables, filing cabinets, and two desks, one so large that we moved it through windows into the room that would serve as an office.

After Hank left, I worked on alone. I unpacked and shelved USIS films and crates of books. The cases provided too many books in English, I thought, but at least they offered me volumes to read in the ongoing isolation of waiting. I got a phone installed. I bought a table and a chair, locally made, and transferred my office from the hotel to the center.

By late November my car arrived. It sat for a week on a barge outside my hotel balcony awaiting the slow off-loading process. My personal effects were still wending their way upriver.

One day André and I climbed above the center ceiling to inspect the building's construction. Rats skittered under our feet. Heat from the corrugated iron roof made us sweat. We saw that we could remove a bathroom and two walls without endangering the ceiling. Those changes would allow the center to have a theater and classroom.

André suggested constructing a projection booth outside the building, an excellent idea. It would create more space for theater seating and eliminate much of the projectors' light and noise. I would have to get Mâitre Herman's agreement in order to start the alterations.

André's electricians installed lighting in the center. It could now be used at night. I entered one evening to find Tata Edouard making love to a woman on the floor. I hurried into the office to give them privacy. She was a woman I had not seen around the place. Edouard later explained that she was his bush wife; the woman in the *boyerie* was his town wife.

Jules André introduced me to the *ex-colon* principals of the construction firm DeLinte & Boudart. It would construct the projection booth. The partners rotated their time in Coq. Jules Boudart had just arrived for his six-month stint. Boudart struck me as being what might be termed an Earth Father. He was rough, loud and profane. He spoke a gravelly, guttural Belgian French that I often had trouble understanding. He looked shrewd and, whether he actually did or not, he seemed to swagger.

If the disintegration of the Congo depressed some, it invigorated Boudart. (Perhaps six months away from Coq every year made invigoration possible.) He told me once that he wished he had lived in the Wild West. In fact, the Congo we inhabited possessed an atmosphere somewhat resembling that. Asked if he would have been a sheriff or a bad guy, he did not answer. Living by his wits, as bad guys do, clearly fascinated him. Still, he had a strong sense of integrity. If his Congolese were working in the sun, neither he nor his European foreman was to stand in the shade.

Boudart oozed the kind of take-no-prisoners virility that often suggested joyous womanizing. Sometimes at the get-togethers we began to have, most of them *chez les Andrés,* he and Janusz Michejda would laugh uproariously, teasing about fixing me up with Anne-Marie, a Congolese women of volcanic sexuality, from whom Boudart claimed to receive favors. Boudart was married. However, Madame did not come to the Congo. She was never mentioned.

Despite the teasing, I had a sense that Boudart did not seek out Congolese women. Or did so only very discreetly. Would I have known? Probably not. But Coq was a small place. Mme André told me about the *ex-colon* lawyer whom I'll call Teriot who had Congolese women as soon as his wife left town. I sensed that acceptance into Mme André's circle—she entertained us often enough to consider it that—required discretion in this department. Boudart was accepted there. He was probably ten years older than André and judged himself to have a much more realistic approach to surviving the ups and downs of the post-independence Congo. The contrast between André and Boudart would fascinate me for months.

Coq, 15 December 1963

Hi,

Yesterday I accompanied Betty Erlewine and Ron Sallade on an all-day trip to Tondo, a small station of the Baptist Mission Society, a British outfit, on the banks of Lake Tumba almost directly south of Coq. We passed through Bikoro (which you can probably find on the map); Tondo is located on the second inlet to the south.

The road into Tondo—in fact, almost the entire road south from Coq—sits on dikes raised out of swamp. The bush grows so thick against the road that one is rarely conscious of the fact that he's moving on a thin line of road drawn through the swamp. Occasionally water appears on both sides and reminds you. There was a bad stretch of mud at one place. Ron dared his luck, got us through both ways—although returning we were sliding slowly into the swamp.

The drive took about three hours each way. The land is flat, swampy, except for three or four incongruous stretches of meadow. The villages do not seem noticeably more primitive than those immediately outside Coq: mud-wattle-and-thatched huts surrounded by hard-swept earth. A few people sitting around under heavily and low-thatched unwalled buildings that seem to serve as community centers or dining areas. Most of the tiny children naked, waving at the passing microbus, grinning, excited. Women and children bathing in the open stretches of water at the roadside, women washing their laundry.

Tondo's a row of old buildings, rather in need of repair, built one story above ground. Missionary furnishings are always spare: a few hard, angular chairs; an ink spot of a rug in a huge room; thin, tiny ascetic cot-beds against the expanse of wall and floor; no decorative or fancy trimmings.

The hospital was dim, nets of cobwebs hanging under the steeply-gabled ceiling, a feeling of uncleanness (dirty clothes, dark people, faint light), a clutter of children hanging around, bare-breasted women cooking in a kitchen area. The wards looked like the movie concept of insanity wards. You had the feeling that these poor missionaries were struggling against overwhelming odds. Mullen, who seemed quite a nice fellow, is the only white man on the station;: he's certainly too busy doctoring to play handyman.

Walking into the village, we saw women carrying pails of water up a steep path from the lake edge and a young bare-breasted woman pounding her wash on a log. I felt rather sorry for her. Each time she pounded, stooping from her hips, her breasts fell, jerked, swung. Seeing the treatment they received one understands why they will soon hang as forlornly on her as they do on most Congolese women.

Lunch, in its very simple way, was rather pleasant. We sat on the porch overlooking the lake, had canned meat and Yorkshire pudding, potatoes and the picnic stuff Betty had brought in case lunch would prove too much on such short notice. Talk was slow, as it often seems to be with missionaries. Jello pudding with fruit for dessert while the Mullens played with their daughter.

Talked Congo social customs and theology, both of which absorbed me, most of the way home. At Beambo a barricade of four metal drums stopped us. We were asked to take sacks of flour and cement to Penzele, the next large village. We dropped these off with a woman who claimed to be the wife (or, we thought later, one of several wives) of the man who was to receive the sacks. He was out in the forest.

Pooped most of today. An all-day ride over bouncy roads really takes it out of me!

Ever since my arrival in Coq, I'd been aware that financial difficulties plagued the province. The Adoula government had devalued the Congolese franc, but that had little impact on me. Merchants were not allowed to raise the prices of goods, but I bought little in the shops.

Then I read a complaint in one of the *stencillés* that the central government had withdrawn a CF 17 million subsidy from the provincial government, half of the province's annual subsidy. I wondered what that was all about.

I appealed for information to Roger Raeys, a *conseiller* with the Internal Affairs Ministry. At the Ancion he lived in the room next to mine with a young *Congolaise*, known locally by her status as *femme d'un blanc* (white man's woman). Since local government officials rarely sought his advice and even more rarely acted on it when received, Raeys felt some of the same frustration with his job that I did with my endless waiting.

Raeys explained that the subsidy in question did not finance provincial operations. Rather it was for teachers' salaries. Teachers in the Cuvette Centrale had not been paid in over a year, he said. As a result, the central government had decided to pay the teachers directly. To do this, it subtracted the funds for teachers' salaries from the provincial subsidy.

Raeys all but stated that the provincial administration was corrupt. Apparently it used the teacher funds to pay people who had abandoned their villages and moved to Coq, but did no work. Properly cultivated, they would serve as a political base in future elections. That being the case, it was not surprising that Internal Affairs Minister Gaston LeBaud did not often seek Raeys' advice. In fact, he suggested, the province was generally going to hell.

Not long afterwards Mutien-Marie Bokele, the governor's protocol chief, tipped me off that roadblocks would be established around town. As we ate breakfast together at the bakery, he mentioned that police and army units would soon be stationed throughout Coq. The provincial government was about to take the unusual austerity measure of reducing by sixty percent the wages of its workers. The army and police would prevent any unrest caused by the reductions.

Soon the roadblocks appeared. At them police checked Congolese for payment of the head tax. By now I had taken possession of my car. I was stopped repeatedly driving to and from the pool. Although I had heard rumors that Portuguese merchants had illegally raised prices in their stores, I did not really understand what was going on.

Early the morning after I returned from Tondo trucks of the *Armée Nationale Congolaise* moved through streets of the town center. Soldiers closed virtually all commercial enterprises in Coq and took up positions outside them. With guards at the entrances, officials, led by Interior Minister LeBaud, entered the stores. They searched the stores' inventories. They confiscated what they deemed to be goods hidden so that post-devaluation prices could be charged for them. They exacted fines. Crowds of excited Congolese stood outside the stores to watch officials emerge from them carrying confiscated goods. The closures lasted a week.

Most Congolese were delighted to see a squeeze put on the merchants, especially the Portuguese with whom they mainly traded. The Europeans were sullen. To them the closures constituted plunder, an attack on all of them, done without any sort of judicial procedure.

Rumors quickly flew around the European community: that safes had been forced open and money taken; that Portuguese merchants were beaten, tossed into jail, and threatened with expulsion from the Congo; that Internal Affairs Minister LeBaud was masterminding the searches and profiting from them.

Ron Sallade witnessed police breaking into both a Portuguese store and the derelict Hotel Leopold II. From the latter they removed hidden bicycles. Having his camera with him, he took pictures. A police officer shouted at him, threatening arrest, and demanded the film. Ron surrendered it to him. Later he learned that he might have been beaten on the spot had it not been for Protestant police in the group. He was advised to stay off the streets.

At the swimming pool that first afternoon Jules André came over to talk, looking very thin in his bathing suit. I was surprised he was there; he rarely swam. He seemed tense and depressed, as if suppressing a fury inside himself. We sat at the edge of the pool, our feet dangling in the water. André looked deeply into it, as if staring at the collapse of his hopes that Coq was coming back, that he and his family could resume their lives in Coq and live out their days in the home he had built, supported by the business it had taken him so long to create.

"Were you searched?" I asked.

He nodded.

"What happened?"

"They held a gun to my head and demanded that I write a check for two hundred thousand francs."

"Write it to whom?"

"The minister."

"Him personally?"

Again he nodded.

After a moment he said, "I gave my men the day off." I wondered if that was because he could not bear to have them see him being humiliated.

"What did they take?"

"Whatever caught their eye. Six radios. Someone now has six radios that once he would have had to buy."

Although André would ruefully admit that he had sufficient stores of light bulbs to illuminate the entire Equateur for a year, it was my impression that he had not been selling items for some time. When

Hank Clifford came to town to rent a center building, he had found André's windows soaped over and his building closed.

André and I sat side by side until mosquitoes made us leave.

That evening I tried to make sense of what had happened. I wished I could do something for André who had been so generous to me. I knew that he often considered getting out of Coq, but really wanted to stay, to enjoy what he'd spent his youth building. If he did leave Coq, he would lose most of the investment he'd worked years to amass. Independence had already stripped most of its value.

Despite all the nostalgic talk of *le métropole* at his wife's dinner parties, André resisted returning to Belgium. Here he was a pillar of society; there he would have to work for another man as an electrician. Life would be harder. He'd be able to offer his children fewer opportunities. He had told me that he shivered throughout his last visit there, in December, 1961, when he'd gone to see his family after they had fled from Coq. He complained of the smallness of the *mentalité belge*. Better to try his luck in Australia. At thirty-five, he was young enough to start over some place. But with a wife and four kids? What a daunting prospect!

That evening I also felt sympathy for the Portuguese merchants. They seemed never to have done more than eke out a living from selling cheap clothing in their poor little stores.

Wanting to understand what was going on, I again sought out Roger Raeys, the *conseiller* with the Internal Affairs Ministry. He explained that at the time of the devaluation merchants were supposed to declare all goods they had on hand. These were to be sold at pre-devaluation prices. Some merchants went short on their inventories. Goods found in their stores that were unlisted on inventories or arrival notices after the date of devaluation would be considered suspect and confiscated.

According to Raeys, the Portuguese merchants had taken advantage of the devaluation to hike prices. He exampled a roll of wax paper; it cost CF 400 before devaluation, but now was selling at CF 2400. In addition, merchants had not waited for the arrival of goods brought in from outside the country to raise prices. They were exploiting the devaluation.

Raeys claimed the Ministry assured him that no merchants were beaten, that Michejda had not gone to the prison to tend a wounded person, that merchants would not be deported. He deplored the Ministry's methods, he said. He would have preferred that the hidden material be laid aside under guard, then sold by the merchants themselves at government controlled prices. The merchants themselves would have handled the transactions.

Theoretically the present system had the government confiscating suspect goods. It was supposed to sell them at controlled, pre-devaluation prices, then return eighty percent of the sales to the merchants. The other twenty percent would be considered fines. That was theory. In practice things did not work that way. The goods disappeared. Officials pocketed the fines.

Coq remained in limbo the entire week of what the *ex-colons* called *le pillage*. The life of the town came to a halt, including, of course, the alterations to the center building that André and Boudart were to undertake.

At the end of the week Jules André came to see me at the center. When I looked up from the desk and saw him park his car, I went to the door to greet him. When we shook hands, I saw that even if he had not been beaten physically, psychologically he had been badly knocked around.

We sat in my office. Late afternoon sunlight slanted into the room. "How goes it?" I asked. He said nothing. Usually an intense and voluble talker, he now stared at his hands. By then I had been a guest in his home often enough to know that he did not drink heavily. But I smelled liquor on his breath. I wondered why he had come.

"I'm sorry I have no refreshments to offer you," I said.

He shrugged.

"It's been a bad week," I observed. "Is it over now?"

He nodded, shrugged again. Then he asked rhetorically, "Is it ever over?" I leaned forward across the desk. He told me again that he had been fined CF 200,000. His friend Bogaerts—he and his mother owned a stationery and office supplies store—had been forced to pay CF 25,000. Then quietly, but with deep anger, he said, "Boudart paid nothing."

"Nothing? How did that happen?"

He raised an eyebrow without looking at me and rubbed his thumb and forefinger together.

We sat for a long moment without speaking. "I spoke to Raeys," I said, "*le conseiller.*" He nodded. I summarized what Raeys had told me.

He snorted scornfully, almost inaudibly. "He is extremely naïve." André told me once again how while he wrote the check a soldier had held a gun on him, how the Congolese who took the check, offered his hand, bowed slightly, and, pocketing the check, said, "*Merci, patron.*"

"This is not a place to raise children," he said. "A year ago we thought it might be and I wanted the family here." He shook his head. "But no longer."

He spoke of Coq as "*ce petit coin*" (this little corner) which had once been such a fine place for a family. But not since independence. In those days, he said, after independence his oldest son Yves, then eight, had seen Congolese soldiers in the streets, laughing, swaggering, bayonets on their rifles. "Always before he had felt safe. But then, no more. Poof! His sense of safety vanished."

For the first time in his life Yves had grown nasty to Congolese, André said. At that time of tensions when everyone was on edge, Yves' outbursts threatened the family's safety. André had been forced to lock Yves in his room. He took him on his lap and tried to explain that the period they were moving through was not just, but it was very dangerous. He tried to assure Yves that he did not lock him in his room to punish him, but to protect the family. Yves became ever more upset. "He used to cry inconsolably. Sometimes I had to shut my ears not to hear him."

André stared at his hands again. "Earlier this week he got nervous the way he used to. I told him we might go to Australia. I didn't know what else to do."

I nodded.

"He saw soldiers in my office with guns and bayonets. When he gets excited, it rattles the other kids." André now gazed fixedly out the window. I wondered again why he had come. Did he need someone to listen? I wished I had refreshment to offer. "I told him that soldiers breaking into stores, confiscating goods: that was not just, not right. I mentioned Australia to give him something to look forward to."

We fell into a silence. It seemed to last forever.

Finally, as if he could no longer hold out against what had made him come, almost in a whisper he blurted out, "You need somewhere to live. I came here to offer you our place."

So that was why the liquor was on his breath. Why it had taken him so long to get it out.

"Your home?" I said. His children's home. His wife's.

He nodded, then hesitated as if the words stuck in his throat. "It would be perfect for you. It's in the center of town. On the main square."

"But it's your home." I could hardly believe that he was offering me his family home.

"I will continue to work there. The office and the work area and all my stores are there."

I did not know what to say. Yes, I needed a place. I badly wanted to get out of the hotel. To stop living out of a suitcase. But to take the home of the only people in Coq to befriend me? How could I agree to that?

"But where will your family live?" I asked. "You've got four children."

Obviously the liquor fortified him to make this offer. "I have charge of a house out by the river," he said. "A bit north of town." It was hard for him to say these words. "It has more room than our house."

I nodded, to help him say what was so hard to say.

"Thérèse keeps saying we need more space. We have three boys in a small bedroom."

I was very unwilling to exploit his need. Had the searches really hurt him this badly?

He explained that he took care of the river house for a friend, acting as his agent in the same way he acted for the firm that owned the flood-damaged house he had shown me. As for their home in town, he recalled that months before he had talked with Hank Clifford about the embassy renting it as a center building with apartment. "It would have been much better than Herman's house," he reminded me.

Still I did not know how to reply. I would be forcing the André children out of the only home they knew in the Congo.

"We have decided to leave the Congo," André said. "The talk about Australia was not simply to soothe Yves." I could hardly believe his words. Madame and the children had been back so short a time. Only a couple of months before everyone had thought things were getting better, that Coq had hit bottom and was coming back.

"This is not a place to raise children," André repeated. "This is not a place to do business." He stared at the floor, hardly able to speak so deep was his anger at what the African pillagers had done and at his impotence to counter them. "They held a gun to my head," he said as if he had not already told me this. "They demanded that I write a check made out not to the government, but to a member of the so-called *comité de vigilance.* It went right into his pocket. Robbery."

I nodded, stunned by the courage and the despair that lay behind the decision to start over.

"This is not a place to bring up children," he said yet again. "In *un petit an* we'll be gone."

I said I would be grateful to live in the house. I understood, of course, that the American Embassy would pay hard currency for the rental and bank it in Belgium. That would be of real benefit to the Andrés. If they truly intended to abandon the Congo, they would need hard currency the next place they went.

The house held pleasant memories for me, I said. I would be glad to have André working every day in the office attached to it. That would mean that I had regular contact with others. It would reduce my sense of isolation.

"Should I take a look at the house?"

"Of course. When can you come?"

He relaxed for the first time that afternoon. He even smiled when we shook hands. I was both distressed and delighted. Housing had seemed an insoluble problem. Now maybe it could be resolved—and in a way that helped the Andrés. It was a win-win situation.

When I went to the house, tiny Martine, maybe six years old, showed me her bedroom with innocence and delight. She had no idea that I would be taking it from her. Once again I said that I would be grateful to live there. I'd have to make arrangements with the embassy.

As it turned out, André had suddenly to fly to Belgium. His father was dying. He was gone three weeks. We would arrange the lease when he returned.

For weeks after it happened, the ex-*colon* and expatriate communities tried to make sense of *le pillage*. A theory that gained currency noted that the confiscations and finings took place two weeks before the end of the year. *Bonne Année* was an occasion much more important to the Congolese than Christmas. It was now thought that the finings financed New Years parties thrown by government ministers who got access to the money. Eventually, it was said, the confiscated goods made their way into the African markets in the *cités* of Coq, their prices marked up even higher than the Portuguese merchants had dared.

FIVE

THE BEGINNING OF 1964 FOUND me a little frustrated:

Coquilhatville, 2 January 1964

Happy New Year!

I have just reread the home letters I've received in the last week and they have really been life-savers. It has been a rather grim four days since last Monday when I woke headachy and woozy . . .

Such an unexpected combination of sensations and frustrations here. Sunday, for instance. Canned roast beef (ick!) at noon, an afternoon nap that I woke from feeling drugged and exhausted, a swim with late afternoon sunlight shooting its glare into your eyes; too hot soup in the evening; after dinner sitting in the heat of the DCCM church with that deathly sweet smell of insect repellent all around you.

Since I last wrote I have gotten a full dosage of exposure to missionaries: Christmas Day, New Year's Eve, New Year's Day, and last Saturday afternoon as well. That's rather a full schedule for a worldly young fellow like me.

It's gradually getting hotter all the time, hot enough now so that you have to have (or at least want to have) the air-conditioner on part of the night so that you scramble from no covers to two light blankets as the air-conditioner gurgles to itself and trembles and rattles like second childhood. And you're beginning to get fed up with a number of things: the fact that you've been living out of a suitcase now for six months, the fact that you haven't seen your personal effects for six months and those goddamned people down in Léopoldville have never told you firmly whether the effects have been sent to Coq or not, the fact that you are more isolated in the Congo than you ever dreamt (because you are not isolated just in Coq, but in Léo as well, where there is no one you want to see and as far as you can tell no one who wants to see you and you're isolated in all of Africa so you have to escape to Europe to get any relief from the African-ness of the place). Etc, etc, etc.

Tuesday noon when I returned to the hotel, I found a young American couple, a pastor from a Brethren Church in Pasadena and his wife, stranded at the hotel. Someone had told them they could fly without difficulty from Kampala to tiny Bangui, capital of Central African Republic, as if it were the New York-Chicago run. They had gone to Stan, from Stan to Coq. Didn't speak French and were surprised that no one at Coq's hotel spoke English.

The contrast they provided made me realize how much I have adapted to Coq. I'm continually grateful for how good the hotel is, for the fact that we do have one restaurant and a decent one at that.

DCCM put them up and delivered them to the Air Congo bus yesterday morning. I went to the airport, thinking they'd need somebody who spoke French if the plane was really crowded. It wasn't and they got off without difficulty. Innocents abroad!

Although her husband was suddenly called away by his father's illness, Mme André gave a previously scheduled dinner party in his absence for Boudart, Dr Michejda (whose wife was out of town), Favosch, a planter who ran a number of plantations between Bikoro and Boende, and me. I appreciated her kindness in not canceling the event and in doing us the honor of wearing an attractive party dress. Her guests did not necessarily return the compliment. Boudart, robust and earthy as always, appeared in the same sport shirt and sandals he always wore.

We discussed race relations. The planter opined that the intellectual difference between blacks and whites was proved by the fact that after a century of American efforts, US blacks lacked a role proportionate to their numbers in the leadership of the country. "I think you may exaggerate our efforts to develop our blacks," I said.

Mme André remarked, "There's an honest man."

Turning to the Congo, Boudart insisted that Belgian authorities had never practiced discrimination against the Congolese. Rather there had been anti-white discrimination. The planter agreed. The *metropole*'s stereotype of the *colon*, he said, pictured him as a ruthless exploiter with a black girl in his bed, a phonograph playing on the table, a bottle of whiskey beside it. Boudart added, "And an African waving a fan." The planter said that he had lived in the forest for nine months, moving about with a caravan of porters. Boudart declared that when he first arrived, he had hauled water twenty kilometers every day.

Mme André once again turned on her Piaf tapes and sang along, *"Dansez, Milord! Dansez!"*

The next day Michejda had the three single men to lunch. Boudart arrived in the usual shirt, sandals and shorts. He looked about the house, asked if there were women around and immediately stripped to the waist. While we awaited lunch, Boudart considered me in a manner I was never fully able to fathom. Did he think me naïve and untested, but having potential? Therefore he would give me help in understanding the Congo. Or did he regard my naiveté (which I readily acknowledged) and my abstinences as fit for jokes and teasing?

He looked at me now and said, "When you came to my house"—I had gone there to discuss the alterations his firm would undertake at the center—"I was careful to hide the African girl who takes care of me. You know what I mean."

"Oh, yeah?" I said, already a little uncertain as to where this was headed.

"Anne-Marie. Shall I send her around?"

The offer may have been on the level. "How does a guy get laid around here?" was an entirely appropriate question in this company. But not for me. I did not want to deal with venereal disease in this place.

"Go ahead and send her," said Michejda. "It's not easy to meet girls in the Congo."

They waited for my answer. I did not want to seem prissy. It was bad enough that I didn't smoke or drink. "No, thanks," I said. I wished for the world that this sort of thing did not embarrass me. My embarrassment was obvious.

So the offer immediately became a joke.

"She's very accomplished," said Boudart, a gleam in his eye.

Michejda caught the gleam and joined the fun. "I can attest to that," he claimed. "I have her when my wife is gone."

"Anne-Marie's happy with Congo francs," Boudart said. "So she's both very good and very cheap."

"*Vive Anne-Marie*! I had her the other night," Michejda said. "Then I sent her on to a friend. We could send her on to you."

I laughed. So did the planter. *Vive Anne-Marie!*

Michejda and Boudart began to describe her specialties, laughing to one another and the Belgian planter, who surely had his woman, and laughing at me. My French gave out at this point, but hand gestures and pantomime made things clear. I was amused, baffled, and embarrassed, all at once.

The talk turned again to the *metropole's* misunderstanding of the colony and the *colons* and the mess that had been made of Congolese independence. I did not participate much in this conversation, but I enjoyed the fact that it was intelligent talk, very good practice for my French, and that my eye was sought as the arguments bounced back and forth.

On a brutally warm day about this time I put on a long-sleeved shirt with cufflinks and, as Coq's official American, went to the cathedral. Governor Engulu was marrying the sixteen-year-old, said around town to have been found for him by nuns in a girls' school, this after three other candidates had failed their probationary periods. The couple had had a "probationary marriage" for several months. The bride got along well with the Governor's six children. The ceremony was the sanctification of their vows.

A reception took place on the lawn of the governor's residence. A lasting impression: a large woman, a guest, dressed in mammy cloth, a bodice and an elaborate head scarf, palavering with men, shaking hands with passersby and drinking beer straight from a quart bottle. Soon empty beer bottles littered the yard. No fights had started by the time I left.

My personal effects arrived. Delighted to see almost forgotten clothes and books again, I had a strange and unexpected feeling of melancholy in unpacking them. I seemed to be dismantling my very happy Brussels life from boxes and trying to reassemble it in an atmosphere entirely foreign to it. I found myself wondering who I was and how I'd arrived at this unlikely place.

Perhaps it was this succession of things: general crankiness, Mme André singing to *Milord*, the offer of Anne-Marie, the governor's wedding, the nostalgia evoked by the arrival of my Brussels life. . . . Perhaps it was these that sent me to the typewriter to write:

Coquilhatville, Republic of the Congo
January 21, 1964

Dear Mrs. P_____,

Having been asked to forward periodic letters from Africa all fall, I suppose it seems strange, doesn't it, to get one addressed to you personally? Although we have never met, I suppose you know that I am the man who saw a great deal of Penny in Brussels and fell in love with her there.

Of course, I don't know how much of that story you already know. I did fall in love—I think we both did—and a number of times we seriously discussed the possibility of our marrying. Naturally I knew about Chris W_____, as he had some idea of me, and I knew that when Penny returned to the States she would have to make some decision about us. Intellectually there always seemed many reasons why she should decide for Chris, but it was difficult to believe emotionally since our falling in love had happened so naturally, harmoniously, right-ly. We got along so well together and had such fun and shared similar values and interests. Penny made me happy in giving myself. She brought me a kind of aliveness I hadn't felt for a long time.

I said that we had discussed the possibility of marriage. When we were at the train together in Paris, just before Penny left for the boat, I told her definitely I wanted us to marry.

Please believe me when I tell you that I wish Penny every happiness and that I want to cause no problems. I have been writing her this past fall because I've wanted her to continue to realize that I still love her and still feel we could make a happy and useful life together. She hasn't answered any of these letters, and I haven't expected her to. Still I'd like to keep some reminder before her—as long as she isn't married.

She said there was a good possibility that, if she chose for Chris, she would marry him by Christmas. After arriving in Africa, I decided to write her occasionally to roar at my fate. If all seemed lost, what more could one lose? Since I had no way of knowing anything except from her, I asked her to send me a wedding announcement when she married. It's late January now, and none has come.

It seems to me too bad that we never met. Penny always said we would get along well and felt certain you'd approve of me as a son-in-law. So I'm going to ask you a favor in the name of the friendship we might have had. Would you be so kind as to drop me a note telling me a couple of things? Has Penny married? If not, do she and Chris intend to marry during spring vacation or at the end of the school year in June? Is she still completely certain that Chris is the man? If not, I'd like to see her and can arrange that without difficulty. And if she has not married and you think my continuing to write her not harmful, could you give me her address in New York?

In closing, let me again assure you of my very best intentions and hopes for Penny. But perhaps you can understand how much I would like to know whether or not she has married.

At the end of January news reached Coq about very disturbing events in Kwilu, a region to the south of us, due east of Léopoldville, and in Lisala, to the north. I kept a record of these happenings, but was careful not to mention them in my letters to my family.

Notes from All Over: Killings in Kwilu and Lisala—1/29/64

At the end of last week, press and radio reported the murder of three Catholic (Flemish) priests in Kwilu. After burying the priests about ten nuns made their way to safety in Kikwit, the provincial capital. Two groups of American missionaries were helicopter-rescued by the UN from the same part of the province after their mission stations were burned. Ron Sallade told me yesterday that the Kwilu death toll had reached eight or nine, all Catholic missionaries, possibly one Protestant. He says a number of Protestant stations have been evacuated.

Trouble seems to have a political base. A Gizenga lieutenant named Muléle, I believe, has been terrorizing the area as a means of bringing some kind of leverage against the provincial regime. And perhaps the Catholics are still associated (in the Gizengist mind) with the Belgian colonial rule, and the Americans with the present Congolese regime.

Reports also come that Europeans have been killed in the last day or two at Lisala, just a day and a half or two days' boat-travel up the river from us. Some dissident group has taken control of the airport radio tower, Lisala's only outside communication link, and no news is coming from the town.

Ron and I drove out to the airport (just for a drive) and he felt Europeans here have to rely on the good will of their African contacts because the police are incapable of offering protection. We both wondered what will happen when the UN troops pull out of this place.

Notes from All Over: Kwilu—1/30/64

From all reports the situation is worsening in Kwilu. Bands of young men are wandering around the countryside spreading an as yet un-checked reign of political terror. Death toll is said to stand at 150 persons. According to Roger Raeys, at least one American missionary, a woman, has been killed, shot in the "face" with an arrow. Her missionary room-mate was wounded in the arm. He reported this as happening at 2:00 AM. Another US missionary woman reportedly maimed, her hands cut off.

Many of the dead in Kwilu are said to have been government workers. Political opposition is attempting to incapacitate provincial government by exterminating those who make it function.

One evening I drove out to Bolenge in a downpour to show USIS films in the auditorium of the DCCM secondary school. Afterwards I went to Faith McCracken's cottage to play Hearts with her and two missionary teachers.

At 9:50 the lights dimmed, warning of the generator's shutdown. Faith brought out kerosene lamps, soft drinks bottled in Léo and pep-permints sent by her living link church in Iowa. The rain stopped, leaving the air cool and heavy with moisture.

Faith showed me an article entitled "Bows and Arrows" in the *Congo Mission News.* Written by an American Protestant missionary, the ar-ticle described the first youth band attack against a mission in Kwilu. Early one morning, the writer reported, he and a colleague were called to a nearby Catholic mission. Arriving, they found three Belgian priests murdered. I read the description of the bodies: "Faces and bodies dis-figured by gashes, legs broken, fingers and hands hacked off, probably to be dried, cured and eaten at witchcraft ceremonies."

I watched a teacher roll peppermints in her fingers. Another drummed her thumbs against the table. Watching them, I kept won-dering if the reports were accurate. Eating cured fingers: it did not seem real.

As other reports came in, it seemed as if there were unrest through-out the country. It grew as the time for promised elections approached. Neither the DCCM's Gary Farmer nor I thought it certain that the elec-tions would actually take place. If they did, rumors warned of troubles in Coq. Soon the elections were cancelled.

We wondered: if there were trouble, would the ANC or police pro-vide effective protection for Coq's inhabitants? The real danger for Europeans lay in the troubles taking an anti-European turn, always a possibility. If there were incidents, could we cope with them? At that time the ineffectiveness, not to say absence, of communication facilities would increase our danger. What about evacuation? If necessary, could we escape?

Then the letter I had been waiting for came from Penny's mother:

January 26, 1964

Dear Fred,

I am glad that you have given me a chance to write to you. I've wanted to every time I forwarded a letter from you to Penny in New York. Fear of intruding myself into a delicate situation kept me from acting.

I'm sorry—sorry is such a meek word—to have to tell you that while Penny is still not married, plans to do so are going steadily forward. We have not as yet announced the engagement publicly, but unless something happens, that will be done at spring vacation time, and the wedding is set for June 20.

The answer to your third question—is Penny still completely certain that Chris is the man—only Penny can answer. My inmost feeling is that she is not, but is being carried forward by the machinery of her surroundings.

Perhaps this idea is only wishful thinking on my part. Penny has always been trusting and giving. She is being handled by an expert. I am as sure as I have ever been of anything that this marriage will be a mistake, but when in desperation, I spoke out about the feelings of both her father and myself, I'm afraid I accomplished nothing but lining up Penny defensively on Chris's side, and now there is a barrier between her and us that there never was before. We don't talk easily any more.

Among other things, I have said to Penny that when we marry we seek a partner, not a child to take care of; we have children for that. Has Penny told you of her pets—even the turtles—and the care she lavished on them?

I think I'd better not say any more. Perhaps you already have talked to Penny in New York? A long distance operator called here for her Friday. I had a strong hunch it might be you.

She gave me Penny's New York phone number and her address. Her letter closed:

Need I add, "Good Luck to you!"? Yes! write to her.
Clue: Penny needs to be needed.

What was I to do about this? My mother was urging me to continue my pursuit. Her mother was urging the same. The Lady Herself was silent. Being of a romantic bent, I decided that I must go see her. On the long afternoons as I sat idle in the center, I spun scenarios about a prospective trip. Perhaps I would just turn up in New York. Penny would sense my presence and start looking for me. She would see me and I'd feign surprise. And. . . . And. . . .

Or: I would go. My journeying half way around the world to see her would serve as proof of my commitment. I would take her in my arms. The music would rise to crescendo. She would forget The Other Guy. And. . . . And. . . .

The scenarios might work as romantic comedy. That's what my play was: two charming, off-beat people living in the history exhibits in New York's Metropolitan Museum and falling in love.

But this was something like real life. I kept wondering if I had the stuff to actually go see her. I did write her that I was coming.

Poor Penny! Here she was in what should have been a euphoric time in her life: the months before she got married. She and her fiancé were away from their families in New York. And here was this lovesick, very lonely jerk in the remotest part of the dreadful Congo, pestering her, determined to interrupt this happy time to offer her what? A chance to join him in the pisshole of the Congo's Equateur where unrest was flourishing. I really was a romantic!

I received the first letter she had written me since breaking off our relationship. Come if you must, she said. But she would see me only in the presence of The Other Man. As her mother wrote, she was being handled by an expert.

The letter was not friendly. I wondered if He looked over her shoulder while she wrote it. Or did they write it together? It said that she would see me only in His presence. I wondered if that would really happen. I examined the possibilities every which way. I decided the prospects of success were not high. I thought about the savings that might be wasted, the vacation time thrown away. Even in the best of circumstances, afterwards I would be here, she would be there and so would He.

I gave it up.

I was furious with myself. The characters in my play could say, "You've got to dare in life," but I lacked the stuff to dare. I felt a little depressed at how small and predictable I was: that in the end I chose to save my money, my bird in the bush, in preference to pursuing happiness.

SIX

As the weeks passed, progress at the center became more evident. Boudart's construction workers, supervised by a M Gaufin, were removing walls in the building and creating a theater for film shows and lectures. They constructed the projection booth on the exterior of the building. Since it would permit the use of two projectors successively, there would be no down time while reels were changed. André installed the electrical equipment the theater needed. Boudart's men also began to lay linoleum tile throughout the building. Gaufin's leaving for several months of off-time in Europe put a deadline on these efforts.

I had been trying to get Mâitre Herman to paint the roof of the center building. He was agreeable to its being painted. USIS ordered paint for the job. But the embassy took the position that Herman should pay for the work and the paint. He balked at that. When finally he agreed, he discovered that the paint ordered by USIS had been sold. He took a sharp tone with me about the possibility that he would have to pay hard currency to bring paint into the country. He was irritated when I told him that, having tried to make arrangements that would please him, I did not consider the situation our fault. He seemed to like me no more than I liked him.

Just as Boudart had returned after six months away, allowing his partner DeLinte to leave, so M Ancion returned. He brought good news, having decided that the hotel should resume offering *petit dejeuner* to its residents. Ancion and the wife much younger than he resumed their marriage. Now that Madame's husband had returned, M Gérard, the father of her son, soon departed.

With the likelihood that I would move into their house in early March, I began to spend more time with the Andrés. They wished not to let *le tout Coq* know of our plan until it was set. We met one afternoon at their home to discuss the lease that the embassy had proposed. Its clauses were very favorable to the embassy. The Andrés suggested changes. I assumed that embassy bureaucrats would be inflexible on some issues, accommodative on others. My goal, of course, was to get out of the hotel and into my own place.

I discovered that Mme André was a hobby painter. If she was not markedly accomplished, oil painting gave her quiet time away from her family and worries about their future. It helped her see beauty around her. Since I was writing a play—although I discussed that fact with no one outside my family—Mme André and I had a shared interest in things artistic. André himself showed no interest in her painting.

One Thursday afternoon she and I went together to see an exposition of paintings by an Italian UN doctor. They were representational, though highly abstracted, depictions of the Congo and its life, done generally in somber colors.

Part of a letter about that outing commented:

One could not help being struck by the violence of the paintings. They seemed a very true portrayal of what is here now, and I was interested in how thoroughly my mind rejected all of it. The violence is everywhere here, and yet you live with it so closely every day that you no longer consider it until something like these paintings throws it at you.

The curious thing about the exhibit is that the doctor couldn't be a milder, kinder person. The color, movement, rhythm, even the application of the paint: all of it was violent. You look at the fellow and wonder where it all comes from—or marvel at the control he has over it and his channel for getting rid of it. Mme André says he sometimes breaks brushes, sometimes even applies the paint with his hands. Hmm. Such a meek fellow.

How very pleasant to go to an art show, to assess the work close-up and far away, my head tilting this way and that, and then to discuss the strengths and weaknesses, all with a woman friend.

It occurred to me that if the Andrés truly intended to start life again in Australia, they would need to learn some English. When André returned from his trip to Belgium—his father had died—I suggested that I could give them English lessons. Mme André delightedly embraced the idea. André seemed less enthusiastic. He had a lot on his mind. He was often exhausted at the end of the day and his commitment to removing to Australia was sometimes strong, sometimes wavering.

Even so we began to meet weekly. I would join the family for dinner. After the children went to bed, we would have an informal lesson. At the end of the lesson we drank tea together.

One evening arriving at the Andrés, I discovered that Boudart was joining us for dinner. Since Boudart exacerbated André's underlying tension, this news surprised me. It turned out that after dinner the two men were going to a special meeting of the Lions Club, an organization of Belgian *ex-colons* that strengthened their bonds. At the meeting the members would draft a report about *le pillage* for the Belgian Embassy.

I knew about the Lions Club. At André's instigation I had given a short talk there. At that meeting my stumbling, heavily accented French undoubtedly persuaded the Lions that this fellow could not possibly be a CIA spy, but was truly opening an improbable cultural center. The event convinced me that the club importantly kept the men's bonds strong.

Boudart appeared in the shirt, the work shorts and the sandals. As usual André wore his after-work outfit: white dress shorts, a white short-sleeved shirt and white knee sox. As we sat drinking, Boudart asked, "Why has Herman insisted on this meeting? A report will do no good now. That's all water over the dam."

André's eyes narrowed. He was certain that Boudart had bribed LeBaud not to inspect his stores. He regarded this as a betrayal of *ex-colons* and their values. It infuriated him.

"We're stuck with LeBaud & Co," Boudart continued. "If they enter your store with guns, you have to let them take what they want."

André bristled. Boudart shrugged.

"One week they rob you," Boudart said. "The next they give you a contract for work. So you rob them. Why run to Belgian officials?"

André shot a glance at his wife. She answered with a slight smile.

"Those officials gave the country away in the first place," Boudart said. "Handed it over to that criminal Lumumba. No use running to them."

Mme André went to call the children to dinner.

"We only have one defense," continued Boudart. He leaned forward, totally absorbed. "Exploit the black, manipulate him—"

"I do not manipulate," said André.

His wife called us to the table.

That lesson was the first one André missed. I wondered if we would be stopping them. But we continued, although often André's thoughts drew him to matters of more immediate concern. At tea-time he was usually too tired to continue. He would excuse himself, sometimes going into the office that adjoined the living room, sometimes retiring upstairs, leaving his wife and me to the part of the evening we most enjoyed. Because André was so distracted, because I spent so much of my time alone, she and I both needed someone to talk to.

One evening Boudart invited some guests for a *moambe* (chicken, rice, manioc greens, palm nut sauce, all garnished with a pepper sauce of liquid fire called pili-pili). The guests included the usual group: the Andrés and the Michejdas with me included as a member of the Andrés' group and now a Boudart client. There was also a visitor to Coq, a M Guillaume, the regional secretary of an organization of Congo and Belgian business firms. The *moambe* was delicious, though probably not prepared by Boudart's friend Anne-Marie. The occasion gave me a chance to assess the colonial polar opposites, André and Boudart.

The Andrés arrived late. After greeting the group of us, André hardly spoke. I had seen him withdrawn at his own home. Usually he maintained appearances outside it. A light whiskey revived him, then he began to nod. He did not speak at all during dinner.

Afterwards we sat around a kidney-shaped coffee table and talked late into the night as the table became ever more weighted with coffee cups, water, liquor and fruit juice glasses, an orange juice maker and ash trays burdened with cigarette butts.

Boudart and Michejda were great talkers. Sometimes André discussed topics with an intensity designed to squeeze the juice out of them, though not this evening. In this company all I had to do was sit back and ask the proper questions. Then off they went. Boudart put on some 45s of music popular the previous year in Belgium. When she tired of the men shouting at one another, Mme André would lean back and sing.

There was more teasing of me about Anne-Marie: her prowess, her abandon, her willingness to accept Congo francs. Michejda kidded his wife about patronizing her when she was away. When Boudart returned after leaving the room, he said he had asked Anne-Marie to be patient.

When I returned after making a stop, Boudart inquired me, "Did you find her?"

"She must have gone to her village," I said.

"She's in the armoire," said Boudart. "She's afraid of white women."

Shouting against Michejda to keep the floor, Boudart told about one of Anne-Marie's clients who wanted to make love in the Cossack style. This involved jumping onto her from a height, only his aim was bad and he broke his leg.

I found this a little ribald in front of the ladies, especially after having spent such a pleasant afternoon at the exhibition with Mme André. I noticed, too, that André was saying nothing. I had never seen him so silent. Now he sat, staring at the floor, as if he were not part of the group.

My letter reporting this evening said:

M André is having a particularly bad time of it just now, what with his father's death, being fined at gunpoint, and deciding to leave Coq. The contrast between him and Boudart couldn't be more pronounced. André's nervous, restless, yet unable to focus his energies. He's idealistic to a fault, and the realities of Congolese life now (the disintegration, the lack of law and order, the exploitation) are making it more and more impossible for him to stay here. Something is eating away inside the man, and it's difficult for his friends and acquaintances to watch. After he and his wife left the other night (around 10:30 which was quite early for a bunch that chatted non-stop till 12:30), Michejda and Guillaume commented on André. Michejda mentioned his forthrightness, his honesty, his inability to act in any manner except the direct one.

As the party was breaking up, Boudart invited me to lunch the next day to finish up the *moambe*.

I arrived *chez Boudart* before he did. Soon afterwards robust, crafty, thoroughly vulgar, he strode into his house in his typical garb. He ripped the shirt off as soon as he entered and did not put it on again until he went back to his car. He ate holding his fork in his clenched fist as if it were a stick and thumbed clumps of food onto it. All in all, he was a kind of life force. I quite liked him—I found rascals fascinating—but I was rather sure I did not trust him.

I trusted André. Probably I idealized him, seeing him as somehow heroic, wrestling with a fate that was crushing him. André, his wife and their four children were the brick and mortar from which a society could be built. Yet how could they stay? The kids would soon need an education that could not be found in Coq. It was possible that the tensions of the times were seriously damaging Yves psychologically; his parents seemed to treat him as if he were a special case. If they left the Congo, they would need the hard currency my rent provided.

I suspected that I assessed André from a privileged position. I doubted that the Andrés had told even these, their closest friends in Coq, that they had decided to pull out. The friends seemed to feel that André's investment in the place chained him to it. The friends thought he was suffering only from the strain on his bruised idealism. By contrast, I knew that he was facing the worries of how to extricate himself and his investment, where and how to start over, wondering probably if he would be able to begin again. The people who came to the Congo and carved something out of nothing had worked *hard*. He had to be wondering if he could do it again.

Boudart and I discussed André as we finished off the *moambe*. Boudart felt that the Congo was no longer a country where one could act directly, forthrightly. He struck me as basically too kind (in a rather tough, cruel way) to scorn André for his failure to adapt to the now-reality of Congo living. Boudart considered direct action something one could employ only from a position of power that Belgian *ex-colons* no longer possessed. I wondered if André had a bourgeois mentality, more Belgian than he might want to admit. That mentality was certainly not the sort of thing that worked any longer in the Congo.

Boudart was a distinct contrast. In reference to a Clark Gable Western shown recently at the UN Club, Boudart said that existence in the mythic Far West was the sort of life he had always wanted to live. There a man was truly free, surviving by his wit and his muscle. Ah, the times of the bandits and the sheriffs!

Boudart certainly loved the opportunities the Congo provided to manipulate his circumstances. At lunch he explained his racial theories in terms of geometry. Axiom 1: There was a difference between the Congolese and the European. Therefore, Axiom 2: One must be stronger than the other. And, therefore, Axiom 3: One must be more intelligent than the other. Boudart considered himself more intelligent because he'd been to school, had learned how to think, and knew some basic psychology.

Before independence, he said, he was stronger because the country was ruled by whites, by white law (if not necessarily for whites). Now he considered himself less strong than the Congolese who was running his own government with enough disregard of white law to render the law of no protection to a white man.

Thus, Boudart felt, the question of surviving had become: Can I be stronger in my weakness through the use of my intelligence than the Congolese is strong through the use of his strength? When the Belgians had both strength and intelligence over the Congolese, it was possible to be direct, idealistic, moral. In other words, like André. Now, that was indulgence. So claimed Boudart.

He pointed to *le pillage* as an example of a situation in which the weak man had to use his intelligence. He had delighted in matching wits with Internal Affairs Minister Gaston LeBaud. That was something André would never have thought of doing. LeBaud was crafty, Boudart said—*le pillage* was an expression of that craftiness—so LeBaud's opponent had to be crafty, too.

The morning the provincial authorities closed all the stores in town at 7:30, Boudart said, he went to see LeBaud at 9:00. "*Monsieur le Ministre*," he claimed he had said, "I know there is going to be a systematic search of all the stores and warehouses. Could you please come to my stores and warehouses first? I have a great deal of work to do and would like to take advantage of the time the stores are closed."

"I did this," he told me, "because if they were going to come anyway, they would find what I had. Taking the initiative gave me room to maneuver."

LeBaud did not visit Delinte & Boudart that morning. Boudart visited him again that afternoon and repeated his request. Then, he said, LeBaud asked him, "Don't you have goods hidden?"

"Oh, yes," Boudart said he answered. "I have things hidden." He listed a number of scarce materials that LeBaud wanted for a couple of houses he was remodeling. LeBaud thought for a moment, then suggested, "*Cachez les bien*" (Hide them well). As it worked out, the Vigilance Committee never visited DeLinte & Boudart.

That, at least, was the way Boudart told the story. His intelligence and knowledge of psychology enabled him to manipulate the situation so that LeBaud himself made the decision that benefited Boudart. Nothing dishonest in that, he felt. Whatever André thought, Boudart could not have bribed LeBaud because LeBaud could take whatever money he wanted from him openly, in fines.

Boudart was crafty and amoral, with a hardness that his Africans understood. Within his own rules, he played fair. But if you stole from him, don't get caught. A hard-working guy, he described D&B's pre-independence hours as 6:00-12:00, 2:00-6:00; 8:00-12;00.

In a survival-of-the-fittest part of the world. Boudart was pleased that he possessed good survival instincts. In contrast to André. At the previous night's party, Boudart claimed, André had eaten no dinner. Was it true? I hadn't noticed. Poor André! He was dealing with a lot!

I had the non-rascal's fascination with rascality. So it was easy to suppose that Boudart had everything figured out. Take sex, for example. Congolese could make love all night, he said. But not Europeans. That's why it was all right to send the mythical Anne-Marie—was she myth?—on to another man after he had finished with her. She was still up for more.

Take history. "History is a meat grinder," Boudart told me. "One turn of the handle the Belgians grind up the Congolese." That was colonialism. "Next turn of the handle, the Congolese grind up the Belgians." That was now, national independence. At the next turn of the handle—Mobutu—Congolese would grind up Congolese, but that was still to come.

If it was refreshing to have lunch with Boudart and receive a non-stop explanation of his approach to life in the Congo, still I was rooting for André. How could I not root for him? My acquaintance with the Andrés had saved me from excruciating loneliness! I was also rooting for my values because André was much closer to those values than Boudart would ever be.

So it was a little unnerving to wonder occasionally if, despite the flexibility of Boudart's honesty, he might in the long run be the more honest of the two men. I was watching André's values under extreme pressure. His approach to surviving in the Congo seemed so rigid, so exacting, and so dependent on the support of law and order that it could not stand up under the strains of this place at this time.

Occasionally I remembered his first coming to me during *le pillage* to offer me the house. That there was liquor on his breath had struck me forcefully at the time as perhaps a dishonest path to a decision. I remembered the betrayer's look in his eyes as his charmingly innocent daughter showed me where she slept, which bed was hers. And I recalled the time I went to André's office, knocked, and was mysteriously allowed to enter. A Bolenge missionary was inside buying four portable radios. The transaction was so secret that it must have been clandestine. I felt there was something compromised in this clandestineness.

Or did I wonder if he were compromised because I was the one who was rigid, exacting and so dependent on a system of order that I was having trouble with the strains of this place at this time?

SEVEN

THE WEEKS PASSED. The hottest season of the year settled on Coq. My letters complained of *"the days' awful sameness, the heat, the boredom, the loneliness."* Still, things slowly improved. Boudart's men completed tiling the floor of the center with linoleum. The roof was painted at last with Herman bearing the cost. André erected letters on the roof that spelled out CENTRE CULTURAL AMERICAIN.

As the weekly English lesson evenings continued at the Andrés, I became better acquainted with the family. Mme André showed me her paintings. They were oils, depicting the landscapes outside Coq and scenes of the river: the sky and water lightly blue, the plant life vibrant and sparkling, with distant piroguemen bending to their oars. "That is the Congo I carry inside me," she said. "The river is calm and blue, the sun shining, the Congolese happy at their work." She tilted her head to and fro as we examined the paintings. "The piroguemen are singing," she said.

"Yes. I can hear their voices faintly across the water."

I also got to know the children. The oldest was Yves, twelve, dark, thin and intense like his father. The upheavals of independence with the first violence occurring in Coq had damaged Yves, so his parents thought, to the extent that they would hold him back in school when the academic year began. By contrast, the blond and steady Benoit, eleven, would go off to Belgium for his education. Yves would join Jean-Luc, nine and also blond, at a school in Léopoldville. Yves always referred to this school as "being sent to China" because he was sure the diet would consist mainly of rice. Martine, *gamine* and six, would remain at home. Her educational talent, quite valuable to me, was to giggle at my mistakes in French and correct them. I was grateful for the tutelage and thought her a fine instructor. Her impudence horrified her mother.

In witnessing the family's interaction, I thought André too often treated his wife abruptly, correcting her or laying down the law. In the marriage I had most closely observed, my parents', that never happened.

I learned respect for women from my father. I assumed European marriages were simply different, the husbands dominating, the wives accepting this situation.

André could also be stern with his children. I knew about his locking Yves in his room during the uncertainties after independence. One evening some disobedience by Martine got under André's skin. At dinner the children were silent, their heads lowered. They ignored Mme André's attempts to lighten the atmosphere with laughter and teasing.

Shortly after the meal began, André laid down his fork and stared at his daughter. "We must learn to obey, Martinette," he said. "It is to make your life easier that we insist." Martine stopped eating and stared at her plate. "*N'est-ce pas, ma petite?*"

"*Oui, Papa.*" Martine whispered.

"It is not easy to insist," André persisted earnestly, trying to smile at the lowered heads. "We do not want to spank you. We do not want to make you cry. But you *must* obey." His voice went severe again. "*N'est-ce pas, Martine?*"

She nodded, but would not look at him. André repeated the question more softly, as if imploring her to look at him. Martine raised her head, her eyes moist and blinking. "*Oui, Papa,*" she said, trying to smile.

"*N'est-ce pas, Yves?*"

"*Oui, Papa.*"

"*N'est-ce pas, Jean-Luc?*"

"*Oui, Papa.*"

"You know this, don't you, Benoit."

"*Oui, Papa,*" the steady Benoit answered timidly.

"Now who wants more fried potatoes?" asked Mme André gaily. "Yves, *mon petit,* how about you?"

But Madame's cheeriness did not lighten the mood. André kept on badgering the children. As soon as the meal was over, they ran outside.

"That is not necessary," Madame said after they had gone. "It only frightens them."

"They must learn to obey. You know how things are." He was referring to the unrest to the south of us that was spreading east across the country.

"Do you want them insulting Congolese again?"

"I must know they will obey!" André said excitedly, raising his voice. "What if there's an emergency? I must know they will obey!" He stalked away from the table.

As a frequent visitor at the Andrés, an observer of how the family worked, I wondered more and more about their earlier lives. I had heard André speak about living in the back of a pickup truck. Had he ventured out to Africa alone? Then how had he come to marry? I concocted scenarios in which he returned to Namur where his family lived and. . . What? Had the family lined up young women who might be willing to take a chance on both him and the Congo?

One evening as we sipped tea after playing at an English lesson—André had gone to his office—I mentioned bureaucratic problems with Léopoldville. "Ah, the teeming capital!" Madame said derisively, her eyes flashing. "We spent our first year there."

"How did you come out here anyway?"

"We were refugees from postwar Europe," she said. "After the improvisations and uncertainties of the war, that difficult time, the old ways were stiffening again. Like rigor mortis. We wanted to escape." She measured my expression. "It was so difficult after what we'd known during the war."

She and André had both grown up during the German occupation, she explained. She had lost her father at the beginning of the war and her mother at the end of it. In their mid-teens, she and her brother found themselves orphans. "That was a period of struggle." She shrugged as if she had no desire to recall it. "For all of us. Jules grew up tinkering with electricity. During the occupation he ran messages for the *maquis*."

"Wasn't that dangerous?"

"Of course!" She shrugged again. "Neighbors gave my brother and me help. We survived." Her eyes brightened and an ironic smile slid across her lips. "We had well-to-do relatives who offered counsel, so much counsel—'Try this, Thérèse! Do this!'—but they never really helped us."

André had been a friend of her brother. Together they shared a yearning to flee postwar Belgium with its cramped perspectives, bourgeois patterns, and the hypocrisy of her relatives. They dreamed of Africa. Immediately after marrying they left for the Congo.

"Jules had a three-year contract with Otraco. Léo. . . ." Again the ironic smile. "What a dreadful place! Longtime *colons* belittled us because we hadn't spent the war there. It was too much Belgium, not enough Africa."

Eventually Otraco transferred André to Coquilhatville. They liked the interior immediately. Because all sorts of building was going on, they decided to open an electrical installation business. "Our friends said we were crazy."

"You had some capital then."

"The decision to try. That was the capital. Not so very much to lose. Except there were three children then." She sipped her tea and stared into the cup. "Jules thought it would be cheaper and easier on the children if I returned to Belgium. He stayed. Lived in the back of his pickup for a time. Later he worked in exchange for lodging."

When she and the children returned, the family lived in a government guesthouse: two rooms with thick earthen walls and outside plumbing. "We made our furniture from crates," Madame said, her eyes glazing over with memory. "We slept in beds cast off from the hospital."

I stared at her with a kind of wonder.

"It was fun!" she insisted brightly. "Before long Jules had sixty employees and jobs throughout the Equateur. We worked full days and built the house I expected to live in for the rest of my days."

I got a glimpse of how astonishing to the people trying to make something of the Congo had been Brussels' decision to abandon it.

"Those were good days," she said. "Yet already I've lived almost three of the intervening years in Belgium. And where will we be next year?"

Military radio guys arrived from the embassy to install a single side band radio in the center. After Dean Claussen's medical emergency, the embassy determined that all posts should have some kind of radio communication. Nothing was ever said to suggest that the radio was a precaution of any kind. The Claussen emergency had happened months before. But now there were pockets of unrest across the country: Kwilu south of us, the Kivu on the country's eastern border, the secession in Katanga still not resolved.

The radio guys erected the necessary antenna in less than three hours. They showed me how to tune the mechanism for optimum reception and how to broadcast on it. Happy to be less isolated for whatever reason, I was soon checking into the embassy network with all outlying posts Mondays, Wednesdays and Fridays at 9:00 AM

As the center drew ever readier to open for business, Léopoldville sent Coq a Congolese assistant. Iwo Pierre had been working at USIS Léo. A man of the Equateur, a product of DCCM schools, he was clearly a good choice for Coq. But he was also expendable in Léo. I heard that he irritated his bosses. "Too big for his britches" was one complaint. Because Iwo had spent a year as a *stagiaire* at USC, his sense of himself was all wrapped up in having lived in the United States. That undoubtedly convinced him that he was superior to most Congolese.

Probably an aspect of his difficulties at USIS Léo was that, because Iwo spoke some English, lazy Americans, uncertain of their French, gave him instructions in their native language. Sometimes Iwo did not fully understand them. But he could not admit this for fear that it would undercut his position as a man who spoke English. I determined that as much as possible I would speak French with him. This would avoid Léo-style problems. But, of course, my not using English would further erode his facility with it.

When I inquired about Iwo at the DCCM, Gary Farmer said, "Oh, yes! We know him. There was a matter of wife-palaver. Not at all what we wanted from one of our teachers." Apparently Iwo had abandoned the family he'd created for a very young girl, had run off, and married her. "We try to inculcate the sanctity of marriage," Farmer said. He shrugged. "I'll admit: young as she was, she was a real knockout."

One Friday evening Iwo, his child-wife, and their two daughters arrived from Léo. They had had a four-day journey up the river on an Otraco boat, enjoying the luxury of a stateroom, even if it was crowded with luggage. Most Congolese rode on the open decks of barges the boat pushed. Accompanying them on the barges were all their worldly possessions: ducks, pigs, chickens, edible parts of crocodiles, and in addition to personal luggage an incredible mass of dried, smoked fish. Standing outside their stateroom, Iwo and his family could gaze at Congolese life going on below as if a barge were a village. Women washed their children, prepared food on little cookstoves, fetched water directly from the river by dropping buckets tied to long ropes. Men sat around, talking and chewing smoked fish.

When I went to meet Iwo, there was a kerfuffle on the dock. The commanding officer of the Coq battalion, a major, had received word that Mulélistes from Kwilu were attempting to infiltrate the Equateur. They might arrive on this boat. As a result, he had filled the dock with ANC soldiers. I succeeded in bringing my car on the dock only because a soldier at the entry checkpoint mistook me for a missionary and gave me a *laissez-passer*.

Finding space among the crowd at the edge of the dock, I watched the Otraco boat draw slowly toward shore, huge and white in the gathering dusk. Billows of African clouds marched across a purpling sky. People on the dock scanned those on the boat and barges. Those on board watched those of us awaiting them. Everyone chattered, waved, and called in the characteristic African screech.

There was excited anticipation from the two still separated groups, the travelers and the greeters. Women crowded the rails, the dusk-subdued colors of their mammy cloths everywhere. Distant sounds of music wafted across the evening air. The stench of Congolese humanity hung on it. Piles of bananas and the blue metal footlockers every traveler seemed to own crowded the decks. Against the sky I saw the silhouette of a leashed monkey running back and forth on a wire mesh parcel locker.

Suddenly people found their friends. They screamed at each other across the water. The boat moved to only a long broad jump from shore. A guy to my right yakked loudly to his pal on board the boat, all the while urinating into the river. Right in the faces of the travelers. Ah, the Congo!

As the boat tied up, I saw standing at a railing on the cabin deck a solitary Congolese, a man of the elite. He surveyed the bustling passengers below with unhurried regality, wearing a tie and eyeglasses, a shirt with French cuff sleeves and the jewelry of a white man: tie clasp, cuff links, watch and ring. All of them were gold as were the eyeglass frames. All of them glinted in the light of the deck lamp.

I jumped aboard and went up to greet this man. Iwo emerged from his cabin wearing a suit coat. He extended his hand and said, *"Bonsoir, Fred."*

"*Bonsoir, Iwo.* You're finally here! Good!"

Now Madame stepped from the cabin. She was small, quite pretty, and appeared hardly past adolescence. "*Bonsoir, Monsieur,*" she said, offering her hand with a sophistication that merited the cabin deck. Iwo beamed. I was impressed with Madame's poise, delighted that she spoke some French and that the accent was good. Still, she looked too young to be a mother. Now the little daughters appeared, the older one about four. The younger one, possibly a year and a half, Mme Iwo lifted into her arms. I welcomed the entire family to Coq.

Iwo had arrived *à la Congolaise.* He had suitcases, rope-tied bundles and baskets wrapped in mammy cloth, twenty pieces in all. Some of them weighed fifty pounds. Iwo and I struggled these onto the dock and made camp on a stretch of concrete near the warehouses. We loaded half of Iwo's luggage into my car. We posted Mme Iwo and the two little girls as *sentinelles.*

As Iwo and I left the dock in my car, I surrendered the *laissez-passer* mistakenly given me by soldiers guarding the entrance. We quickly stored the first load of luggage at the center, charging Edouard to guard it, and returned to the dock.

When soldiers at the checkpoint saw Iwo in the car with me, they refused to allow the car to enter despite the fact that a white man and a black man in white man's garb were unlikely Mulélistes. Iwo got out to parley with the soldiers in Lingala. I heard the word "*Muléliste*" bandied back and forth. Iwo went off to see the major. He returned with the necessary whatever. We drove onto the dock, loaded Mme Iwo and the girls as well as a bit more of the luggage, soldiers hustling us the entire time.

Iwo said, "I'll see you in the morning."

"Aren't you coming?"

"No. You are allowed to go, but I must stay."

"This is ridiculous!" I said. What would I do with Madame and the children? I was supposed to be playing cards with missionaries.

"If I don't guard the luggage, it will disappear."

"*Allez! Allez!*" shouted the soldiers.

Hardly before I knew it I had driven off the dock.

When I turned toward Mme Iwo in the back seat with her daughters, she clutched the little girls. She was no longer the sophisticated young woman who had so confidently offered her hand on the cabin deck. Now she was a young, terrified teenaged mother, awkward in European clothes. Never before, I supposed, had she been alone with a white man. All the warnings her mother and village aunties had given her about the depravities of white men must have flashed through her mind. I felt certain she wished she were back with her own kind, bedding down on the hard and blissfully safe concrete of the Otraco dock.

When I spoke to her, she could not answer. She had lost her French. Perhaps she possessed hardly more than *"Bonsoir, Monsieur."* I turned back to the wheel, unable to endure the look of fear in her eyes. What to do with her?

I took her and the girls to the Oasis. Most regulars at the restaurant had at one time or another dined Congolese women before taking them to their rooms. Mme Iwo was the first *Congolaise* who had come to the restaurant with me. I might have gotten points for bringing such a beauty, but she was also the first girl-for-the-night ever to drag children along with her. The restaurant regulars grinned at our procession. I nodded to them. I seated my charges, told the waiters to bring them whatever they ordered, and left to find them lodging.

At the Ancion Hotel I implored the receptionist to remove the barlock from the telephone dial. I called M Ancion and explained that I needed lodging for a woman. "I'm sorry, M Oontaire," he said, "we have nothing for an American woman."

"This woman is Congolese."

There was a long silence on the line. He was wondering if I wanted a special room for a dalliance. "But, Monsieur, take her to your room."

"She's my assistant's wife." I explained the situation.

It turned out that Ancion owned another hotel, patronized mainly by Congolese. He gave instructions to a *tata* who gathered bedding and drove with me to a building in the center of town.

While the *tata* prepared the room, I returned to the restaurant. Food had revived Madame's spirits. She was happily chatting with a waiter. However, when I took her and the girls to the hotel and entered the room with her, her spirits sank again. While she steeled herself to be raped in front of her children, I busily—absurdly like a bellhop! —circled the room, flicking light switches on and off, opening closets, and indicating the bathroom.

Leaving the room, I turned back to say that I was glad she and Iwo

had arrived. I saw fear widen her eyes. I could not remember ever terrifying anyone. I reached out my hand in friendship, to assure her that
I was a new kind of white man who meant no harm, who looked to her
husband for help. The extended hand increased her discomfort. She
cringed and pushed against a wall.

"*Bonsoir, Madame,*" I said.

Relief brought back her French. "*Bonsoir, Monsieur.*"

On the threshold outside the room I turned back to smile. The door
closed in my face. I heard the bolt slide home.

Iwo survived his night on the dock. The luggage got all sorted out.
Having Iwo at the center proved to be a great help. I got him working on a card catalog of the English language collection, a tiresome,
clerical task.

USIS Léo authorized me to hire a second local employee. Having two
men on staff would mean that both the library and film activities
would be staffed. Parades of job applicants passed through the center.
I winnowed the likely candidates down to two. The first seemed intelligent and had work experience. But his craven obsequiousness made
me turn away in his presence. The other candidate, named N'Djoku
Pierre, had a pleasant, rather casual carriage and presented himself
well. I was not sure how bright he was, but how bright need he be to
operate film projectors and help patrons check out books? N'Djoku
meant "elephant" in the local language. N'Djoku sometimes signed
his name simply "Elephant." I may have liked the idea of having an
elephant on staff.

I engaged N'Djoku on the condition that he agree to a trial period
of four to six weeks. He seemed flummoxed at filling out the necessary employment application and I wondered if I had made the right
choice. Many Congolese did not know where or when they were born.
But N'Djoku had trouble remembering when he was in school, when
he was in Léopoldville, who exactly were his parents: the couple in the
bush village or the people in Brazzaville.

Only later would I come to understand the Congolese bafflement
with questions and the hesitation to respond to them. This was especially so with N'Djoku. Eventually I learned that his slowness was not
caused by lack of wit, but rather by a process of testing the question

from all possible angles and wondering: What does he want to hear? Which answer will serve me best?

I asked Iwo to sort out the matter of N'Djoku's parentage. He came to a Congolese conclusion: N'Djoku had two sets of parents.

With two assistants on board I opened the center as a reading room. As soon as all the books were catalogued and shelved, the library started functioning. I insisted that every applicant for a library card listen to me explain that books must be returned within two weeks. Then they repeated the rule to me. When the theater was finished, we began to show USIS films every afternoon, a project Iwo took care of. It swelled library usage.

Although I complained of isolation, wanderers in the remotest Congo did occasionally drift through Coquilhatville. Nick Sapieha made me yearn to join him on treks into the deeper Equateur. He was a young American of Polish descent. He aspired to be a National Geographic photographer while officially making an inspection tour of Catholic missions for Catholic Relief Services. The weekend he passed through we did the Coq diversions—a drive and a swim—and I wondered if he were wise to drive into territories full of political unrest. His priest boss had assured him that he could go wherever CRS food went. Also that his religious education had been neglected. The priest advised him to spend three days contemplating death.

One evening four men, obviously Americans, entered the Oasis dining room in black trousers, black shoes and white socks. Hmm. The waiter said they'd been drinking whiskey in the bar. That ruled out missionaries.

I went over to say hello. They were four US Air Force men, two officers, two EMs, crewing the DC-3 President Kennedy had given General Joseph Mobutu. (This was months before Mobutu became the Congo's President, but he was obviously a comer.) Mobutu wanted something grander than a DC-3, but nothing grander was able to land on short airstrips. Since the Congo lacked pilots, Uncle Sam provided the crew. They were staying at the Ancion. We chatted in my room till midnight.

The next day I arranged for them a black market exchange of dollars for Congolese francs. The exchange rate in Coq was 400 Congolese francs per dollar in check form. (In Léo 365 to 1 for cash, 350 to 1 for check; 280 to 1 in Brazzaville dealing through a bank.) I presented my-self and the officers at the back of a Portuguese store where the family lived. As the money and check changed hands, the Portuguese mer-chant, unshaven in a dirty tank top, commented, "It's very hot today." Beads of sweat on his arms glinted in the light. His family watched the officers deal with the bundles of francs.

"Yes, very hot," I agreed.

"I've never known it to be so hot in all my years in the Equateur." The officers counted their money.

"Really? How long have you been here?"

"Eighteen years."

The officers were satisfied with the transaction. We thanked the merchant, nodded to his family, and departed.

Once refueled with bush-cheap Congolese francs, the major and his pals flew off in what may have been the world's best-decorated DC-3. The plane was worth $100,000. Reconditioning it for Mobutu cost twice that much. I returned to the tranquility of trying to operate what may have been the world's least likely American Cultural Center.

The happy day finally arrived when I moved out of the hotel and into the André house. What heaven to have a place of my own!

André worked most days in the office adjacent to the living room. Madame was often in and out. I did not object to having them around. In fact, their company pleased me. They were gone by nightfall and I had the house to myself. The river house where they moved, a bit north of town on the Congo, gave them more space and they soon happily spread into it.

As for me, what a delight to have my own living/dining room! With an adjacent kitchen and a small office nook! And even better to have a bedroom upstairs. I chose the bedroom that overlooked the town square. Down the street outside, I could almost see the center. I read in that room before going to bed. There was air-conditioning downstairs, none in the bedrooms. I slept with all the windows open.

If I had felt lonely and at loose ends at the hotel, I could be cozy all by myself in the André living room. I moved the center's phonograph there. That made an evening of reading even more pleasant. One week-end I ensconced myself in that room and read without interruption a volume that had arrived for the library: the recently published French translation of Ernest Hemingway's posthumous *A Moveable Feast.*

I unloaded the suitcases out of which I had been living since I left Belgium. That seemed a century ago. Like most Foreign Service people in remote posts, I had ordered a crate of food from Denmark, mainly canned goods. It had arrived and I savored the opportunity of arranging cans in the *magasin.* Since I'd gotten a water purifier, I could make myself a cup of instant coffee any time I wanted.

At this time I installed in the house the woman I would live with in the Congo. She came to the center one day in an expensively printed Christmas advertising brochure from Brussels: a Memling Madonna holding a Christ-child on her lap, offering him an apple held delicately between the thumb and index finger of her left hand. I first met this woman at the St. John's Hospital in Bruges. I responded immediately to the special modesty of her eyes. She had a flattish, long-nosed face. Her manner and presence exuded virtue.

Discovering the reproduction of the Madonna in the brochure, I cut it out and mounted it on cardboard. She had been with me in my room at the Ancion Hotel. Now I placed her in the *cabinet de toilette* adjacent to the bedroom where I slept. I saw her first thing in the morning and several other times during the day. She was, in fact, too beautiful and refined for the room she was assigned. The name *Notre Dame de la Toilette* was not as genteel as she deserved, but it was not a genteel country. She resided in the *cabinet* until abruptly I had to leave Coq. She stayed in my personal effects, left the Congo, travelled to California, and is with me as I write.

At the André house I began to cook for myself, an activity that gave me scant pleasure, even after not having a chance to do it for so long a stretch. I washed the vegetables with soap, lathering cabbage leaves, for example, until they squeaked. Marketing proved time-consuming. The baker was good at his trade, but opened only when he felt like it. There was a simple pleasure at the meat market—I bought *haché,* ground meat—because the young woman behind the counter gave me a smile. I realized I needed to find a capable Congolese to take care of household chores.

André found a *sentinelle* for both the house and the work yard/court-yard strewn with refrigerators, air conditioners and other appliances in need of repair. After a night or two on the job, the *sentinelle* moved his family onto the premises. This compromised my privacy. The man's wife rose early in the morning and went about her chores trilling sing-song chants. The *sentinelle* let friends into the courtyard. I looked up one evening from working in the *magasin* to find a young man staring at me through a window. I wondered how long he'd been watching me. A job-seeker, he pushed a paper to the window, a long-ago reference from the DCCM.

Another evening—I was contentedly reading *Roots of Heaven* about elephants in Chad—when a rapping sounded at the courtyard door. I looked up to see a woman, fluttering her fingers flirtatiously and offering pleasures. I waved her off. Eventually I got my needs for privacy worked out with André's for security. And I realized that a lot of Congolese were keeping tabs on me: where I lived, where I worked, the company I kept.

Soon I engaged a servant, called a *boy* in a parlance that must have begun in British colonies. He was Mbuli Joseph, a mature and efficient fellow, pleasant, but by no means obsequious (thank heavens!). He did my marketing and laundry, kept the place clean, arrived early enough to make me an omelet for breakfast and a main midday meal. He left about mid-afternoon and made sure there was a something light for supper.

For months I had accepted hospitality all over town. Now it was possible for me to have a few people in for lunch.

As a result of my moving into their house and of the weekly English lesson evenings, the Andrés and I made a jump into acknowledging friendship. We took fumbling steps toward addressing each other by our given names: Jules, Thérèse and Fred (generally pronounced Fret by Jules). The French language is structured so that it is easy to address acquaintances as Monsieur or Madame. Even people who've known each other for years—people Americans would consider friends—continue this mode of address. As a result, the move to given names became a conscious step, a declaration of friendship. And friendship was not the casual relationship Americans might have. Friendship meant commitment, loyalty.

Thérèse instigated this venture into new territory. She was very attuned to the presence in Coq of foreigners, most of them UN people. Unlike most Belgians she enjoyed reaching out to them. As an American, it struck me as a little strange that we were so gingerly about using given names. Thérèse and I easily adapted; we had a genuine rapport. It always distressed me when Jules would start to call me Monsieur and then realize he should say Fred. But Jules had to deal with many distractions in those days.

I now saw the couple daily at the house since Jules' office was part of the same building. I had dinner *chez André* at least weekly. Often I joined them on Sundays for picnics or outings on the river. With the worries that kept gnawing at Jules, it was useful for Thérèse to have a friend she trusted and could talk to.

One evening as we were having tea after the faux English lesson, there was only the single lamp between us on the table. André had gone upstairs to take a sleeping pill. Everything was quiet, hushed. Thérèse and I could almost hear the eternal Congo sliding past outside.

"Boudart must get lonely out here," I said. A smile moved across Thérèse's lips. "Was there never a Madame Boudart?"

The smile quickly faded from her lips. She watched me across the quiet as if I had asked her to open for me a secret door. Finally she said, "Yes, there was."

"Was there a family?"

Thérèse said finally, "Two daughters."

"He never talks about them?"

Thérèse shrugged.

"Are he and Madame divorced?"

Thérèse shook her head. She looked from me into her cup of tea.

"Did she die?"

Again she shook her head.

"She never comes to the Congo?"

Finally Thérèse looked up. She said, "They all lived here. Perhaps ten years." Thérèse glanced off, as if remembering Mme Boudart. "A beautiful woman."

I waited. There had to be more.

"Then on holiday in Europe he and Madame had an accident. He was driving. She lost an arm and badly injured her head." I nodded. "Plastic surgery restored her face, but it's not *her* face anymore."

Thérèse looked down at her book.

"Has Madame never come back?"

"Boudart returned before she was completely well. They've lived apart ever since."

"He sees them on vacation, right?"

"Mainly he travels. Alone."

We both gazed into our tea. I thought, Poor Boudart! I hoped that there was an Anne-Marie and that she took good care of him.

I finally said, "Sometimes I think the Congo affects him less than anyone. That he's mocking the rest of us."

"That's because he's here so recently," Thérèse replied. "Even less time than you. He returns, laughing and confident. But he's alone too much. He worries, thinks of the past. Pressure builds. It gets a little harder each day. DeLinte comes back earlier every year. You'll see how it plays out."

I felt as if Thérèse had revealed a secret that could only be shared with a trusted friend. I was glad we could be together these evenings. I was sure Thérèse was grateful for a friend to whom she could talk about things her husband would not listen to. For my part it was wonderful to have an attractive woman friend to whom I could open myself and ask for secrets. For me Thérèse represented what was essential for most men: the Female Principle.

Was there an attraction between us? Yes. Were we aware of it? Yes. Was it something either of us would act on? No. Jules understood this. When things grew a great deal more tense, as they eventually did, he would leave Thérèse and me together without concerns about our relationship. That lack of concern was no great compliment to his assessment of my virility. But Thérèse was a good woman. And I was a good boy, immensely grateful for their friendship. It seemed to have saved my life in Coq.

In response to my letters about the Andrés, my mother wrote, noting that one did not repay a friendship by interfering with a marriage. That never happened, and I did not need the caution.

EIGHT

THE SINGLE SIDE BAND RADIO QUICKLY PROVED ITS VALUE. Thanks to it, I learned of the decision to upgrade Congo cultural centers to two-officer posts. A man whom I'll call Tom Madison, a thirteen-year veteran of the USIS Foreign Service, was being rushed from the Philippines to take charge of the center I had almost opened. He had served there two and a half years. I did not regard the assigning of a more senior officer to supervise the Coq operation as indicating dissatisfaction with my work. The upgrades were country-wide. I assumed they were being made because policy tea-leaf readers saw a likelihood that the Congo would fall apart.

I understood immediately that I must have Coq's *Centre Culturel Américain* up and running before Madison set foot in the Equateur. I wanted there to be no question about who had established the post. It was not clear when Madison would arrive. When he did, however, I wanted to make sure he found a fully functioning operation. Achieving this did not require marching orders or a full court press. In fact, the center was almost there with its library loaning and circulating books and the small theater offering film shows every afternoon. USIS publications were circulating in the community.

To my distress there seemed to be animosity between the two Pierres, Iwo and N'Djoku. They were very different: Iwo smarter, ostensibly shrewder, in a more solid position and eager to appear dominant; N'Djoku, presentable, capable of performing learned routines, and just a nice easy-going guy. They hailed from neighboring and apparently unfriendly tribes. Iwo struck me as intent on diminishing N'Djoku. He told me that N'Djoku had submitted a false employment attestation. I was uncertain what to do about that. I hoped it would not blow up into something serious.

The next project for the center, one I was very keen on, was film shows in the hinterland. Coq was a residue of Belgian commerce. The Real Africa lay out beyond it. I wanted to have explored it before Madison arrived.

Leaving Iwo in charge of the center, N'Djoku and I drove south to Ingende where the only road out of Coq crossed the Ruki. I contacted the Congolese in charge of the town and gave him a sweetener, USIS publications to distribute. Such things had not been seen in the bush for a long time. As a result, they represented a kind of wealth. He agreed that in the evening we could show movies at an open stretch of ground. We set up the translucent screen. While I took care of the projector, N'Djoku drove around, shouting out news of the showing. It went off without a hitch to a grateful and excited audience.

N'Djoku found his own lodging for the night. I slept in what remained of the Ingende *gîte d'étape*, an abandoned colonial era bungalow without furniture. I waxed a candle to the floor, ate something and slept in blankets on concrete, pleased to have proved to myself that bush film showings would work. They would be much easier when the promised Dodge Power Wagon arrived. In the morning someone brought me a bucket of water and I was able to wash. N'Djoku and I headed back to Coq, the people of Ingende waving gratefully to us as we left.

A few weeks later, thanks to the radio, I discovered some surprising news. An excerpt from the letter of 21 April 1964 takes up the tale:

Last Friday morning, began the letter, *I was unable to get through to Léo on the radio, but heard Léo talking to Bukavu. Léo said that Coq was going to be surprised on Sunday morning when visitors dropped in to see him. I figured AID people might be coming and would want reservations at the Ancion.*

I'd set aside most of the day to get final reports written before Tom Madison's arrival the following Monday: my monthly report, a short thing on the USIS-sponsored chamber music concert given in Coq the previous evening by the Dorian Quintet, and a piece about the downfall of local Interior Minister Gaston LeBaud. Having masterminded the merchant searches in December, he had apparently gathered too much power and bounty to himself. Engulu got rid of him.

Later that afternoon I went over to the post office to see if I could phone and find out who was coming. I did. Charlotte Loris, USIS admin officer, and I screamed across three hundred miles and I discovered that Ambassador G. McMurtrie "Mac" Godley and an entourage of twelve people, including the British Ambassador and Tom Madison would arrive in thirty-six hours. I would have to bed them down, feed them, and arrange meetings for the ambassador with local government leaders.

By a stroke of incredible luck, M Ancion had enough room for everyone at the hotel—even enough so that Ambassadors Godley and Rose were given rooms to themselves. (Godley had the one I lived in for four and a half months.) The Oasis, despite being closed on Sundays, agreed to give the group a noon meal (which turned out to be the world's toughest chicken). The Hacienda, the town's newly opened restaurant, did the evening meal in real style: tablecloths, bits of greenery and napkins specially folded in the drinking glasses.

Loris said Godley wanted to see US missionaries. So very late Friday afternoon Barbara Farmer and I drove out to Bolenge to arrange an early Sunday afternoon meeting with the Gary Farmers and Dick Taylors. I drove over to see Governor Engulu, but no one was at the Presidential mansion. With lodging taken care of, I spent most of Friday evening at the Michejdas. Left around 10:00, went home and began writing briefing papers.

Saturday morning I got cookies ordered for a soirée at the center that I'd decided to attempt. Found Mutien Bokele, Engulu's protocol chief, who took me to Engulu. He has begun to use an office in the house where the Ministry of Finances is located. Yes, he would see the ambassador at 4:30 in the afternoon; he would put off his trip to Léo at least a day and would attend the soirée at the center.

Got André who has gotten me out of SO MANY jams here to move the refrigerator in my pantry into the center, install a light bulb in the center's bathroom and get the portable generator working so that we could show movies in the center even if the normal electrical current were too uneven to run a projector. Thérèse André checked the wording of the invitation to the soirée.

Bokele, N'Djoku, Iwo and I wrote out the invitations, then Bokele and I ran around town delivering them to the ministers in Engulu's cabinet, the president of the provincial assembly and the premier bourgmestre. (It was the first time I'd met a lot of these guys and I tried to get a really good look at them in order to be able to introduce them the next evening.) Iwo and I worked out a list of men who'd gone to the US on AID-financed training "stages." After writing more invitations, we ran around to try to find these guys, too.

Saturday afternoon I helped Edouard get the center cleaned up, ran out to Bolenge to deliver an invitation and to firm up the time of the missionary visit. Saturday evening dined on a moambe *at the Andrés' new house out by the river. Left early to return to more report writing, this after pumping the usual crowd for the story of exactly what happened to LeBaud.*

Sunday morning I finished the briefing papers (missionary visit, political situation, biographical notes on Engulu, schedule of the day, and a guest list for the soirée), carried drinks to the center, got the new vehicle out to the airport, and returned to town with Nick Sapieha who was still wandering around. I was washing my car when I realized the plane would arrive in twenty-five minutes. Frantic rush to get changed. Got to the airport in time to park both vehicles on that section of the runway where planes are left and stuff briefing papers into individual envelopes.

The missionary visit went off fine. We had a briefing before the ambassador saw Engulu. Engulu spoke highly of Major Itambo, the local gendarmerie commander, who had arrested some Mulélists infiltrating from Lac Léopold II. The next morning I arranged a meeting for the ambassador with him.

You can't blame the Congolese if they don't know how to act at the kind of party we were giving. I had no dinner, but stayed to fix up the center and get drinks servers under control. The guests invited for 8:00 arrived at 7:30. We let them sit around looking at picture books until we were ready to do something with them. (I was in the office trying desperately to remember the names and titles of the ministers. Iwo tested me and I did a fair job of remembering. But as one minister came in, I looked at Iwo for help and he said in a fairly loud voice, grinning at the minister, a friend: "Don't you know who he is?")

We got as many as we could to meet the ambassador. (Those whose names I could remember I would take over to meet him.) The Congolese don't know what to say; they are scared [American Ambassadors had been virtually running the Congo for several years]; they want to run away; they try to melt into the bookshelves. Once we got them inside the theater we were all right. They saw three films. The ambassador made a little speech. I told the guests after the speech that brochures would be awaiting each of them as they left.

In a way the visit was better done under extreme time pressure. There wasn't any time for timid hanging back. We've needed to get top government people into the center. This was an ideal occasion. I am still tired after the running around. Had eleven hours sleep last night and could use more now.

Ambassador Godley graciously wrote a letter of commendation about me to the head of USIA in Washington. (To clarify: USIA, the agency, served as stateside headquarters of USIS, the information service, operating overseas.)

Tom Madison arrived with the ambassador's party and took over supervision of the center. He was a tall, dark-haired officer in his mid-forties, originally from San Francisco where he had a married son. His wife was finishing a master's degree program at a university in the Philippines and would not be joining him for several weeks. There would be adjustments to his taking over the supervision of the post. My job was to get along with him.

Madison's arrival and his assuming control of the post's program took from me the most interesting aspects of the job. I stood back to let Tom get to know the potentialities, the employees, the equipment, what had and had not been accomplished. Not surprisingly, he expressed irritation at Washington's totally disrupting his life under conditions of maximum hurry to send him to this no-place where nothing much was going on. He claimed that the world average of local employees to American officers was 8 to 1. It was about 5 to 1 in Brussels. In Coq it was 1 to 1.

At the outset it did not appear that as individuals we would have much rapport. Madison had no interest in Africa, even as a place full of various cultures, ethnicities, and adventures where he'd never been before. He did not share my desire to see the country.

Madison really must have wondered how the calamity of the Coquilhatville posting had befallen him. When I looked about, I saw only progress. André, Boudart, their workers, and I had transformed the center building. The center now had a fully operating library and films service. Patrons crowded the reading room each day; they lined up for our afternoon film shows. The center had two local employees who were handling their jobs satisfactorily although I sensed tensions between them.

When Tom Madison looked around, he must have been horrified. Evenings standing on the balcony of his room at the Ancion, staring out at that muddy river with the huge clouds billowing off across endless swamp, he must have wondered: Who did I cross? What did I say?

Will Sally want a divorce? How did I get sent here?

He was a man with considerable USIS overseas experience. He had been doing important work in Manila, doing it with success. And Washington as a matter of urgency had plucked him out of meaningful work in that archipelago to plunk him down at the edge of the jungle in a tiny Congo backwater, generally regarded in Léopoldville as a hell hole. That backwater had no commercial center and the building designated as the cultural center was clearly too small for it. The office he shared with me was way too small for both of us. There was only one typewriter for the two of us, a definite inconvenience to me because I used it both to write letters and work on my play. Madison thought the operation ought to have five locals instead of the two authorized for it. Hard for him not to see the assignment as a demotion; its circumstances under-ranked him.

One of his first preoccupations was: How do I get out of here? He wrote a memo expressing the opinion that the miniscule Congo stations should be one-year posts. I told him I had been yelled at for making a similar suggestion. When his wife arrived in Léo, he planned to take a week away from Coq to welcome her. Having served two and a half years in Manila, he was due for home leave after six months service in Coq. That would get him out of the Equateur by late October or early November. He planned to stretch that with annual leave well into March.

When he returned maybe he could wangle a job in Léo where his services would be of more value to USIS. He also talked about leaving the service entirely, hinting that a job awaited him in New York. Or he might transfer to the CIA; that kind of work had always interested him.

Those first days Madison must have found as excruciatingly lonely in his way as I had in mine. As I was to learn, he was a man very attached to his absent wife. He was also very attached to his little poodle, his "man's best friend." Tom described the poodle as a "terribly shy mutt who suffered runt-trauma" in his early days. Called Shadow, he followed someone at all times. He provided Madison company. "The little mutt has real insecurities," Tom told me. "And now he's been caged for a week or more." I expected to meet a psycho pooch, assuming he survived his quarantine in Léo.

Madison's mind, unlike mine, took a technical turn. He enjoyed being a ham radio operator. The single side band radio accommodated that hobby. He spent the evenings in what he called the radio shack, a closet in the center where the transmitter had been installed. He tried to connect with ham radio operators who could set up telephone patches either to Sally in Manila or to his son and daughter-in-law in San Francisco. Atmospheric conditions were such, he explained to me, that he succeeded in this effort only after midnight.

Finding him a place to live was the first order of business. He had written me a letter from Manila, suggesting that during the four or five weeks before Sally arrived he bunk at the André house. This idea raised all kinds of terrors for me. I knew that Hank Clifford—who seemed in my paranoid state about housing to do everything he could to thwart me—had encouraged Madison to pull rank and force me out of the André house. I rejected his notion of staying with me to prevent his deciding that the place would do just fine as his lodging, thus forcing me back to the hotel.

I did invite Madison to lunch several times—Mbuli Joseph was proving a more than satisfactory houseboy—and he had a chance then to look over the André house. Perhaps he did not want to share space with a business and warehouse. Perhaps he saw how much the place meant to me and realized that a good way to poison our relationship would be to displace me. It took all my self-possession to keep from reacting to any suggestion that he might appropriate the house. Somehow I managed.

With incredible luck we found Madison and his wife a pleasant, nicely landscaped, two-bedroom house with a living/dining room and a small office. It was the sort of thing one might come upon in a modest San Francisco suburb, truly a find for Coq. We located this place within a week. Given the ease with which this happened, I wondered why it had taken me so long to find housing. Was it that a single man's lifestyle suggested Congolese women of dubious reputation running in and out at all hours? Or was it that I'd gotten to know some people in town and, more importantly, they had gotten to know me—and had finally decided that the center was really not a CIA front after all?

About this time friends and people I knew casually began to leave

Coq: UN technicians I spoke to on movie nights at the UN Club; men I saw regularly at the bakery when I went for morning rolls. The couple who owned and ran the Oasis Restaurant decided they'd had enough of Africa and were returning to Belgium. Ron Sallade went for a month in South Africa prior to leaving for the States. Janusz and Barbara Michejda departed for jobs with the World Health Organization in Dahomey. A *moambe* at the Andrés' new river house gave me a chance to say goodbye.

As others were leaving, we welcomed a new arrival. Shadow, Madison's little poodle, flew in from his quarantine in Léo. He was as advertised a very dependent dog. The journey from Manila had only increased his neediness. Madison delighted in his company. Shadow came to the office every day and followed Madison everywhere. If Madison went from one room of the center to another, Shadow followed at his heels. They went outside together every couple of hours for doggie calls of nature. Shadow lay at Madison's feet during his long hours in the radio shack. At a time when USIA seemed to belittle Madison, Shadow offered him adoration. Madison became more content.

Shortly after Madison took charge of the center, Mme Engulu surprised us with a very welcome program request. The governor's wife wanted to entertain the wives of some of his ministers with a film show. Could that be arranged?

Then Tom offered Engulu a Leader Grant to visit the States. Within forty-five minutes the governor eagerly returned the bio-data form by messenger. He wanted particularly to see the World's Fair in New York and had become interested in learning English. We assured ourselves that he was not only bright and intelligent, capable and hard-headed; he was also quite a personable and likable guy, maybe not entirely untainted by corruption, but less corrupt than ministers like LeBaud. N'Djoku and I went to the Présidence to set up the film show. We installed equipment between 5:30 and 6:00. N'Djoku stayed to run the show, starting at 7:00.

It was probably not a good idea to leave N'Djoku unattended at the governor's mansion. The next morning he did not come to work. Eventually we learned that he was in jail, arrested in a bar, accused of twice stealing glassware from the governor's home: one glass the previous evening while showing our films; two glasses during the public reception of the governor's marriage. So many glasses had been stolen during that reception that Engulu made a public plea for their return.

I went to the jail to try to sort out N'Djoku's arrest. Yes, he had taken glasses, he admitted, but only broken ones. This was obviously unlikely. Even so, I got him released in order for us to go together to the Commissariat of Police in a former *colon's* house; there he would be held if he were not released. We spent much of the morning there, waiting for the *commissaire* to return. He was out getting his car repaired.

I caught up with the *commissaire en chef* in the early afternoon. His office was a dark, high-ceilinged room, bare of furniture except for his desk and two chairs, with a poster called *Actualités Congolaises et Mondiales*—produced by USIS Léo for the central government—crookedly masking-taped to a wall of flaking plaster. A cord for the telephone dangled down from a rafter to the *commissaire's* desk. He sat at it, wearing a hat, but bare to the waist. As I waited, he offered me the typical performance for a European visitor. He hemmed and hawed; discussed matters with subordinates; ignored the visitor; sized him up; shouted at him in order to demonstrate his wisdom, authority and capability.

Eventually N'Djoku was led forth, also bare to the waist. There ensued an exchange of insults and accusations. N'Djoku shouted something about the *commissaire's* wife and was led away, screaming *"Ne l'écoutez pas, patron. Il est contre moi!"* ("Don't listen to him, boss. He's against me!"). He was remanded to a holding tank, the pantry of the former house, where he stood jammed in among other miscreants. By this time he had assured himself of a couple of meal-less days in jail. There was nothing I could do for him.

In the afternoon two days later N'Djoku appeared at the center, liberated and smiling. Iwo greeted him as if he had suffered police brutality. Madison went next door to the recently opened Hacienda Restaurant to buy champagne glasses for return to the Présidence. The Hacienda was regularly borrowing USIS films to show its patrons. We agreed so long as the films were not shown in the bar itself. The restaurant converted an extra room into a theater. At the restaurant Tom discovered that N'Djoku had been charging meals there on the center's account.

A week or two later N'Djoku went to the restaurant to change a part in a projector we had loaned the place. He asked the barman for CF 100 for the service and was given the money. Madison and I shook our heads. N'Djoku must have come from a hunting tribe, from people trained to take. Later that week an inspection discovered a Coleman lantern missing. Tata Edouard found the lantern's carton; it was empty. Madison exploded. Suddenly the lantern itself was found, shoved off into a corner where it would have disappeared if no one had missed it.

As far as N'Djoku was concerned, easy-going though he was, I became ever more convinced that I should have hired the obsequious man.

One lesson night at the Andrés—it was late and Jules had hours before gone upstairs to bed—Thérèse and I talked and talked: about the children, about Coq, about her painting, about the center, about Madison. I told her that in watching Madison adjust to his new posting, I realized that I had become a *coquin*. In French a *coquin* is a rascal, a rogue, a scoundrel, a Boudart. I was certainly not one of those. But a *coquin* was also someone who belonged in Coq and I seemed to qualify. Thérèse smiled and said, "Congratulations!"

NINE

SHORTLY AFTER TOM MADISON took charge of the cultural center, I learned that DCCM doctor Bob Bowers would be driving to a mission station in the deep interior. Eager to take a look at the bush, I inquired about tagging along and wangled an invitation to accompany him. I convinced Madison that the trip offered an unusual opportunity for me to make contacts at Ingende and Boende, river towns, and to show films at mission stations. He was probably glad to have me out of town for a week.

We decided that he (and, of course, Shadow who would tag along) should have Mbuli Joseph provide him lunch every day. He could relax in the house if he wanted. Although he had already met Jules and Thérèse, I got them reacquainted. Tom heard me address them by their given names and followed suit. Since he knew some French, I assumed he might realize that *politesse* strongly suggested that he begin with *Monsieur* and *Madame*. His assumed familiarity embarrassed the Andrés, but one had to accept Americans as they came. When the Madisons began calling Thérèse Terry, she felt disconcerted. They never noticed.

Bob Bowers and I drove east along the watershed of a river known variously as the Ruki, the Busira or the Tshuapa depending on where it flowed in relation to tributaries. We drove on roads once well maintained. Now, almost four years into independence, they were deteriorating. Rain carved deep ruts into their surfaces. Now that overhanging vegetation was no longer cut back, the orange-colored roads did not dry quickly after rain. Passing vehicles dug holes in them.

The road would rise to a ridge, then descend to a watercourse. Over the watercourse lay a bridge of logs. Bob would stop the VW microbus and I would get out to check that the bridge was solid. I would guide him across and remount on the other side and we would start toward another low ridge. The river we drove beside was old. It doubled back and forth, changing course. It meandered, formed horseshoe lakes, drained water from vegetation that was intensely green.

Occasionally we passed through villages, brown clearings where clusters of thatched huts and dirt dooryards lined the roads. Naked children rushed out to wave. Adults watched us pass, men sitting in dooryards, swept clean of vegetation as a protection against snakes, women ambling between huts, wearing only strips of cloth between their legs, these held in place by strings or thongs tied at their hips.

At every village animals darted across our path: goats and chickens, ducks and dogs. It was important not to hit them because then there would be long palavers about compensation. But avoiding them was not easy. Goats seemed mesmerized by the microbus as if its motion required an answering one. They raced across the road at the last moment as if testing their daring and speed.

We never hit a goat or dog. Chickens were not so lucky. Once three fled into the road just in front of the vehicle, squawking and flapping wings unaccustomed to flight. We hit them broadside. They seemed to be coming through the windshield, feathers flying, the birds landing on top of the roof and bouncing, bouncing backwards, until they landed again on the road, nothing but their dignity damaged.

At our lunch break Bob parked at the side of the road. We ate, not bothering to converse, until a small man, well short of five feet, appeared out of the jungle. He was naked except for a pair of old, torn shorts. He carried a *panga*, a long knife, and jumped, startled, when he saw us.

"Batwa," the doctor said. "Pygmy."

I studied the little man. He examined both of us, then started talking.

"Or pygmoid, to be precise," the doctor added. "He's a mixture of pygmy and other strains. The Mongos don't regard Batwa as human." The Mongos were the main tribe of the area. "Of course, they were here before the Mongos arrived." The doctor scrutinized him. "He's been smoking hemp."

As we continued to eat, the man kept up his flow of words. He harangued us, whimpered, sat on the ground, frustratedly threw down his knife, beat the earth. "What's he saying?" I asked.

"Gimme hundred francs. . . Gimme fifty francs. . ."

The pleas went on and on. Bob opened a small can of turkey and ate it with a metal fork. "Gimme twenty francs," Bob said, translating the pgymy's demands. "Ten francs, five francs. . . . Gimme a shirt."

When Bob finished his lunch, he wiped the fork on a napkin and set the bottom of the turkey can within easy reach of the pygmy. "Lots of uses for a can like that in the forest," he said.

As we prepared to leave, the man hurried forward, picked up the can and sat down within two feet of the vehicle. He went on whimpering. When we got back into the microbus, he shouted at us. "Hey! Where's my five francs? You promised me five francs!" We drove off. I watched the man sitting on the road, mumbling to himself, and examining the can.

We passed Mondombe station and reached Monieka just before dark. There I met Bob Bowers' colleague whom I'll call Dr Rob Davis. He invited me to his surgery the next morning where, among others, he was performing a hernia operation. "We do a lot of those out here," he said. "It must be something genetic among the Bantu." In the surgery three Congolese nurses attended him, two of them male. The female nurse said a prayer.

As the operation began, I watched Rob insert a nerve-deadening agent into the vertebra at the small of a patient's back. Rob was not fat, but loose flesh hung over the top of his shorts. The patient was a man older than Rob. But there was not a scrap of fat on him. Rob had the mental development and skill with instruments that the Congolese lacked. The Congolese had the physical development Rob lacked.

I had seen remarkable physiques among the Congolese. And no wonder. Paddling pirogues on rivers is hard work. It produces tremendous shoulder, back, chest, arm, and leg development. Women had amazing posture and muscular development at the neck and shoulders from carrying loads on their heads. I watched a woman picking potatoes in front of Rob's house the next day. She was naked to the waist. When she stood, her back to me, I could not tell if she were a man or a woman.

As Rob worked, he asked about the movies I would show that evening. The casualness of this surprised me, but I was not surprised that watching the operation made me light-headed. I left the surgery and sat on its steps with my head between my legs. When I looked up, a crowd of Congolese was studying the *mondele*.

Rob could not have been nicer to me. Still, as I watched him work,

I saw that he did not possess the sort of personal warmth that would have immediately attracted people to him, the kind of warmth that many evangelizing missionaries boasted in abundance.

His wife was shy, reserved, a quietly pretty girl who wore glasses. She was cautious with people, not outgoing and open as it behooves missionaries to be. She served tuna casserole to her family at the dinner I ate with them. Rob kidded her about the meal. She admitted to me—and later even showed me—that she had pantry shelves stacked high with cans of tuna. And a small box filled with tuna recipes.

So her reserve extended to eating carefully, to living in a place that could easily be seen as forbidding, among people who were not only physically, but also seemed metaphorically, dark. She acknowledged that she worried about her kids. I sensed a disquiet between her and Rob. Perhaps they were too much alike.

I wondered if he knew how to woo her, if there were romantic moments late at night—balmy air moving from the darkness into the screened bedroom, candles, soft music from a radio, the regular breathing of children down the hall, the tastes of kisses on their lips—when Rob lifted the glasses from her and told her she was beautiful. Perhaps. Movies could show a guy how to do that. But Rob was too serious to have bothered with them in med school. Sweet-talking, even at so rudimentary a level, did not seem his style. Still, I suspected that a high priority on a mission station was keeping a marriage in good repair.

Rob took me on a short jaunt to Bokote. He introduced me to a Catholic priest, a docile old gray-beard in the Congo almost forty years. He'd just wakened from his *sieste,* entered sleepily in a threadbare white soutane, and reminded me of a teddy bear. He had a gentle, patient sense of humor, a kind of hands-thrown-up attitude toward the Congolese and their future. The Catholic priests did not strike me as participating in the life process in the same way that the Protestants did with all their kids. The Congolese for whom procreation and children were such vital parts of life must have felt baffled by the priests.

Rob liked the people. After I said I'd like to see how villagers lived, we stopped at the hut of a Congolese. He and the householder greeted one another affably. I peeked inside the hut. The host asked if I'd like to try my hand at shooting the arrows they used for hunting. I obliged. My awkwardness amused him. I bought a rattle with bottle caps inside it.

I came to feel a real sense of respect and even friendship for Rob Davis. When he told me about his work as a missionary doctor, he spoke without the self-importance that some doctors assume about themselves and without the self-dramatizing of those missionaries who always mentioned that they were serving in a "benighted land," in "the heart of darkness." After six years in the Congo he felt he was reaching his maximum usefulness. He handled the doctoring without difficulty, he said. He knew enough of the local language and customs to work effectively with Congolese.

I told Rob that he seemed perfectly cut out for the work he was doing. I wished I felt as much purpose in my work. After a moment he admitted that his wife was lonely. Her life on the station did not give her sufficient social outlets. She worried about the children. So, Rob assumed, the next time they went home on leave, they probably would not return. That likelihood distressed him. He did not want to go back to a kind of doctoring where his professional conversations with colleagues centered on investments, on getting rich.

Although I had expected back-country missionary life to be full of hardship, I did not find that to be the case. The Congo bush seemed to me a place of renewal for the world-weary. Yes, real limitations characterized that missionary life, limitations of creature comforts and distractions, of intellectual stimulation. But the stations struck me as places of real interest, of great leisure, and sometimes of incredible beauty. On the stations I swam in slow-moving rivers, read, played cards and other parlor games, took walks, went canoeing on the river and into nearby swamps, watched monkeys, chattering, playing, feeding in the tall trees at dusk. The life did not seem taxing in the sense that the daily grind of city living could be. Nature could bring refreshment, much of it splendid.

As we retraced our route, returning to Coq, Bob Bowers told stories. He mentioned a man he'd examined at Lotumbe. While the patient complained of leg pains, Bob detected nothing wrong. Nor did another doctor consulted for a second opinion. The patient insisted he was sick. He grew progressively worse. Finally he walked about using two canes, then with women holding him on either side. Soon the women were preparing him special food. He was reduced to sitting all day. At last he went back to his home village, prepared to die.

But he did not die. Instead he consulted a witchdoctor. Bob discovered this months later when he was traveling near the man's home village. A church member asked him for three thousand Congolese francs, at the time about $60. "Who needs so much money?" Bob asked.

"A friend is badly in debt to the *nganga*," the woman said. "Here he comes now." She pointed to a man carrying a huge log. He was the man Bob had examined. He was now working off the debt he owed the witchdoctor.

"How was he cured?" Bob asked.

"The *nganga* had him buried up to his neck," the woman said. "Then he dug holes nearby. He started fires in the holes."

"And that cured him?"

"He begged to be unburied and has walked ever since," the woman said.

Bob laughed, driving along. "Get well or get roasted! And he's walking okay now. We should take lessons from these guys."

During my absence in the bush, Tom Madison came upon unexpected visitors at the Ancion: a party led by the American Ambassador to the Central African Republic, posted in Bangui north of us. A storm had forced the ambassador's plane to land in Coq. He was en route to Léopoldville with his wife, his senior USIS man and his wife. In Léo they would attend regional meetings to confer with G. Mennen (Soapy) Williams, the US Assistant Secretary of State for African Affairs. Tom learned that a Congolese *sureté* official at the Coq airport had cited Ambassador Tony Ross over some infraction.

Ross shrugged it off. Colonial officials had treated Africans that way in the old days. Some Africans followed their example. No problem.

Madison was new to Africa. He had little sense of the colonial influence. He may also have felt that he needed to show that he had taken command in Coq. So, despite his lack of experience with Africans, he rushed off to Governor Engulu to demand both a written apology from him and a public one from the *sureté* official.

Relating the story to me, Tom seemed pleased with himself. I wondered if humiliating an official and demanding a favor from the governor advanced our program goals. But I said nothing. Tom seemed to want people in Léo to know that he was on top of things in his new post.

Unexpectedly Ambassador Ross, PAO Welch and their wives returned to Coq. Once more bad weather prevented their completing their flight. I invited the party to stay with me. (Not that I had much choice; the Ancion was full.) Because there was air-conditioning downstairs (but not upstairs where I slept comfortably every night), they all decided to sleep barracks style in my living room.

We all went to dinner at the Hacienda Restaurant, Coq's only eatery now that the Oasis had closed its doors. The host charmed us, impressed at feeding an ambassador. Quite graciously Mrs Ross told him, "Every town has its charms." The diplomatic visitors from Bangui made that sentiment true for one evening.

From a letter dated Tuesday, 19 May 1964:

Just a quick flash before the work day starts here.

All hell seems to be breaking loose up near Bukavu on the Congo's eastern border. The Mulélists have occupied the town of Uvira, south of Bukavu. The rebels control an important segment of the fine road between Bukavu and Usumbura. Yesterday they captured a sugar plantation in the area. The plantation manager reports having seen a Chinese among the rebel troops. So far this activity has not taken on an anti-white aspect.

I came down here to the center at 4:00 PM to listen with Tom Madison to a broadcast. Hilltop (Bukavu) was talking to Tomcat (Embassy Léo) and Bourbon (home of Mobutu's US Army pilot). There Cyrille Adoula [the Congolese prime minister] was listening with occasional relays through River Rat (Stanleyville) where the chief regional ANC commander was.

Congolese naturally do not know how to use this single side band equipment. Only one person can talk at a time. It's a kick to hear both men chattering away at each other in Swahili, both on the air, then to have them finish and together say, 'Ovaire.'

Bukavu's new consul took an inspection tour in a UN plane yesterday. Saw three abandoned trucks on the main road with bodies lying around them. Plane was fired on, but undamaged. There is also said to be increased

Mulélist activity in Kasai, east of the rebels' Kwilu stronghold.

No sweat, kids. Coq's a long way away—it's like there being trouble in Seattle when you're in LA—and nobody (myself included) thinks anything is going to happen here.

Suddenly a number of good things occurred. Tom Madison left the Ancion and moved into his house. Reichling, the restauranteur who established the Hacienda, succeeded in getting a shipment of vegetables into Coq. A letter rhapsodized: *"Cauliflower, green beans, potatoes, rhubarb, tomatoes, Brussels sprouts. We haven't seen anything like that since I arrived here."* I cooked some cauliflower for myself and baked a cake from a mix sent in a food order from Denmark. Buildings were being painted. I hoped that meant Coq had hit bottom and was reviving.

At the same time—this was the Congo, after all—there were opposite signs as well. A real question was: What would happen when the UN withdrew its troops and technicians at the end of June? Rebels continued active in Kwilu and the Kivu. Rebel sympathizers were said to be infiltrating south of us across the river from Congo-Brazzaville. The blues—*crise de cafards*—occasionally assailed me. When Thérèse assured me these hit everyone in the tropics, I decided to buck up.

One evening when Thérèse and I had been having an English lesson, Jules came in agitated by a meeting he and other *ex-colon* businessmen had attended with the local Minister of Economic Affairs. The minister told the Europeans that they must concoct schemes to engineer Coq's economic recovery. The Europeans had attempted, so Jules reported, to explain that all the wealth in the Congolese community traveled within a very small circle of government officials, their friends and families. These elites had bars and enterprises. They hounded out of business any Congolese with initiative who might offer competition. The minister was uninterested in this analysis of economic problems.

The minister also announced that every firm with more than thirty employees must soon organize a *Conseil de Travail*. In them elected workers would participate in the management of the firm. Jules was concerned that rabble rousers among the employees of his brick-making business would get themselves elected by intimidating fellow workers and then tell him how to run his enterprise. He would reduce the number of his employees in preference to allowing that to happen. Thérèse listened patiently—and tiredly—knowing that Jules always reacted excitedly to this sort of situation.

Tom Madison's wife's arrival in Léo where there was now a 6:00 PM to 6:00 AM curfew gave him a chance to escape the Equateur. He found the Coq posting so disagreeable—I heard a lot of anti-agency, anti-Congolese, anti-underdeveloped countries bitching—that he had already written Léo that he intended to take a four-month combination of home-and-annual leave in mid-November, not returning until mid-March. After six weeks of bachelorhood, of grumbling about the rushed transfer, about Coq, and our miserable little center, plenty of time in bed with his wife struck me as just what the doctor prescribed.

A few days before his trip he asked me, "Would you mind taking Shadow while I'm in Léo? Or shall I make other arrangements?"

The blooming pooch! What other arrangements did he have in mind?

"Sure, Tom," said I. "Glad to do it."

I knew that Shadow's deep-rooted insecurities caused him to need constant reassurance. But I did not know what that was like in the living.

Aptly named, the pooch followed me step for step. I often paced when I wrote and at home I was working on my play. If I moved back and forth while trying to think, I was accompanied by the clitter-clitter of doggie toenails. If I sat on the toilet, I heard adoring sniffs beneath the door as the consoling whiff of me assured Shadow that he was not alone. When shut up in the kitchen at night, he yowled. The poor little guy was stupid, dependent, unkempt, unclipped, tick-ridden, and odoriferous. He smelled awful.

Shadow had to be urinated every couple of hours. He lifted his left leg, always the leftie, and could make four stops in five minutes so that other animals would know he'd passed. The baker thought it endearing that he made a stop every morning on his front step. He rewarded him with petit fours. His other *besoin* was taken care of every second day. It had to be primed by chasing a ball or some rocks. With his teeth tight around a rock and in unleashed freedom where he could concentrate, he crouched. Shaking like a rat expelling a beach ball, he delivered the goods. Tom would announce, "The dog has shat." When Sally Madison arrived, Shadow's little tail shook like a leaf in a high wind.

Sally Madison proved to be a calming influence on her husband. For a remote and isolated post she was well provided for. Lucky Sally! Her house was all ready for her. She did not have to wait for the household effects to arrive. They needed only to be arranged and a house servant trained to her satisfaction.

She landed on her feet. Thanks to a neighbor, she got the Madisons and me introduced into the fresh food supply system from the Catholic mission at Bamania, something I had never heard of. Passing muster with the priests, she was shown how to order meat from Bamania. Meat was often available in town, but pork and veal from Bamania were especially tasty. Sally took charge of a shipment of furniture that arrived from Léo and supervised our two households sharing it.

Thérèse André offered Sally ready female company, a real plus in a town like Coq, particularly since Sally showed little interest in friendships with missionaries. "Does she drink a lot?" Ron Sallade asked me after he returned from South Africa. That question seemed to say more about him and his missionary colleagues than it did about her. But that was apparently a question they had all asked themselves.

Now that Sally had arrived, Tom was more relaxed. He smiled oftener. I heard less complaining about the post, both because there was less to complain about and because he shared his complaints with her. Despite the master's degree she had just earned in the Philippines, she gave little evidence of having cultural or intellectual interests.

Tom had mentioned that Sally had been a showgirl, dancing in a chorus line somewhere. One didn't know quite what to make of this information. Perhaps it was offered to credential Tom as having, before Foreign Service, moved in a faster lane than had colleagues whose wives had degrees in history, political science, or sociology. Sally was a year or two older than Tom, mid-forties. She was at a time when a woman needed to pay attention to her figure—which Sally did—if she intended to keep it. "Look at how tiny she is!" Sally once said of Thérèse André "And she's had four children!" Sally was an embassy wife in a post without an embassy.

Sally and Tom were definitely a team. They supported one another. I did not get the feeling that they shared a great romance, but that was asking a lot of a couple that had been married for more than two decades.

Sally and I never completely hit it off. Maybe that was because I had set up the post and therefore had more of an investment in it than Tom did, an investment that might somehow jeopardize Tom's emerging from Coq service "smelling like a rose," as he repeatedly said. Maybe because my Coq friends became theirs and a kind of obligation was implicit in that. But without ever discussing the matter, Sally and I decided to make the best of our being thrown together. I was pleased to have her in Coq.

While Tom returned from Léo sobered by the extent of unrest across the country, he happily reported one distinct advantage of the Equateur. He exultantly announced: "Coq is the safest place in the Congo!"

Ten

QUITE UNEXPECTEDLY BIG NEWS CAME OUT OF LÉOPOLDVILLE. Moise Tshombe, leader of the failed Katanga secession, arrived in the capital and set off a storm of speculation about his possible role in the central government. Then Cyrille Adoula, the prime minster, resigned, forced out by the machinations of the American embassy. Tshombe became prime minister just at a time when anti-government rebels grew increasingly active around Albertville, a Lake Tanganyika port town in northern Katanga. There was concern that those rebels would join forces with Mulélistes in the Kivu.

It was a political season, even in Coq. Most of Governor Engulu's ministers charged him with misappropriating government funds. Engulu called ANC soldiers into the streets. Tom Madison was eager for the cultural center to extend its reach to opinion leaders in Coq. He talked up the possibility of the center's forming a Congolese-American Friendship Society. But political considerations prevented that. Until the standoff was resolved, Tom decided hands off politicians.

I focused my efforts on setting up a regular schedule of film shows in Coq's *cités indigènes*.

The Madisons dealt with a reversal. Shadow fell ill. I was present when the veterinarian arrived, a Congolese. He diagnosed the case, clearly intimidated by Tom Madison: his being European, his worry, his obvious lack of confidence in the vet. Tom paced as the dog whimpered. He grew impatient with the vet's procedure and yelled at him: "Do something! Hurry! Can't you see the dog's in pain?" The vet hastily gave Shadow a shot. The dog burst back to health. We smiled, relaxed, laughed. Then Shadow collapsed and died.

Tom and Sally were disconsolate. "Obviously incompetent," Tom declared of the vet. "What can you expect in a place like this? That little mutt was our best friend here." Tom was sure that in his incompetence the vet had given Shadow a dosage of medicine meant not for a dog, but a cow. Even as I commiserated with the Madisons, I wondered what might have happened if Tom had not yelled at the vet.

About this time the Belgians' national day occurred. When I was invited to represent the United States at the annual cocktail party, Tom said, "You have to go, Fred. I couldn't be happier." I realized he was miffed. He was now, after all, the senior official American in Coq.

Not wanting this to become a problem, I appealed to Thérèse. When I brought her a pail of eggs from the DCCM, I asked if she could wangle the Madisons an invitation. She consulted the dean of the Belgian community. He refused. It was the custom to invite only one person of each foreign nationality to the annual party.

On the day itself Thérèse found some reason to turn up at the center. Jules was also there, fixing a generator. He was surprised when she insisted he go to the house to get her some keys, but he went. Then she mentioned to Tom, "Ah, it's our national fête today."

"Yes, that's what I understand," he replied.

"Are you coming to our cocktail?"

"No, Fred has been invited instead of me."

"Ah, but of course," she said. "It's tradition to invite the person who's been longest in the community."

"Oh, is that how it works?" asked Tom.

"Yes. Strange custom, isn't it, when you are more senior."

On our next lesson night Thérèse was very pleased with herself. "I really should have been a diplomat," she told Jules and me. "I made all that up and Tom swallowed it." She turned to Jules. "The only tricky part was getting you out of the center so that you wouldn't contradict me!"

One day at the house a Congolese woman came to the door peddling pineapples. Because Thérèse was there, she did the negotiating in Lingala. The merchant acknowledged that she would sell Thérèse pineapples at a much cheaper rate than she would sell them to me. Thérèse relayed this information to me in French. When we were together a few evenings later, she referred to this negotiation in making points about Americans in Coq. "I am *une Ancienne*," she explained. "I've been here a dozen years. I speak Lingala. They know me."

"So you get the better rate."

"Of course. You are not *un Ancien*. Tom Madison is even less of one." She shrugged. "They don't know you. Our workmen laugh about you."

"They do?"

She nodded. "I'm sure your employees have two names for you. One admirable, one scornful. But they'll never admit it."

The question, of course, was: How could our work be effective as long as we were unknown quantities? Especially when no American would ever stay in Coq long enough to become *un Ancien*.

A provincial minister appeared one day at the center. We fell all over ourselves greeting him. After some introductory chitchat, he asked if he could obtain a movie projector from us. He wanted to use it for campaigning. His idea was that we would obtain it for him from the States. Getting it through diplomatic channels, he could avoid paying import duties. We reluctantly explained that this was not possible.

We asked if we could set up a film showing for the top people at his ministry. He suggested a film showing at his home. Justin Bomboko, the Equateur's national politician, would be visiting. We delightedly agreed and sent N'Djoku with films and a projector to his home. The show turned out to be an evening's entertainment for his wife and children. The minister did not attend; neither did Bomboko. Moral of the story? We were not *Anciens.* Congolese did not know what to make of us. Madison and I were disappointed, though not surprised, that the contact did not advance our program goals.

One of our problems was trying to define whom we were trying to reach. Given local uncertainties, it did not seem possible to reach political leaders. Film showings in the *cités* were scattershot rather than targeted. But at least we could reach young Congolese who would eventually take over in the community.

Was there any point at all in trying to reach villagers outside of Coq? Madison thought not. He did not want to leave the town. Wanting to see the Real Africa, I thought yes. I emphasized the opportunities of opening to villagers glimpses of a world they had never imagined.

I discussed village film shows with the Andrés. Jules shook his head. Thérèse thought we should try to reach women. "They are the basis of the whole society," she said. "You won't get anywhere till you do something to reach them."

I set up a schedule of local film shows. We selected nine sites in and around Coq. Two men—a host and a projectionist—would go to three sites each week. We'd hit each site every three weeks. The showings were to take two hours, 6:00 PM to 8:00 PM. Each man working a show would get two hours of compensatory time. We selected three films and I wrote introductions to them in French. Iwo translated them into Lingala. The host was to read the intro before the film to help audiences understand what they were seeing.

The first Monday and Tuesday nights the guys (as I thought of them) had trouble with the generator that ran the projector. Wednesday night the site we'd chosen was not available to us. Thursday night the sound mechanism on the projector failed; wisely, the guys had brought a backup. As expected, we had things to learn. Practice would make perfect.

I also devised a schedule of bush showings. We'd make a bush trip once a week, usually Thursday evening. I stressed that each member of the team was expected to help with the set up and the take down. The sites were the towns of Bikoro and Ingende; Flandria, a plantation near Ingende; and large villages at Bokatola-Bomembe and Kalamba-Penzele.

At a trial run at Penzele Iwo proved unwilling to drive around the community announcing the show. As an educated man, he was also reluctant to do anything that looked like manual labor. In addition, he did not read the intro text. Instead, he half-narrated the film in Lingala; that meant I had no idea what he was telling the audience. The host providing a kind of narration might serve better than reading an intro. But we would have to watch the films with the hosts to be sure they understood the points the films were making.

We hired two more men to help with the showings: Raphael, a driver-projectionist, and Denis Ahenga, the man whose seeming obsequiousness had caused me to hire N'Djoku. Once he became an employee, the obsequiousness fell away. He proved to be intelligent, willing to work, and had better French than Iwo.

Sadly, the longer Tom Madison and I worked with Iwo Pierre the more complicated the relationship became. Iwo would have said that we did not take cognizance of his being both extraordinary and quite different from the other Congolese. We would have said that the problem stemmed from his failure to make that differentness work for him. Instead of an advantage, he made it a liability. DCCM people said the problem was *mpifo*, prestige.

As Iwo saw the matter, he was not merely a man of the Equateur;

he was a man of the world. He had lived in the United States. He had studied at USC. He had worked at the USIS office in Léopoldville. He spoke Lingala and Lonkundo, French and English. Every day he wore slacks and a dress shirt, a tie and oxfords to work. Unlike many Congolese, he ate three meals a day. He had too much education to work with his hands. He had ambition and standards. He strived to better himself. The totality of all this merited *mpifo*.

He could not stand to be corrected in front of the others. Since I'd had limited experience in directing employees, I made mistakes in doing this. I soon learned that all corrections must be given to him in the office that Madison and I shared out of the hearing of the others. Iwo claimed to speak English, but his command of it was limited and fading. I saw that this distressed him, but how could it be otherwise? Tom often gave him instructions in English. When he did not understand them, he couldn't follow them. But *mpifo* made it difficult for Iwo to acknowledge that he did not understand.

Iwo was also reluctant to admit that he didn't know things. If we asked, "Do you know how to operate this machine?"—a movie projector, for example—he would say that he did, even if he had never touched the thing before. The other Congolese employees tended to answer the same way. Since we expected more from Iwo and were willing to train him, the evasions strained our patience.

Bosses often drive staffers crazy. Things Madison and I did must have seemed equally baffling and frustrating to our Congolese. Of course, part of serving overseas was learning how other people did things and being tolerant of them, even delighted by them. But having to continually step carefully around Iwo's *mpifo* sensitivity led us a merry dance.

Madison and I wished that Iwo could relax, that he could make peace with being a Congolese, even take pride in being an unusual one, and stop trying to be a white man. His ambitions tied him in knots. He always seemed tense. Recognition of his *mpifo* seemed his goal in life. We could well have used him as the best, the Number 1, of our Congolese. Unfortunately, he wanted to be the Number 3 of the Americans.

I had hoped Iwo would take ownership of the bush film shows. We could give them to him as his special responsibility. To test out bush film shows, I took a couple of overnight excursions to Bikoro and environs with Iwo and Raphael. I learned that Congolese would not watch movies on grass, as I had assumed they'd prefer to do. No, there were snakes and bugs in grass. They tended to watch the film shows standing. Who wanted to sit in dust? That meant audience members at the rear of a crowd had a limited view of the screen. Mounting the screen on the cab of the film truck increased visibility. It also meant more work in setting up a show. On the outings I saw that, if sent out with a projectionist, Iwo would do no manual labor. The projectionist would have to do it all. Even in my presence Iwo hardly carried anything.

He seemed to feel that local people would spread word of the film shows. When we drove around, announcing a show, Iwo was reluctant to be seen with us. His attitude made me scratch my head; surely advertising a show was a crucial part of making it a success. Why was Iwo so hesitant?

I came up with an idea that I considered little short of brilliant. In the old days Congolese had widely communicated by what were known as talking drums. I had seen one at the DCCM; it fascinated me. It was a tree trunk, four or five feet long, with a depression carved its length leaving a curved ridge on either side. Each ridge had its own tone. When beaten properly, a well-made talking drum could be heard for five miles. It talked by replicating the rhythm and tonal differences of Congolese speech.

What if we called villagers to our film shows by playing such a drum?

What a terrific idea! Our means of calling Africans to the film shows would be of Africa. It would be both efficient and salute African tradition, tradition that villagers might enthusiastically recall. Eventually villagers would hear the drum, know it meant a film show, and come running.

Moreover, I assumed, our using it would delight our bosses in Washington. They would immediately grasp its PR potential: "In the deepest Congo jungle villagers know the call of USIS," that sort of thing. I thought the process of finding the right tree trunk and the right carver would be an education in African tradition.

Iwo was aghast. Talking drum use, he assured Tom and me, would result in "*mauvaise propagande.*" Anti-US elements would claim it harked back to the Belgian colonial era. Villagers would mock us. Hmm. Tom seemed somewhat swayed. I tried the idea out on missionaries and the Andrés. The missionaries thought the idea might be worth a try.

Jules in his overexcited way assured me that I would never understand anything about the Congo. "Your man doesn't want that talking drum around because he thinks it's savage. It's a threat to his *mpifo*. When he went to the States, he put all that behind him."

I was not very happy with the notion that I would never understand anything.

"We none of us understand anything," said Thérèse. "I've been here a dozen years and I admit I don't understand them. The missionaries will tell you the same thing."

I told Tom that I considered Iwo the wrong man to take charge of the bush film showings. Perhaps Ahenga could be trained for that. He was working out well and, if he had complexes, we had not yet discovered them.

Tom broke the news that my enthusiasm for bush showings was probably misplaced. He had been driving the Dodge Power Wagon and detected a shimmy in the steering wheel at forty miles per hour. Less sensitive to shimmies, I had never noticed it—and, in fact, I never did. Tom had decided that it was unsafe to take the vehicle outside of Coq. Until the problem was repaired—that might take months—we'd have to put hinterland film shows on indefinite hold.

As for Iwo, Tom advised patience in working with him. We could keep building him up and, if necessary, slapping him down. "He may end up running this place someday," Tom said.

At this time rebels were being trained in camps in Congo-Brazzaville across the Congo River. Thousands of Communist advisors were said to be assisting them in the camps. Suddenly the rebels crossed the river, attacked, and captured the towns of Bolobo and Mushie, 120 to 150 miles south of Coq. Reports came that the rebels at Mushie had cut off river traffic on the Kasai, a major river. I found it a little difficult to take seriously the notion of a rebel threat from a place called Mushie, especially when the hapless ANC was reported to have quickly retaken Bolobo. But since rebels continued to gain territory in the eastern Congo, Tom and Sally Madison took the threat seriously.

One evening at the Andrés Boudart gave an account of what he had heard about the ANC at Bolobo. "Imagine the battle," he said, standing to give a performance. "Early afternoon, Bolobo at siesta. The heat like a furnace, shimmering off the airport runway. The ANC flies in. Within minutes it secures the airport. The soldiers creep toward town. Every few yards they skirmish—with fears of magic. Bravely they move on. And then. . ." He paused for effect. "They discover that the rebels have already returned across the river."

I laughed. "You mean there was no battle at all?"

"No battle? No, no! It was a stunning victory!"

"Did the rebels cross the river just to give people a scare?" I asked.

"The ANC reclaims a town? There must be a celebration!" Boudart was outdoing himself in his performance. "So the soldiers rounded up all rebel sympathizers. Of course, there were mistakes. This is ANC. There are always mistakes. They got some loyalists and people without political ties. Forced them to dig a deep hole. Bound the captives and shoved them into the hole. Drenched them with gasoline."

"Stop! Don't go on!" Thérèse implored. But Boudart was full of steam.

"What courage, eh?" he shouted. "Picture the pit: its sides drying to powder, the struggling victims gray with fear, the smell of their sweat. Imagine the gasoline: its scent, its shimmer in the heat. Imagine the brave soldiers giggling with excitement. They toss matches at the gasoline. It explodes with a blinding whoosh. Screams rise with the stench of burning flesh."

We could not look at one another.

"With the ANC," said Boudart, "it's better that they run than win."

I checked out this account with Raeys. He termed it substantially correct.

The UN presence in Coquilhatville began to diminish. The UN pulled its troops out of the country. The school year ended and UN teachers were leaving. So were technical advisors.

Ron Sallade said goodbye. Since he was virtually the only person to whom I could be absolutely frank, I was very sorry to see him go. The Andrés held a farewell dinner for him, complicated as always by his lack of French. Another guest was the Spanish doctor who had replaced the recently departed Janusz Michejda. The Spaniard spoke French as if it were his native language. The "j" in "*je*" was pronounced like an "h", the "e" like an "ay". As a result his *"je"* sounded like "hay." Conversing with him required a delay of several seconds for sound translation.

Boudart announced his departure. He expected to be gone for a year. I would miss him: his buccaneer style, his energy, his rough wit. After all Boudart had done for the center, the Madisons and I felt loath to send him off without ceremony. In spite of the bluster he could be sensitive.

The Madisons invited him for drinks with the Andrés and me the evening before he left. He and Jules were relaxed. With no strain eating at them, it was great fun. Sally Madison got tipsy. She told Boudart, "You have a commercial mentality." The charge did not faze him. Tom expressed the opinion that Congolese had the mental capacities of dogs. Sally put a dish of pretzels in the place where Tom had just lifted his glass. When he put the glass down, it spilled its contents onto the carpet. Tom gave Sally a sharp rebuke. I whispered to Thérèse, seated beside me, that she must not spill a drink *chez Madison*. We giggled together.

The next day we all saw Boudart off at the airport.

I went out on the Congo one Sunday afternoon with Jules and Thérèse and the children. The quietness of the river gave Jules distance from the tensions that assailed him. He joyously chased the children across the night tracks of crocodiles and took them fishing at the end of the sandbar on which we'd run the boat. At the other end Thérèse set up her easel and painted a river scene. While Jules fished alone, I swam with the kids, being careful that we did not get caught in the current.

When I went to admire the painting, something was said about Boudart planning to visit the Michejdas in Dahomey.

"A year is a long time away," I said.

Thérèse smiled privately. She knew how long it could be.

"I remember you said he would leave early."

I glanced over at Jules fishing. Boudart was absent from the Congo for longer periods than he was present. He could rest and restore himself with travel. By contrast, Jules had remained in the Congo almost continually from the time he and Thérèse first arrived. I wondered if a long vacation in Europe would produce buccaneer traits in him.

In the late afternoon we reloaded the boat and pushed off the sandbar without starting the motor. Beyond the shallows we caught the current. In the stern Jean-Luc steered with an oar. We drifted on the silence of the river.

Soon a breeze brought voices to us. Two fishermen chanted from their pirogues as they worked their paddles in unison, reaching with them, pushing against the current, withdrawing, and reaching again. We watched as they crouched, fixing a net between them. One of them sang as he began to paddle again.

"It's about us," Thérèse whispered. She hushed the children as the song came clearly across the water.

"What's he saying?" I asked.

"Do you see the *mendele*?" Jules translated, chanting almost the way the fisherman did.

"He's singing to his net," Thérèse explained to the kids. "Asking if it sees us."

Jules translated again: "See the *mondele mama?* She has four children. . . It is good when the *mendele* have children. . . "

The fisherman pulled his pirogue abreast of us, twenty yards off. We waved. He continued to sing. Jules translated.

"I wish I had fish to sell the *mendele.* . . . There are many of them. . . . I would have good business. . . ."

The space between us widened. The fisherman moved on, praising his net, instructing it to take a large catch.

The sun turned red in the western sky. It drifted toward the horizon through air just as we drifted on the surface through water.

At last Jules started the motor. We made a wide half-circle on the river, heading the boat back toward Coq. I stood on the prow, watching the wake give form to the river's flatness, smelling the clean scent of the water, and feeling the beginning coolness of evening.

As the sun touched the horizon's edge, Jules turned off the motor. Watching the sun set, we drifted on the river's immense silence. The sky grew pink, the river dark silver. The trees on shore became black twilight forms. Nothing could be more peaceful, I thought, nor more remote from danger.

ELEVEN

Aᴛᴛᴇʀ ᴛʜᴇ ɪɴᴄɪᴅᴇɴᴛ ᴀᴛ Bᴏʟᴏʙᴏ ᴅᴇᴘᴇɴᴅᴇɴᴛꜱ of UN personnel in the Equateur were told quietly to leave. Madison began
to discuss the possibility that we, too, would have to do this. Since
he and Sally wanted to go, they were happy to consider evacuation
plans. Tom pointed out that USIS work accomplished little in turbu-
lent times.

I doubted that we would need to evacuate and felt certain that ap-
pearing over-eager to do so would be a mistake. I found it difficult to
work at the center with the Madisons itching to go.

On lesson night, as we sat talking before the lesson began, I mentioned to the Andrés that the Madisons were already speculating about
the possibility of our leaving Coq.

"It's too early for that kind of talk," Jules observed excitedly.

"Madison sees how the rebellion is spreading," I said.

"First, it's talk like that," said Jules. "Then it's running from house
to house. The seeds of panic get sown."

"Then," added Thérèse, "it's people going to Léo to see a dentist and
never returning."

"I don't want to go through that again," said Jules. He looked over
at Thérèse. She stared at her own thoughts, playing with a thread that
had gone loose in the placemat that lay before her. "Hold out against
panic. That's the only way to stay sane."

"It gets more like independence every day," said Thérèse.

"There was panic at independence?" I knew there had been, but I
wanted them to talk about that time.

"Hunh!" muttered Jules. "It gripped the whole country. You say, 'I'm
not giving in to it.' But still it catches you."

"Because we were all afraid," explained Thérèse. "Europeans were
afraid of Congolese, even our houseboys. Soldiers had killed strikers in
Coq. There were mutinies south of Léo. Reports came daily of whites
being raped and beaten, robbed and murdered. Congolese were afraid
of us. Afraid we would leave them to run this country they realized
they didn't know how to run."

"We were like fathers to them," Jules said, "and the fathers were running away, abandoning their children."

"You've heard the story of the most terrible night," said Thérèse.

"No. What was that?"

"So many people had run from house to house that we were all in the grip of panic," said Jules. "Every man thought, 'I must get my wife and children out of Coq.'" I nodded. Certainly Jules had been thinking that. "If there was a boat," he added. "That was by no means certain." He shrugged. "We had called for paracommandos. Belgians. They were to drop at the airport at dawn. The paras were to hold the airport and get the Europeans out by plane. If there was to be a fight, that's where it would be."

"The trick was to get out before the paras arrived," said Thérèse. "Before the soldiers discovered the game." She began to stare in her mind at that time. "After dinner—" She turned to Jules. "Where had you gone?"

"To help the Italians. Remember?" Thérèse tried to recall them. "They were new. She'd just had a baby and her old father had come from Rome."

Thérèse nodded and smiled. "I was bathing the children. It was dark. Windy. I'd gotten them all taken care of except Yves." She concentrated further on that night. "Palm fronds scratched at the windows like thieves trying to enter. A pounding came at the door. I was terrified."

"Who was it?" I asked.

"A friend. 'Quick! Get the kids!' he shouted through the door. 'What's happening?' I asked. 'Where's Jules?' He yelled, 'Quick! There's a boat. Get the kids!'

"Panic took hold of me," said Thérèse. "I flew upstairs. Yves was still in the tub. The others were dressed for bed. I pulled Yves out." Thérèse laughed. "I didn't let him dry off. He was aghast to get into his clothes dripping wet."

Jules and I smiled at that picture. I thought of the boat that had brought Iwo and his family to Coq. Thérèse must have been talking about that kind of boat.

"We got downstairs," she continued. "The friend rushed us to the docks. It was something out of Dante there: a boat at the quai with passengers crowding the decks. But not a single light. And no sound. Forms darted across the dock, scurried up the gangway with their valuables. And no sound, no sound. The plan was to leave before the soldiers found out.

"I pushed the children onto the boat. Impossible to move! I looked for Jules, but it was only women and children and the old man from Rome. 'Where's my husband?' I whispered to him. But he only twitched his head, shivering in his shirt."

"The Italians said a boat was leaving." Jules took up the story. "I didn't believe it and ran to check. By the time I got home, the family was gone. I hurried to the dock.

"Army trucks were in the streets, rushing soldiers to the port. When they saw me running, they spat at me. Shouted insults. I prayed to God the boat had left. I cut through by the warehouse, got over the fence, and onto the dock just as the truck crashed through gates. I hid. Cries rose from the boat as soldiers rushed the quai."

"It hadn't left?"

"It started to pull away from the dock. But a cable held it. Crewmen tried to snap it with an axe, but it held. Soldiers lined the edge of the dock, insulting the women, waving rifles."

"It was terrifying on board," said Thérèse. "Too dark and crowded to see. I held on to the kids. We heard the soldiers cocking their rifles. Everyone pushed away from the soldiers to the river side of the boat. It began to list. If we aren't shot, I thought, we'll capsize and drown."

"At last ministers of the new government arrived," said Jules. "They went among the soldiers and finally quieted them. The boat came back to shore.

"Our families would have to stay on board till morning, I saw that," Jules went on. "Then I remembered the paras. You see what would happen. The soldiers would hear the planes. They'd see the paras drop against the dawn sky. And if they panicked? Or wanted to settle the score? They'd massacre the women and children. Or take them hostage. I rushed out to Bolenge."

I thought of what Thérèse always said of Jules: *Toujours la réaction vive.*

"Reverend Daly and I broadcast for hours," he said, "trying to get the drop called off. Léo, Brazza, Bangui. Not a single contact.

"About an hour before dawn there was a downpour, thick as a curtain. The paras didn't come. The soldiers ran off. As soon as they were gone, we collected our families and walked home in that rain."

For a long time no one spoke. Thérèse went back to playing with the loose thread on the placemat. "Will it happen again?" she asked.

"Don't let anyone talk you into a panic," Jules advised. "That's the key."

From a letter, dated Coquilhatville, 8 August 1964

As newspapers have undoubtedly informed you, Stanleyville was over-run Tuesday by rebels. All but three Americans evacuated from our consulate and USIS post. Those three are the consul, his radio and commo man, and probably the "spook" (CIA type). As far as we know, both USIS men were evacuated.

The battle of Bukavu continues to seesaw back and forth as it has now for two and a half months. The news Sunday was that the town was all but abandoned, that a fifth column of rebel sympathizers inside the town was presumed ready to emerge, and that the town was nearer to falling into rebel hands than it had ever been in May.

You are probably wondering where that leaves us in Coq. Thursday reports from Stan indicated that the rebels had pushed past Stan and were heading out along the two roads that lead eventually west: a north road curving toward Bumba and Lisala in Moyen Congo province at the height of the river's curve and a southwest road leading toward Ikela. Large helicopters have been whirring at low altitudes over Coq for the last couple of days. They are evacuating Europeans and missionaries from Moyen Congo and Ubangi provinces. . . .

The concern of the Cuvette Centrale provincial government is reflected in the fact that the usually unarmed police and military were issued weapons yesterday. To me this introduces a new element of danger. There's enough coercion and exploitation of the civilian population when the gendarmerie is unarmed. More soldiers walk around town than I have seen since my arrival. Now that they have weapons they strut, swagger, roll with importance, helmets drawn low over their eyes.

Will we have to evacuate? It's certainly difficult to say. One would think that the rebels would pause for a moment in Stan to consolidate their gains, open firm supply routes, and rest before pushing on. But this is not a disciplined movement.

Despite this sobering news, the following weekend was festive in Coq. In order to see if Sally's new servant was up to handling a party, the Madisons invited the Andrés and me to dinner Friday evening. After a slow start—the servant had some breaking in to do—we talked till 2:00 AM

The next morning we met again at my house with the André kids for coffee and pastry and to form our group into three teams for the Lions Club's annual *Rallye-Paper*, a kind of scavenger hunt for the European community. Our teams consisted of the Madisons and Thérèse; Jules and his sons Benoit and Jean-Luc; and Yves, Martine (who wanted to ride in the Power Wagon) and me.

We started in the town center, wearing funny hats, ran around town discovering the number of rooms in the hospital, the present population of the prison (432), and other useful information. We ended at the Botanic Gardens at Eala overlooking the Ruki. There our three teams had a picnic dinner. At a *soirée* in town the winners were announced: Jules & Co placed third, the Madisons fourth while Yves, Martine and I came in twelfth. Tom Madison won the prize for the best tie, something Sally had fashioned out of a 100 franc note.

Sunday afternoon I spent on the river with the Andrés.

Late one afternoon after the center had closed—Tom and I were finishing up—Iwo came into our office looking sheepish, yet so oddly pleased with himself that he could barely suppress his smiles. He put his hands to his head, swayed from side to side, and kept saying, "What a great problem, what a problem!" Then he announced that he had accepted a position with the DCCM as the director of the primary school at a place called Kiri, formerly a mission station but no longer staffed by missionaries. He would also be in charge of all back-country primary schools in the area. We congratulated him. He seemed pleased with the appointment and allowed that many intellectuals had come begging him to take the job.

After he left, Tom and I congratulated each other on having a personnel problem lifted out of our hands. We were genuinely pleased for

Iwo—there was a little staff goodbye party for him later in the week—and felt certain that in terms of *mpifo* he had made the right choice: to be the biggest fish in a very small pond.

Coquilhatville, 26 August 1964 Wednesday

Hi,

Madison left in a great hurry Monday morning for Léopoldville, catching a ride on a C-130 that passed through to leave four jeeps for the local military. He sent a message yesterday morning (in a code he'd worked out) saying to expect evacuation by military aircraft within ten days. Some Europeans have been leaving quietly. Thérèse says this is exactly the way it started in 1960, people fabricating excuses and then pulling out. Is it necessary we leave so soon?

Coq has been a hotbed of rumors since Stan was taken. Rebels seem to have moved into the Bumba area early last week. The ANC fled, as usual, and the Congolese population disappeared into the villages, an infallible sign that they figure there's trouble.

Henry Dugan, doctor at the DCCM station at Mondombe, radioed last night that ANC elements were retreating past the station toward Boende and that he was about to operate on a soldier with a bullet wound (indicating rebels armed with guns). The Congolese with whom he works recommended that he leave immediately. He operated on the soldier and left this morning by microbus to Monieka. DCCM is evacuating Wema station today (women and children by plane, the two men, an evangelist and a doctor, coming later with baggage in a microbus). Missionaries will have left everything east of Boende by tomorrow. Dugan tried to talk ANC soldiers out of the idea that there were Chinese among the advancing rebels, but the soldiers stuck to their conviction, insisting that there were. Who knows?

I went over to Coq's military HQ yesterday to see what news Major Kwima (who's new here) and his S-1 lieutenant had. They were in a highly excited state of frustration, a prelude to the agitation and hysteria that will increase as the rebel forces draw nearer. They asked me to radio for reinforcements: pursuit planes, armored cars, even food for the troops.

We are, of course, unsettled by the probability of evacuating. For all of Coq's disadvantages we have begun to carve out a life for ourselves here. The Madisons are enjoying the peace of a tiny post after too many

years of two cocktail parties every night and I feel that I'm just begin-
ning to find a place for myself, especially in my developing friendship
with the Andrés.

Thérèse and Benoit (who leaves tomorrow to start boarding school near
Namur in Belgium) came by Sunday morning about 10:00 to invite me
to spend the day with the family in the canot, *their boat. We got into our*
bathing suits, crossed the Congo and went back into the swamps north-
east of Coq where there's a shallow-bottomed lake. Jules and Benoit fished,
Thérèse steered, Yves, Jean-Luc, Martine and I amused ourselves as pas-
sengers. (Jules reacted to Thérèse's steering with short-tempered grumblings.
"I don't say it to criticize," he claimed, "but to instruct," and she, a good
European wife, whimper-grumbled low in her throat, knowing that then
was no time to call him on it. She teases him about being sharp with her
when he's in relaxed moods.) We had a picnic lunch on the banks, left
Thérèse at a likely spot for sketching, then trolled close into shore. Later we
all went swimming in water that was no deeper than my chin.

When we left, the sky had darkened. The winds that precede tropical
storms began to blow across the lake. Slash-and-burn fires were aflame
all around the lake. We came off it bouncing on wind-blown waves. The
swamp channels were better, fewer waves despite fishing nets everywhere.
It grew cold, then began to rain. Brrr! I had Martine and Jean-Luc, aged
six and ten, up front with me. At times Martine becomes a little wants
machine: I'm hungry, thirsty, cold, got to go pipi. *If these needs are not satis-*
fied, tears brink over the eyelids and everyone is miserable. Fortunately, she
was wrapped up in towels, a sweater and a blanket and gritted her teeth
with admirable six-year-old bravery.

The worst cold lasted only about fifteen minutes, but what a miserable
time that was! Thérèse, stood steering, in only a thin jersey and shorts; Jules
standing at the motor wore only a polo shirt and bathing suit. Both of them
sang into the wind. When we hit channels dammed up with water hya-
cinths, I paddled us through and jumped into one channel, shoulder deep,
to cut a path through the plants. Now and then the three adults would
burst out laughing at our predicament and sing louder.

When we got out into the main river, waves were blowing so high that
we didn't dare try a direct crossing. We huddled along the matiti *(the tall*
grasses) and finally crossed down the Ruki. It was much quieter.

While we were in the matiti *an Otraco boat appeared out of the rain*
and mist. It moved on down the river without making the routine stop at

Coq. The ANC had commandeered the boat in Lisala; it was full of soldiers fleeing rumors. Under Engulu's orders it was not permitted to land at Coq. Armed troops without food or shelter were the last thing we needed here.

To me the evacuation Tom is so eagerly planning seems a desertion of the Andrés. They have been so good to us. I admire their guts and perseverance and independence, their charm and cheerfulness and helpfulness under extremely trying conditions. It's difficult to watch people for whom you wish absolutely the best get mangled by fate. It seems clear to us who have made no investment of years or work or emotions here that there is no future in this country. Somehow the Andrés seem unable to reach this conclusion. They reject Belgium: the bourgeois tradition, narrowness of mental horizons, formality, a social and economic structure not conducive to the kinds of freedom they've been used to here. There is little opportunity in Belgium (as once there was here) to carve something out for yourself, to work hard, and see the results of your work, no room for pioneering.

They've been wonderful friends to me at a time when I needed friends. I hate to think we may be deserting them when, in the face of a worsening situation, they may need friends.

Returning from Léo, Tom Madison flew into Coq in the army attaché plane, known as Bugsmasher. With him were two military attachés and the newly arrived Public Affairs Officer, the top USIS man in the country. He was John Mowinckel, a tall, thick-boned fellow of Norwegian stock with a budding pot-belly and an earthy manner. He responded enthusiastically to Africa. He had some of the temperament of a beer-loving lumberjack, a sort of broad-hipped walk, his toes pointing sharply outward and his feet spread about a foot from each other.

As we toured Coq, he insisted I was driving too fast. He marveled at the "virility" of the river, at the beauty of the pirogues on its beige surface at high noon (sunset was the time to see the color), and kept talking about trying to get the *real feel* of Africa. What a contrast to Madison who failed to thrill at any of this.

Mowinckel seemed pleased with the challenges of the Congo assignment. Certainly he had arrived at an interesting time! After the jaded, temperamental Steve Baldanza and the bitching of Tom Madison, Mowinckel was distinctly refreshing. He seemed capable of making fast decisions and of making them himself. I wondered how a man so right for Africa could have also been right for France where he'd served for six years.

It must have been clear to John Mowinckel that Tom Madison wanted out of Coq. Tom had vented his frustrations in Léo and had conferred at length with the Branch PAO from Stanleyville who fled on the last plane out carrying a single suitcase. The Stan consulate's intelligence about the rebels had been solid up until three days before the town's fall. Then the rebels outran the intel.

Obviously Tom did not want him and Sally and me in that situation. He felt we could not do our cultural center job as things deteriorated. He had stressed to Mowinckel that we had virtually no reliable intelligence in Coq. As the rebels drew nearer, ever more exaggerated rumors flew around the town. Mowinckel agreed that Tom should have *carte blanche* to do whatever he felt best served US interests in Coq.

The question, of course, was: How dangerous was our situation? The visiting military attachés put together an assessment. By working hard and fast, using their findings, the center published a newssheet that reported that there were no rebels in the Cuvette Centrale, our province, none at Lisala, none moving toward Ikela and probably no Chinese advisors with youth elements.

Moreover, Coq had sufficient supplies and men to counter a rebel attack, if it possessed the will. It was hard to know if the newssheet actually calmed any fears. Radio Stan broadcast warnings to the people of Coq. These excited apprehensions difficult to counter, especially when the intelligence at Stanleyville had proved faulty.

If Madison had received an okay to do whatever he felt best served US interests in Coq, I was concerned that he might misread what served those interests in order to serve his own interests. Tom kept talking about evacuating us and expensive equipment. We did not want to get caught, of course, but running too soon would damage our reputation.

If we were able to return to Coq after evacuating, it would be very tough going if the townspeople thought we had inflamed panic by prematurely evacuating rather than displaying some courage until things were clearly bad. And was there any real reason to worry about expensive equipment? Wasn't evacuating equipment a way of dismantling the center I'd worked so hard to establish?

Rebel broadcasts from Radio Stan threatened reprisals against

Americans because of American aid to the Central Government. They also encouraged acts, specifically against Americans. With everything in flux, which meant Congolese might see chances for gain or opportunity, the missionaries found that even some of their own people eyed their material possessions, salivating at the prospect that looting would begin. A missionary at Bolenge was warned by his servant to leave because "the people here hate you and they want your possessions."

Henry Dugan found it rough evacuating Mondombe by microbus. Fleeing solders stopped him several times along the way. At one point an armed Congolese ordered him to drive him to Coq. As the man moved around the microbus to get in, Henry gunned it and took off, only to have *jeunesse*, youth rebels, run out of the forest along the side of the road. He was very shaken when I saw him later at the mission offices. It was not rebels now so much as *jeunesse* (which meant local bands of discontented and unemployed youth) that menaced the region.

The afternoon that we went out to the airport to meet Bugsmasher after the attachés had flown over Lisala, Bumba and Basoko, we found Benoit André dressed in a charcoal gray flannel suit with short pants, a tie and a white shirt. He was about to leave home to seek his fortune in the world, quite an undertaking at age eleven. Thérèse urged him to take off the coat. He refused because everyone would see the spots on his shirt. He was to fly that afternoon to Léo where an André friend would meet him and put him on the night plane to Brussels via Athens.

Thérèse told him that when he arrived in Athens he must look for the *"Acropole qui est tres visible de l'air,"* that he must buy some postcards for people in Coq. But would Belgian money buy him postcards? Would he have to change it into drachmas? Who knew? I asked Madison (who always carried "green") to give Benoit a dollar for postcards.

"This is good anywhere in the world," Tom told him.

Benoit stared at the dollar, obviously just the thing to give him. "I have the feeling he won't spend it," Thérèse said later. Perhaps he put it somewhere safe where he could take it out to impress his friends and comfort himself with when he felt lonely. He seemed both excited and sad. The sadness and the challenge he faced almost got the better of him as the end of the waiting drew near. When his plane was announced he looked as if he might cry, but he didn't.

That evening Colonel Raudstein, the military attaché, asked me to hunt up Major Kwima, the Coq ANC commander. I went out to the Wangata Military Camp, found Kwima, and got him and Raudstein together at a meeting that included the power elite of the Coq military plus a stellar attraction, the regional ANC commander responsible for the flight from Lisala. As the meeting progressed, this officer kept interrupting Raudstein in Lingala to undermine what he was saying. To bolster Raudstein's French, I acted as translator. Raudstein tried to convince the officers that there were enough men and enough equipment to hold out against an attacking force, particularly if rebels coming up from Ikela were cut off from the ferry at Ingende.

The Congolese didn't want to believe it. They considered the rebels to be invincible. Witchdoctors immunized them from bullets, they had heard. Bullets turned to water when they hit rebel chests. Numbers seemed the only thing that mattered to the Congolese military: reinforcements and complicated machinery. I left the meeting quite depressed about what seemed to me the inevitable loss of Coq.

But you couldn't blame the Congolese. Their kind of warfare was different from ours. Ours was lethal and we kept sending them arms. In addition, they seemed incredibly ignorant, without analytical skills. Moreover, they were stationed outside the tribal areas where they had loyalties and they lived in a spirit-filled world incomprehensible to us. They talked in good faith about fighting to the death. They might mean it, I thought—until bullets flew over their heads. Then it was something else again.

Raudstein told his assistant that in the Congo he'd learned patience and prejudice. Yes, you learned something about patience. But prejudice, as he meant it, struck me as a stupid reaction to what we encountered. Sometimes, however, it was tempting to think: "Hell, let's give it to the Chinese to see what they can make of it."

I was looking forward to escaping Coq for a while. But not as a refugee. In fifteen days I was scheduled to go to Europe on vacation. I would be meeting a young woman in Munich.

TWELVE

Coquilhatville, 2 September 1964

Hi,

As usual The Situation is as complicated and fluid as ever. Sunday an Air Congo plane was shot at trying to land in Lisala and was forced to seek another airfield. Monday a C-130 passed through here on its way north to Gemena in the Ubangi to leave ANC reinforcements. Radio Tomcat (Embassy Léo) relayed a message from the ambassador that Sally Madison should return to Léo "on consultation." This at 11:00 for a 2:30 departure.

"I have nothing to tell the ambassador," said Sally and she has stayed. But the Madisons sent out two large footlockers and their VW. I sent out a crate of my "valuables." Three missionary women and their children also went on the plane.

Yesterday Tom decided that we should leave next Monday, in five days. The idea is to get a C-130 up here to take out us and our belongings and the most valuable center equipment. We had a short meeting with the staff late yesterday. Today we began to pack movie projectors and speakers, the addressograph machine. This morning we delivered the bulk of our Nouveaux Horizons books to local schools (although this project was already scheduled).

It's now 5:15 Thursday morning. I couldn't stay awake last night. We seem to do nothing all day but listen to the radio and try to piece out bases for intelligent decisions. It's wearying, although not physically.

I am beginning to realize how itchily ready to get out of here Madison has been for several weeks. When he went to Léo ten days ago, I thought it was to clarify things about our operations. I wonder now if Tom may not have been seeking permission to leave. "I can't make your decisions for you!" the Deputy Chief of Mission was supposed to have shouted at him.

Madison lays greater stress on monetary considerations than I do. He keeps wanting to get the equipment out. He suggested yesterday that I go through our library collections and withdraw all "expensive books." I can imagine those "expensive books" getting tossed around a Léo warehouse, covered with dust and cobwebs, forgotten in a corner, sitting in water during the rainy season. I told Tom I thought it a good suggestion when its priority came around, which we agreed would be late.

Yesterday when things turned critical in the Ubangi, Tom came back into the office feeling pleased with himself, feeling exonerated. He said: "I'm going to get my skin and your skin and Sal's skin out whole and I'm going to get out some of the equipment!"

Tom has checked with me right along to see if I agreed with his decisions and I do agree that as a USIS post we have all but lost our usefulness. We know that there is no will to defend Coq from the rebels. It's said that the town is full of jeunesse, armed with smuggled weapons. I doubt the likelihood of some sudden combustion of these elements. I don't think they'll explode until they can work in conjunction with rebel army elements moving toward Coq. Past experience suggests that the jeunesse aided rebel troops, but not before they were fairly close to a town. Tom stresses the advisability of a "graceful withdrawal." That seems a funny way to describe an evacuation.

I told Tom yesterday that I thought it was a bit too early for us to make an evacuation, that it could do him professional harm. You "come out smelling like a rose" (to use his term) if you evacuate, particularly if with a suitcase and a few singed hairs. But if you get out too early, you can look silly, regardless of how many machines you bring with you. Maybe people oughtn't to think this way, but they do. His response was: "The professional harm is nothing compared to the physical harm of waiting too long." Of course, there is no answer to that.

I'm concerned that Tom will pull us out before the missionaries go. "I've been acting like a consul up here," he whines. "Like an intelligence officer." To me, that seems a strange way to react to opportunity. "We have no diplomatic status," he says. "It's not my job to get these people out." I've been over this ground with both him and Sally, explaining my opinion that we are people working for our government and that our govt now needs us to do a consular job. I don't care what the title is!

I told Tom I'd volunteer to stay on, standing by the radio. "If you stay, I can stay," he said. I told him I thought it would simplify things if Sally left. So she'll probably start considering me a threat to her marriage. The thing that kills me about not looking at this situation as an opportunity is that it is exactly what Madison needs to get this promotion he bitches about. It's the kind of opportunity that kicks a man one step up the line. He should be grateful for it.

Sally is collecting all lamps and rugs and govt linens for shipment to Léo. Strangely but truly, rugs have come to represent for me the dividing line between decent and intolerable living in Coq. When I balked about having to give mine up, she agreed to "imagine" them in a trunk.

"Where's the second lamp?" she asked.

"I'm using it."

"Oh." You get the picture.

We got to talking about The Situation and I reiterated my feeling that we can't leave before the missionaries. "I'm not leaving before anybody else," she said, as if I had suggested that she and Tom were running away. Poor distraught woman.

Calling Sally distraught is perhaps unfair. I have so little to worry about except for my skin. I keep forgetting there are differences in viewpoint and resiliency and adjustability between thirty and forty-six. Sally has done a good, good job of keeping her figure (and I'm sure this is one of her Great Values). Sally still looks great in slacks and girlish dresses and one throws a compliment her way every now and then in recognition of the preservation effort. I'm sure the missionaries find Sally pretty high style. The facial preservation has not been as successful as the other. Sometimes she looks her age, wrinkles chronicling the crises she's battled through. The lines were out in full force yesterday. Enough nastiness.

Yesterday people in Gemena in Ubangi to the north of us began to realize their danger. The National Savior, the ANC, commandeered the Air Congo flight out of the town leaving a number of civilians stranded at the airport. Only in the Congo is Army flight more important than civilian evacuation. Two additional Air Congo planes promised for Gemena yesterday never arrived. People are there waiting to evacuate, people from Lisala and plantations as well as Catholic and Protestant missionaries. Fortunately, the Gemena problems have given Dick Taylor the shove he's needed to realize it's time to get his missionary dependents out of Coq. While there

(The letter ends in mid-sentence. Events overtook me while typing it. The next page of the letter is dated Léo, Sunday 6 September 1964. Continuing, it recounts events of the previous days. I kept a record of our evacuation. As a refugee I had time to do that at the USIS office.)

Tuesday evening, language study night. Dinner as usual chez les Andrés. Jules and Thérèse in fine form. All went well at dinner; no outbursts from

Jules, no scoldings of Thérèse. Jokes about the College where Jean-Luc and Yves start school next week. Jules asks the names of the priests at the school. Jean-Luc knows them only as le Père Prefet, le Père *this,* le Père *that. All titles. Jules inquires: "Do you know* le Père Pétuel*?" The guys shake their heads. "Le Père Ceptive?" Jules asks. The adults laugh behind their napkins and the kids finally get it.*

After dinner we three adults discuss wine ceremonies of la vielle Europe. *I laugh at the formality of it all and Thérèse, on edge and suddenly offended, leaves the table, saying she will not discuss it further in my presence. "What can one do if he has an ironic smile?" I ask her, alluding to her tale of being given demerits at school simply for smiling at the teacher. She returns to the table.*

Jules recounts wine formalities with his usual enthusiasm and involvement: the cave, *the cushion of earth on its floor, the testing and tasting, home-bottling, securing the right kinds of cork. Jules tells of the* curé *who knew the origin of every wine. How he would pour wine into his hands and sniff. And as he tells his story, Jules sits there: pouring, rubbing wine into his palms, taking deep sniffs.*

And I sit there feeling an obligation to warn these friends of Tom's decision to evacuate. I finally tell them. An abrupt change of mood. Thérèse puts her head down on the back of her chair, sitting sideways in it, and says nothing, worried, fearful, feeling abandoned. Immediately agitated, Jules paces back and forth, bending down to me to make a point, words spilling out. I'm next to Thérèse also sideways in my seat. At last he sits.

Thérèse stares at three huge beetles, long as a man's finger. The kids have hung them on a bar of the small table lamp, their wings as glossy as hard shells. The stingers work (and even look rather) like a thumb and forefinger and the beetles hang from them. Before dinner Jules referred to the beetles as Yves, Jean-Luc and Benoit. Now Thérèse taps one after the other and says: "A. N. C." She laughs like a mischievous girl and begins to break up a little wooden match-box, arranging the pieces in a circle.

Jules says to Thérèse: "If we have to go this time, it's finished." He speaks of Australia. No, he won't go back to the small-mindedness of Belgium. Thérèse's head remains on the chairback. Jules says Belgium and the US are crazy ever to have mixed into an inter-African squabble. We have different objectives, take war more seriously, Africans like to palaver, the whole thing might have arranged itself. Our intervention has not helped. Perhaps. But

US policy forces intervention because, whereas we talk continually of non-intervention, intervention is our real policy.

He concludes by saying that if we must leave, he hopes that it will not be too soon. I say I'm afraid it will be. Suddenly exhausted, he says goodnight. He goes upstairs to take a sleeping pill and leaves me with his wife. Thérèse and I start to work on English. A regular lengthy lesson, late starting, followed by tea. It's mostly talk which she and I both need. I return home at 1:15 AM. Late for Coq.

Wednesday there seemed no reason for a precipitate departure. That evening some packing for the C-130 scheduled to take out some of our belongings. Also wanted to write down a log of what has been happening. But too tired.

Thursday morning. Nothing pressing at the office. I suggest to Tom that I go pack since we are thinking in terms of living out of suitcases. I get Joseph out of the house, asking him to wash the car, and work leisurely, cleaning out the upstairs bedroom I've used as a storeroom.

I find Thérèse outside the André office as I am putting the typewriter in the car. She tells me that she passed by the Duriers the previous evening and stayed a moment. Coopmans also there. They all asked her if the Americans were planning to leave. She hesitated. What could she say? But she has always proved an accomplished evader of direct questions. She told them: "You can't imagine the amount of stuff Americans bring to a place like Coq." And it is true that she has been flabbergasted at all the junk that Sally has. "They are getting out some of their excess," she explained. She laughs to me, pleased at this cunning evasion.

Packing finished, I do some errands. Stop at Bogaerts to order a new tire for the car (the spare is no longer good). Over to missionary Ruth Reed's to pick up eggs for Thérèse and me. Ruth puts her entire collection of eggs into a large basket. "Give these all to Mme André," she says.

"All of them?" I ask. "Why?"

"Aren't you leaving today?" Ruth asks me.

"Are you leaving today?" I ask, amazed. This is the first news I've heard of it.

"I heard everyone was leaving today," says she.

Glugg.

I hurry to the center. Engulu, finally returned from Léo, is in the office. Tom stands at the door of the radio room. I ask him: "Are we leaving today?" He begins to explain. But this is no time for explanations. I ask only for the order. He says that Engulu sees no possibility of defending Coq. Tom has called for a C-130. The plane will be in at 2:30. Things are in a high state of nervousness.

I zoom out to see Thérèse and Jules. Jules, doing brick-making business this morning, is off in the chantier *trying to fix the dredge half-sunk in sand. Break the news to Thérèse and give her Ruth Reed's eggs. I tell her that, if she wishes, she and the children can accompany us to Léo on this evacuation flight. Momentarily she's tempted. "No, if I start running, I will never stop," she says. I know exactly what she means.*

Leaving, I pass our man Raphael who has a note for Thérèse from Sally. I take her the note; it asks her to come immediately to the Madisons. Thérèse offers to come explain to Joseph in Lingala that I must leave, but first she will pack the valise I've offered to send down along with my stuff.

Go out to see Jules at the dredge. He has filthy hands and offers me his wrist to shake. I tell him that Tom has ordered our evacuation. "This is a mistake," he says. "The Congolese will think you're abandoning them." He asks me to come for lunch if there is time. I ask him to come to the airport.

At the house I start Joseph wrapping the dishware. I pack suitcases. Thérèse arrives with the footlocker for the Léo pied-à-terre. In typical André style only one of the two hasps works. But bound with filament tape the footlocker stays closed. Thérèse explains all to Joseph and I give him a month's salary (CF 2500), the ticket for the bike tires I've ordered for him from Bouks (due at the end of July, they have not yet arrived), and some old clothes. Thérèse goes off to help Sally.

I finish packing by 12:30 and return to the office to pay the boys. We've told them to stay through the lunch hour, but two have gone out. Pay Ahenga, Raphael and Edouard, making out petty cash receipts for each. Pay each two periods in advance.

Pass by the Madisons to pick up a sandwich and rendezvous with Tom before going to the airport. Everything is more or less chaos chez les M. *Thérèse is the only person working in an organized, nerveless fashion. Tom screams at everyone. Sally is packing, the place a mess, her houseboys running every which way trying to get things done. Once again she has thrown everything all over the living room. She's indulging an innate sense of drama. No wonder the boys are upset, scared, panicky; they take their cue from her. I get instructions and zip out to the airport. The plane roars over just as I am leaving the Ms.*

The C-130 crew wonders what is happening. They've been deflected from a flight going from Katanga into Luluabourg to come get us. How many people? Who will they be? What's the local military situation? The only report I've heard all morning is that eight truckloads of rebels passed Mondombe earlier in the day. There's also been talk of rebels only a little east of Boende.

Go back to the Madisons. Tom has returned to the center. Sally asks me to boost his morale, to reassure him he's done the right thing. In deciding earlier in the day not to question his decisions (in a crisis a superior deserves at least that much support from an underling), I've suspended my sense of analysis. At the center we are still trying to pay the boys. My job. Tom collects our pertinent files.

Everyone being paid, there is nothing more to do at the office. I take the truck and get my stuff out to the airfield and loaded onto the C-130. Missionaries begin to arrive. I talk to Betty Erlewine, asking if Dick Taylor and the other men have decided to go. She doesn't know; it's still up in the air.

Back in town we finally get the Madisons organized. Both the André pick-up and the center's Power Wagon are loaded to the gills with tiny boxes of God only knows what, every conceivable thing. It seems strange that coupled with this hurried decision to evacuate there should be this unwillingness to leave the tiniest thing behind. If we are really so concerned about the burden of the American lives that hangs so heavily on us in our unwonted consular function, why are we so concerned about saving plastic plates? Why so preoccupied with sending out the center equipment? The ambassador himself has said, "Screw the equipment!"

Sally emerges. My god! she looks dressed to call on an ambassador's wife. She's in one of those girlish dresses that attest to her preservation. Bien-coiffed. The switch that's peroxide-streaked just like her own hair rests on her head like a crown. The wrinkles that made her look so overcome by events yesterday are under control; she's taken ten years off her age. Fresh lipstick. Even the God-damned green mascara. What is this: an evacuation or a social occasion? Next to her Therese looks tired, worried. Who has really done the packing?

"Sally," I tell her, "I have never seen anyone looking so nice for an evacuation!" Shame on me! But I don't approve of anyone looking so modish in a crisis. If her husband really needs assurance that we are leaving A Dangerous Situation, why does she look like something out of Vogue? As my irony-edged compliment reaches her, Sally turns on her high heels and her

face lights up with such pleasure at what she a woman (almost fifty) can still do to a man (hardly thirty). How can you disapprove, even in a crisis, of someone so easy to make happy?

We begin to get people and their belongings onto the plane. De Chalan from the Hevea plantation in Bikoro has a Dutch woman with an injured leg and an infant he wants sent out. He also gives me a letter urging light plane evacuation of the other women in Bikoro. The Hobgoods and a British family of four in from Basankusu evacuate with us.

Will Dick Taylor go? I'm concerned that if he doesn't, Tom won't, and Sally in her turn will refuse to go. Is it that Sally refuses to leave without Tom? Or that Tom won't stay without Sally? Dick's aware of this; I've made sure that he is. Fortunately, everyone is to go.

Jules André is nowhere to be found. I go search for him. The waiting room is as crowded as it was the afternoon Benoit left. Two planes come in this afternoon. A concerned-looking Herman calls to me, his reaction obvious on his face: "How dare you Americans leave without telling your landlord!" I can't find Jules anywhere. I say hello to the taciturn Houzé. "Vous partez?" he asks me.

"Oui." We say nothing more. His expression hardly changes and he does not look at me so much as at the huge plane out on the tarmac.

Still that small exchange makes me realize what the Europeans will think: that we've fled (for I feel that is what Houzé would call it).

Unable to find Jules, I seek out Herman. He's concerned about his building; I explain the set-up: Rent continues as usual, Edouard has the keys. We will correspond with him, when necessary, through regular channels until they are cut off, then through his bank. Tom went over this with me earlier in the day, wanting to push the Herman visit off on me. Herman tells me, "There are one hundred women and children who should be gotten out of here." He's obviously concerned about his family. He says that Jules has gone into town to write a letter to the Belgian Embassy seeking evacuation facilities for Belgians. He does not return before the plane leaves.

THIRTEEN

AFTER WE ARRIVED IN Léo, Tom and I drove in to give a report to the embassy's Political Section. There was "surprise" that we had come out so soon. Tom began justifying himself, bad tactics in my judgment. Dick Matheron, down on consultation from Bukavu, asked me if I'd like to come up to USIS Bukavu. I encouraged his interest (why not?) although I said I was taking off for Europe as soon as possible. A C-130 was scheduled to fly into Coq the next day (9/4) and I decided to hitch a ride in order to help any Belgian women and children who wanted to evacuate. Sent a radio message via UN radio to Jules.

Next day up to Gemena with a planeload of ANC reinforcements for the Ubangi. We flew over endless miles of scrub country under a dark sky and found Gemena, a tiny town in the middle of nowhere. The pilot suddenly sighted the airstrip and heading in, barrelled in low and fast over the runway to check that it was safe to land. Then we circled, came in and put down just long enough to get the troops off.

I sought out the MEU representative, an African-American missionary. "How're things up here?"

"Everything's pretty calm."

"Your people getting out to Bangui?"

"Most of 'em. I'm staying on for a while."

Wished we could have had a real chat. As we left Gemena, Congolese tried to rush onto the loading ramp. Paratroop guards pointed rifles at them to discourage their excitement.

At the Coq airport no Europeans were waiting to get out. That meant our departure had provoked no eagerness to leave, just doubts about our courage. The Andrés' white BMW was there with Thérèse and the kids all ready to go. Since there was time, we returned to their house and had lunch together. The kids seemed excited about flying in the big plane, but had no sense of danger. The flight was just a convenient way to get to Léo. Thérèse was to have taken the kids down via Air Congo the next day anyway to put Jean-Luc and Yves into school.

During lunch I realized that my message of the night before had compromised Jules' stature among the *ex-colons*. It seemed to designate him as a kind of evacuation coordinator. He complained, "Portuguese kept coming this morning, saying: 'We understand that we have to see you, M André, to get a place on the plane.'" Very important in the *colon* mind not to be the first to run.

Jules was sympathetic to my situation. He spoke of *brave types* suffering in '60, yanked out by panicky bosses. He felt that, having pulled out too early, too hastily, we'd have difficulty returning at a later time to re-establish ourselves. The Congolese and Belgians would not respect our values, he felt. They would think we ran too fast. After this lunch I felt Tom and I (or one of us) should return to Coq to man the center and act as a listening post until the town is more obviously threatened.

During dessert Maitre Herman appeared. He was offered a beer which he took and stood around like a child who haunts another family's house at meal times. Seeing me, he gestured thumbs-up. We shook hands and the depth of his gratitude for American rescue planes seemed embarrassingly close to the surface. What a contrast to the implied criticism he'd leveled at me yesterday.

Herman had come to plead for a favor from Thérèse. He now asked to speak to her privately, wanting to beg her to keep an eye on his wife. Finally they returned. We'd known all along why he'd come. Even so, Thérèse looked as if she'd been attacked. Herman smiled, relieved, and shook hands all around. In parting he once again gestured thumbs up to me.

After he left, we laughed about that final gesture. "Today it's thumbs up for the Americans," said Jules.

"And yesterday it was thumbs down!" I added.

Thérèse seemed surprised she'd survived the encounter. She kept grumbling about *"cette personne"* (Mme Herman) and her *"crise de nerfs."* At least it was *"crise de nerfs"* before the children.

At the airfield Mme Herman was sloppy drunk. She had never struck me as the sort of woman who belonged in the Congo. Her mind was too sharp, too *raffiné*. Trained as a lawyer herself, she worked up her husband's briefs. But the Congo seemed to unbalance her unusually alert mind, to deprive her of the needed adaptability. She was a well-known victim of *"crise de nerfs,"* as it was euphemistically called in town. I'd heard whispers about the problem. Now she could hardly talk.

She kept walking around, her hair frizzy and sticking out on all sides. Dragging a coat, she complained loudly to her husband that she had left out of her suitcases "the new blue blouse that you've never seen." Herman called after her ineffectually, imploring her to remain at the car until the crew was ready to load passengers.

Their two children, smart-alecky in this crisis, alert but undisciplined, danced around getting in the way. The little girl approached me five times a minute to shake hands, calling out, *"Bonjour, Monsieur!"* in a sing-song voice. Poor kids, probably embarrassed to death. At one point after take-off the boy finally said, "Shut up, *Maman*."

In handling refugees one grew accustomed to people stripped of all defenses. Fortunately everyone made the best of the situation Mme Herman created. The officers and crew members were solicitous, walked her onto the plane, assured her that all baggage would be taken care of.

We boarded fathers and sisters from the Catholic Mission in Lisala, trying to get their names and nationalities so they could be radioed to the various consular officers in Léo. Most of these missionaries were Flemish, blond, with faces right out of Van Eyck, Memling and Breughel. Stubborn and contrary. Finally we boarded them all.

Meanwhile, a crowd of Congolese pushed forward to board the plane. As the only American who spoke French, I was charged with selecting and loading passengers. Gripped by fear, many Congolese became nasty when I refused to allow them to board. They insisted: "These are our planes! These planes are under the control of the Congolese government!" Or "It is not right to evacuate Europeans when there are Congolese wanting to leave!" And finally: "This proves that the US is a racist country."

I assured them that another C-130 was coming in. They didn't believe me. Fortunately, as the first one was preparing to take-off, the second arrived. We boarded most anybody with a legitimate reason to go: Army people, more European evacuees. Among them was the governor of Moyen Congo province and two of his ministers. Dressed in a sport shirt and slacks, he looked like a college student. Those clothes, he told me, were all he managed to take out of Lisala. The second C-130 also took the wife of a local provincial minister. She carried an infant and a huge washtub full of possessions, the whole business wrapped up in mammy cloth.

As I finished with these refugees, the Herman kid came zipping out at his mother's request in a final effort to find the new blue blouse. I got him back on board and took a head check. Thérèse sat in the dark front of the plane, *"cette personne"* beside her, talking confusedly to herself. Thérèse clutched Martine, Jean-Luc and Yves and stared straight ahead. All seats were filled; some men sat on the floor. On take-off and landing they grabbed onto the freight that lined the center of the plane.

Flying back to Léo, I became more and more convinced that Jules was right. If we did not return almost immediately to Coq—even if it meant living out of packed suitcases and doing nothing but tend the radio—we might jeopardize our entire investment in the town. An American presence must be there, I felt, until the danger grew a great deal worse than it was at present. Tom radioed the plane from Léo, wanting to know if he could pick me up at the airport. I suggested he come without Sally so that we could seriously discuss the possibility of a return.

But when we arrived, Sally was there with him. Madison was handling himself badly, without the self-confidence needed to bring off his decision to evacuate. He dismissed my suggestion of a return. I argued that unless we returned, we would jeopardize what we'd built there. Sally shot me hostile looks. I saw that Tom needed reassurance that he'd done the right thing. Sally was there to keep me from undermining whatever confidence he had. I began to suspect that Tom did not want to get out of Coq only to protect Sally. Despite his protests—"I can get along just fine in Coq. What do I care if the job's below my capabilities?"—probably he'd wanted to get out all along.

I tried to suggest that he play things differently, that he not justify his decision. As the man on the spot he knew better than Léo people what was best for our personal safety. Justification only placed questions in listeners' minds. But assuming a positive stance, exuding confidence, took more political savvy, more brazennness than Tom possessed. Instead, he wanted every sympathetic ear to hear the story. He'd even begun to say: "I've been criticized."

"Oh, no!" his listeners would reply to his face. Then they'd go away, mulling what the criticism might be. Sometimes Tom obligingly detailed the charges.

When I got into Léo from the airport, I hoped to see Mowinckel to tell him we must get back. If I could get to the office, I might catch him there. But I could not get there. Instead I was swept up in settling Thérèse and the kids into the *pied-à-terre*. By the time we'd delivered luggage and gotten keys and made certain that Mme Herman was set up, it was well past 7:30. I'd missed Mowinckel. Even so, I was happy at last to be of service to the Andrés.

Nor was I able to see Mowinckel the next day. He was entertaining USIA bigwigs from Washington. Tom told me that Mowinckel had been informed of my feelings. He wanted to hold off for now. Thwarted at USIS, I went over to the embassy, hoping to sell the idea of a return to the Political Section. A young woman in Personnel greeted me cheerily: "You guys were afraid up there, weren't you?" That comment stung me.

As I gave my pitch to Political, Tom walked in on other business. (Truth to tell, he deserved credit for being so patient with a subordinate who was both undermining his confidence and his reputation at the embassy.) We left POL together. He said nothing until we'd driven to USIS. Then he counseled: "I don't think it's wise to talk to POL about a return. State has different objectives than USIS. Let them send their own man."

Sunday night there was a cocktail party for the USIA visitors at Mowinckel's apartment. Due to a rumor that Boende had fallen to the rebels, Tom's spirits had somewhat revived. "There's nothing like experience, old boy," he told me with an exonerated closed-mouth smile that reduced his eyelids to slits. Even so, he looked edgy. Worry showed in his face. His skin had gone flabby, pasty. He was sleeping badly. Still he smiled obligingly to everyone, courting support wherever he could find it.

At the end of the party Mowinkel took me aside. He'd heard I wanted to go back, he said. With the air of a parent soothing an excited child, he advised, "Calm down. Let's not think about it now." And I thought: to hell with the whole thing.

I left Mowinckel's cocktail with the Madisons and suggested that I buy them and Thérèse a dinner. We collected Thérèse at the André's *pied-à-terre*. The kids were asleep. We left them under the care of Thérèse's neighbor who was glad to see her going out with friends. We went to a very nice penthouse restaurant overlooking the river where *fondue bourguignonne* was a speciality.

Ever since our evacuation Sally had been feeling nervous and tired, her nervousness exacerbating her fatigue and vice versa. After she had a martini and some wine, I observed the same tipsiness that I had first noticed on Boudart's last evening in Coq when she told him that he had a "commercial mentality."

As we were finishing our fondue, Sally said, "Terry, my dear, you absolutely must stop letting Fred give you English lessons."

Thérèse was always embarrassed when one of the Madisons called her Terry. Now she cocked her head as if to be sure she had heard correctly.

This matter was no business of the Madisons. I glanced at Tom to caution Sally. I felt sure he had heard the slur in her speech. But Tom only smiled, as if enchanted.

"Fred is going to teach you a masculine and pedantic English," Sally went on. "I assure you."

"I'm well known for masculine English," I said to keep it light.

Sally looked at me as if contemplating a rejoinder, but did not succumb to the temptation. "I'm serious," she continued. "You should definitely learn English from a woman."

"*Vraiment?*" Thérèse said as if she were not sure what Sally was talking about.

"And why is that?" I asked, trying to keep it banter, although I now realized I should never have let the Madisons know that we did the lessons. It would require no great perspicacity for Sally to understand that the lessons were important to me for they provided Thérèse and me a chance to be together.

"Why? Because Terry is so delicate and feminine and you might—" She stopped before going further.

I spoke to Madison in French that Sally would not understand. "*J'en ai marre de tout ça.*" (I've had enough of this.)

Tom smiled one of his indulgent smiles at Sally and made no comment.

"You might do to the English you give her what you do to French." Sally giggled. "I mean, my dear, you absolutely mangle French." More giggles. "Maybe you do communicate, but you do *mangle* it so."

I made a neutral gesture. It had always been a source of secret sustenance to me that Thérèse judged my accent better than Tom's—at least when I was at my best. I was aware that some days were better than others.

Sally got on to me about showing the wrong attitude toward USIS, about my negativity and cynicism, about my having given nothing to the work instead demanding everything, about my being unable to bear up under hardships. I could indulge her in this, partly because it had started as banter and partly because it so obviously listed the complaints that could be made about her husband.

But it stopped being banter and got ever rougher. "I sometimes think cry-babies like you should be sent home to your mother." She smiled to herself. "And you think you're going to be a writer." I wished the isolation of Coq had never tricked me into telling either of them anything about me or my aspirations. "What're you gonna write about, mama's boy?"

"This is getting pretty rough," I commented to Tom.

He shrugged. "Oh, you know," he said. "One really has to be tolerant with women." He must have been glad to hear it said.

Thérèse was embarrassed. I doubted that she understood much of what was being said, for it was all in English. But there was no mistaking Sally's tone and intention. Thérèse ordered coffee. For a few moments we talked about other things. Then Sally started in again.

"Tom gives so much every day to this little nothing post we've been sent to," Sally said. She looked sneeringly at me. "The embassy must have known you couldn't handle it alone. Why else would they have sent an officer of Tom's achievements and capabilities to take charge of the mess you'd made?"

It went on like this, getting worse and worse, Sally leaning over the table. Finally I got up, found the waiter, and paid the bill.

When we left the restaurant, the Madisons went off. I walked Thérèse back to the *pied-à-terre*. "*In vino veritas,*" Thérèse commented.

"*Un moment, s'il vous plaît!* She was saying nasty things about me."

"She's very worried. She knows they came out of Coq too early and that it will hurt Tom's career."

"It could have been a real opportunity if he'd played it right."

"Will you go back?"

"If I can. It doesn't look like they'll let me."

"Jules has so much respect for Tom," she said. "All the places he's served. He's seen a lot of places, yes, I say. But he's learned nothing."

When we reached the *pied-à-terre,* Thérèse could not find her key. In the confusion of our leaving, she had left it in the apartment. We knocked at the door of the neighbor who had found no reason to check the children. Thérèse was locked out. Only a wall separated the neighbor's apartment and the Andrés'. It turned out that the windows opened in such a way that, because the André window was ajar, I could climb on the outside of the building and gain access to the André apartment. I did this and let Thérèse in without ever waking the kids.

I spent the night in the apartment sleeping on an air mattress on the floor. During periods of wakefulness I thought about what Sally had said. Was there any truth to it? Or was it just a woman's way of attacking a man, her husband's underling who had become his nemesis? For that must have been how she saw things. Her words afforded me a chance to glimpse the me that others saw. Madison, I acknowledged, had been very patient with a subordinate who was jeopardizing his reputation. I thought, too, that I could learn a couple of useful truths about life in the Foreign Service: (1) Have a tough skin and (2) Never tell anyone anything.

The next time I encountered Sally Madison, she apologized profusely. She excused herself for having made a fool of herself, apologizing for the hurt she had done herself rather than that she had done me. I told her it was forgotten. However, I'd steer clear of her when she was having a *crise de nerfs.*

The next evening when I stopped by Thérèse's *pied-à-terre*, the kids were asleep on the floor, stretched out on air mattresses. With Thérèse were M and Mme Nizet. He was a *conseiller* working closely with Justin Bomboko, the Equateur's independence-era politician who still had influence. The Nizets had spent much time in the Equateur; Monsieur wanted detailed information about the situation in Coq. We got out a map and detailed what we knew. Nizet felt that the Central Government must act to save Coq. Bomboko was the logical man to push for the aid. Not that Coq was particularly worth saving in itself, Nizet admitted. But it was the gateway to Léo. Its fall would have tremendous psychological impact.

Nizet and I quit the *pied-à-terre* together. He left his wife at home and I followed him out beyond the city into the suburb of Djelo Binza. Nizet had a casual appointment there with Bomboko, but he was not home. The night guard didn't know where he might be. Nizet entered the house to call around. Ten minutes later he returned, having found no one.

We waited, chatting. Nizet said it was always like this. Much important business was conducted at night, at midnight conferences such as this one would be, but often ministers went out leaving no word of their destination. Finally—it was almost midnight—there seemed no more point in waiting. I tried to reassure Nizet of my willingness to help in any way. We drove back into town.

Early Tuesday I received a phone call from California, where it was 3:00 AM. Tootie (my mother), Dad and my twin brother Bob had tried all night and most of Labor Day to get the call through. Plans were all set for me to meet Tootie and Dad in Rome. They all seemed relieved I was out of Coq, Tootie especially. She was glad I would be in Paris tomorrow. They could get ready for their trip in peace. Not to have them worried about me compensated in part for my disappointment at leaving Coq.

That day I concentrated on getting the Wednesday evening plane to Europe. When I accompanied Charlotte Loris, the USIS admin officer, to the APO to pick up mail, I distinctly sensed that she, who had always seemed so supportive, was casting off her moorings to me. Suddenly I realized that Tom's premature decision had sticky fingers. It might attach itself to me. The thinking would be: "Well, Hunter was there. Surely they must have talked it over." Or: "Why didn't Hunter stay, then if he thought the evacuation was premature?"

Suddenly I glimpsed a fact of bureaucratic maneuvering: survival and success were achieved partially by dissociating yourself from the mistakes of others. This glimpse produced a sick feeling in my stomach. I realized that all my work in Coq, my struggles, loneliness, and hard times, could count for naught in the stigma of this criticism. I discussed the matter briefly with Charlotte. We talked turkey. She advised me to make it clear to Mowinckel that I had no part in the decision to leave.

My opportunity came later that morning when John called me into his office. He asked me to sit down and said: "I'm wondering what you want to do when you come back from leave, Fred."

"It doesn't matter particularly," I told him. "I'd rather have a project than be assigned to odd jobs."

"I thought we'd put you to work in Press."

"That's fine." But it sounded like odd jobs. Phil Mayhew, my evacuated counterpart from Stan, had been writing picture captions for about a month.

Nervously I started: "Say, John, I—" I glanced at my hands, "I want you to know that I wasn't consulted in the decision that brought us out of Coq."

"Oh, I understand that."

"You know I think we ought to return."

"Well, I couldn't go to the ambassador with that the day after you evacuated. He'd have gone through the roof."

"I'd like to go back. I'm afraid we may lose everything we've put in there. We can't expect our audiences to accept our information if they don't respect us."

"What's this with Madison? He won't go back without his wife?"

"Something like that."

"You go on to Europe. You've been looking forward to this vacation."

A solitary lunch. The idea that the Coq experience should end in failure and vague disgrace depressed me. I was nervous as I ate. Back at the office I approach Mowinckel. "Look, John, why don't you let me postpone my vacation?"

"What about your plans?"

"I haven't any specific plans until mid-October when I meet my parents in Rome. What if I went back up until, say, October 10?" That would put me in Coq for a month. Its fate would be clarified by then.

Mowinckel looked interested. He said, "Let me check this out with the Country Team." He called Colonel Raudstein with whom I had met Coq's ANC command. Mowinkel quoted him as saying: "Hunter can do a better job than that horse's ass you've got in charge up there." Mowinckel said he would discuss the matter with the ambassador and let me know the outcome.

I went to the André *pied-à-terre* to have dinner with Thérèse and Martine. They had received a message that I was to call Hank

Clifford. When I phoned him, he said that Ambassador Godley had approved my return to Coq. I would hitch a ride the next morning on Bugsmasher. Military attachés were flying to the Equateur to get a situation report on Boende. I was delighted: relieved to feel the worry drop away, pleased to have another chance to prove myself in Coq.

Even so, at times in Léo I had noticed a tiny, almost secret feeling of relief that I no longer had to face the Coq uncertainties. Now I would be facing them again and without a radio. Madison, wishing to bring out everything expensive, had made sure we carried the radio with us. Still, despite that tiny secret relief, I truly did not want to feel that I had run the first time in my life that I confronted danger. Was that a too-young-to-be-sensible notion? A too-many-movies reaction? Did I see myself a tin-star hero? I hoped not.

A refugees' dinner with Thérèse and a whiny Martine. Thérèse ordered her an avocado and a Pepsi and she was momentarily happy, flirty-smiling, looking about her, her legs dangling from the restaurant chair. When her order arrived, she grinned, her eyes almost as big as the avocado itself. Contentedly she began to spread the avocado onto a piece of bread. She sipped at her Pepsi with a *gamine* grin. But before we adults had finished, she was wiggly and tired. Half the avocado lay untouched on her plate. Thérèse had to speak to her: *"Sois sage, ma fille-fille,"* Thérèse implored. *"Viens, ma poulette; sois sage pour Maman."*

Twice Martine's face crumbled at these encouragements. She looked into her lap and dissolved into tears. Poor little kid. It was terrible to watch. There was no frustration, no fight, in her tears. They were abject, worn-out beyond fighting. It was worse for her now that her brothers had gone to school, as Yves would say, to China. Sometimes she played with little girls she didn't know or got dragged along on errands or traipsed at the end of Thérèse's arm to the hotel rooms of other Coq refugees. But mostly she stayed shut up in the *pied-à-terre* looking at pictures in the fashion magazines Barbara Michejda had left behind.

It was also quite hard on Thérèse. Late one afternoon I had passed by to say hello. Martine answered the door. There was no light on inside. Thérèse was sitting beside the tape recorder, staring into the darkness, listening to music I had heard her sing to at parties. I had never seen her this way: depressed, worrying, wondering if Jules were all right, if Coq were safe, wondering what would become of them and of all they'd tried to do in the Congo. She and Martine were not sleeping well. They'd brought no blankets and after Coq Léo seemed chilly at night. In addition, Thérèse had had headaches. I had dropped in several times without detecting them. She always dissembled. That afternoon after I came in, she perked up, turned on the lights, gave me a cup of tea. As we drank tea, she showed me once more the snapshots of the house and the kids in Namur.

At times my relationship with Thérèse became confused. It was something we were both aware of, something both of us controlled. Often I was grateful for Martine's presence. I knew that what I was able to do for Thérèse and Martine meant a great deal to the Andrés. I wished Jules were sharing in it. And that the other didn't intrude.

But now, in the restaurant, despite Martine, Thérèse was in good form, pleased I was returning to Coq. Happy that I was getting the chance so many of their friends in '60 did not get, that of proving my-self—even if the proving was only to oneself. I told her of my concern that I would be in Coq when Tootie thought me safe in Europe. She smiled and cocked her head. She commented: "As Jules' mother says: 'It causes me worry, but I'm glad to have sons like that.'" She gave me a letter for Jules, asking for his approval, she told me, of her plan to return to Coq on Friday.

Back at the Cliffords, my refugee lodging in Léo, Hank followed me downstairs to the basement apartment where I was hardly more than a package awaiting shipment. I had just said goodnight. I had thanked him and Dee for their hospitality to a refugee under the per-plexing circumstances of their sixth baby's arrival and their efforts to pack effects to return to the States.

Hank chose this time to discuss my efficiency rating. I knew he had been very critical of Madison, whom he rated, so critical that Deputy PAO Martin Ackerman had rewritten the rating. Hank had the task of reviewing Tom's rating of me and had apparently toned down Tom's rating.

I wondered: Was this really the time to go over this business? But I kept silent. Hank said he'd suggested that the agency might want to wait another year before awarding me what was generally considered an automatic promotion from the lowest rank to the next lowest. This was quintessential Clifford. Always a friendly insertion of the knife. He asked for my comments. I attempted a couple of hesitant, careful beginnings. He squashed them immediately. I let it go at that.

An absolutely horrible night. I felt utterly discouraged by the interview with Hank. What did one have to do to get ahead in this accursed agency? I had just talked my way into risking my life for the damn outfit only to be told I might have to wait a year for promotion. I tried to think well of Hank. After all, resentment would hurt me, not him. By the time I finished packing, I was thinking of other things.

Still a horrible night. No water in the apartment's cold water bathroom. The alarm clock clicked like a metronome in an echo chamber. A whisper of it remained even after I set it on the stairs leading to the bathroom. Hank had boasted that the new baby was "already sleeping clear through till morning." Like hell. It cried sporadically throughout the night. Eventually I did pushups to tire my body and bring on sleep.

Whereas that morning I had thought I could not live with the sense of disgrace I was feeling, that night I could not rest because of fears. What would happen, I wondered, if I got caught in Coq by the rebels? What if I were held hostage like those guys in Stanleyville? No word had been heard from them for weeks. The fear was like a heavy weight along my back.

I was concerned that the family should think me in Europe. I wanted to feel the support of their thoughts. I prayed, reciting quotations I'd learned as a child. At times it seemed like a trance. Repeating quotations, I sank into slumber, then got jarred out of it by the feeling that I must continue to repeat. I got up before the alarm clock sounded, feeling better in the gray, beginning light of dawn. No sweat. I looked forward to getting back to Coq. I wondered at what it was inside me that caused the emotional somersaults in the dark. Maybe it was partly Léo. I hadn't slept calmly since I arrived.

A long low flight to Coq. Besides Maj. Kohlbrand, the Assistant Army Attaché, and his crewman, we were three: an embassy political officer, the Léo-based manager of Sédec stores, and me. The Sédec man had very kindly agreed to instruct his people that I was to have a space on a steamboat they had hidden on the river as a means of escape if the airport got cut off. If that happened, the river would be the only way out.

Fourteen

WHEN WE SET DOWN ON THE COQ TARMAC in Bugsmasher, provincial officials met us, notably Finance Minister Paul Efambe, decked out in the garb of officialdom: dark suits and ties. They came expecting to greet Governor Engulu who followed the evacuating Americans to Léo. When Efambe realized that Engulu had not returned, a look of abandonment spread across his face. He and the officials abruptly left us alone on the tarmac.

From the shade of the airport terrace about fifty yards away a group of dejected Belgians studied us. They knew of our arrival through the Sédec radio net. Examining the group I saw that the entire Lions Club appeared to be there, all except Jules. Worry had changed their faces, the way they stood. The commercial confidence of their earlier reactions to the rebel advance—"Rebels have to eat and buy just like everyone else"—had disappeared.

We left the plane and started toward them. The men did not talk among themselves. Alone or in pairs, they watched us as—so it seemed to me—they had watched all American activity since I arrived in Coq. With neither affection nor open hostility.

A figure broke from the group and moved quickly toward us: M DeWalsch, *conseiller technique* to the Governor. I had not known him well, but always liked him. His red hair and ruddy Flemish face shone in the sun as he approached, his squat frame carried along on his activist's stride, clad as usual in white: shirt, shorts, knee-socks. A smile burst through his concern as he stretched out a hand to greet us.

He related the latest developments. Rebels had besieged Boende. They now held the riverbank north of the town. The ANC had retreated into the town itself and gave no evidence of a will to defend it. By now Boende had probably fallen.

He reminded us that the Ruki ferry crossing at Ingende lay only seven hours drive from Boende. Once across the Ruki, the rebels could reach Coq in three hours. The road was good. The ANC checkpoint at Kalamba would mean nothing. There was a new atmosphere in Coq. The town was growing ever riper for change.

Once rebels held the road from Ingende they would control the only land escape from Coq. If they entered the town, they could quickly cut off escape by the shipping firm Otraco. And by air. They would place barricades across the long spur of road that led to the airport and put oil drums on the airstrip. Then Coq residents would have only two options: stay in the town or attempt escape in small boats on the Congo.

That was why the men on the airport terrace looked so worried.

The logical place to make a stand was at the ferry crossing at Ingende. The gendarmerie had been assigned this position. Could it hold there? Did it have the will? The proper arms? Fortunately, a Belgian would have command, the technical adviser Marcus. He was a man who with his wife had often swum laps beside me in the pool at dusk. His top assistant was the only Congolese who seemed unafraid among the frightened men at the war council I attended with Col. Raudstein. The will to defend Ingende would be crucial. Congolese generally lacked that will.

Would Coq's ANC garrison hold the road into town? Would it make a stand at the Wangata Army Camp just outside Coq? Major Kwima suddenly appeared. He marched out onto the tarmac to join our talk of Boende. As usual his slight frame floated inside clothes that were much too big for him. Except for petulance and tattoos his face was unlined; he looked no older than sixteen. He possessed a quality more dangerous than simple incompetence: unpredictability. That quality had grown wilder and more violent as the rebels advanced. It had made Tom and me tag him "the juvenile delinquent."

Sizing-up Kwima, Major Kohlbrand looked amused, as if he did not quite believe his eyes. Nonetheless, he agreed to include Kwima on the reconnaissance flight over Boende that he and DeWalsch had just arranged. How, I wondered, would Kwima act under attack? He who had talked so easily of *"jusqu'à la mort"* (until death). Could Coq rely on him? Governor Engulu, for one, did not think so. He had tried to issue arms to Europeans. To a man they refused to accept them. Even for a stand at the airport. After this refusal, Engulu left for Léo.

Kohlbrand, DeWalsch and Kwima took off to overfly Boende.

Near the *Sûreté* counter inside the airport building the Belgians crowded around us, full of questions. Why such inaction from Léo? Did Léo know what's happening in the Equateur? Did the Belgian Embassy know? Did Bomboko? Would mercenaries come? Where was Engulu? Would the Belgian or American embassies do something about evacuating Europeans?

The danger to Boende had worked its change. Five days ago when Jules informed these same men that a C-130 would be available, the answer was always the same: "There is no question, M André, of my leaving Coq."

The Lions Club gathered around the Sédec man seeking one of their own nationality. Nearby Maître Herman wandered, hands in pockets. Then he advanced and attached himself to me. As Jules noted in a letter to Thérèse, part of which she read to me, Herman clings like a liana vine. He supports himself by holding onto something strong just as a liana attaches itself to a tree.

Herman had always struck me as too intelligent to cope with the present day Congo. He was not coping now. He stood fidgeting, the budding belly straining over his belt. His chubby gray face was full of concern. I did not like playing the tree to his vine, but pity proved stronger than irritation. The poor guy was apprehensive. He had nothing to do. His wife and children had gone. He could not practice law in a region rushing headlong into chaos. He wanted desperately to leave. But he could not live with the disgrace of being the first Lion to go.

Herman examined me as I stood beside my gear: the typewriter, the cashbox and my suitcase. I felt silly carrying them into this group of worried men. I smiled to Herman to explain their presence. "I have come back to stay," I told him.

"Mais comment?" he asked, incredulous. "We are doomed. The rebels are at Boende."

"Then I will stay as long as I can."

When the Sédec man left for town, siphoning off the majority of the Belgians, only a few of us were left at the airport. Herman offered me a ride into town in the car of his lawyer colleague Maître Teriot. They took me to the house and parked before the gates next to Jules' office.

Even before getting out I heard banging and Jules' voice, life going on as usual behind the gates. Teriot honked. When the gate opened, Jules peered up from supervising a couple of his men. Great to see him again. He gave me a grin and came forward, hand outstretched. "Allo, Fret," he said in English. "Ow or you?"

During the troubles in 1960, as he had told me several times, Jules removed himself from the community. He worked by day in the courtyard, staying close to the house at night. That, he believed, was why he suffered so few annoyances and was able to stay. I realized that he had begun to live the same way again. After greeting me, he glanced distrustfully at Teriot and Herman. "At a time like this," he told them, "there are two good things: to have work and to have gates to work behind." His tone was challenging, answering unspoken criticisms. Having gotten his family to safety, he wanted only to be left to hang on.

After Herman and Teriot left, Jules showed me into the office. He told me that he would be returning to the river house shortly after noon. With typical generosity he automatically assumed that I would take my meals with him. Thus he did not bother to invite me. He gave me the keys to the house and my car, which I'd already noticed parked as I left it in the courtyard. He gave me a little news of the center. "Your boys took down the sign," he said.

Returning to the house was like re-entering a stopped moment of time. Nothing had been touched. A book waited open on the lamp table. A chair cushion lay overturned as if still falling to the floor. Someone's ashes sat cold in the glass tray. Mason jars Thérèse lent for drinking glasses when I first moved in clustered on the dining table. They stood where left when I told Joseph not to pack them, some still wrapped in newspaper. Strange to glimpse in this mirror its retained image of Thursday's rush and disorganization. "After you left," Jules explained, seeing but misreading my curiosity, "Thérèse was so tired from helping Sally pack that she did not clean up. Then the next day. . . ."

So no one inventoried the house with Joseph as I had hoped they might. No matter. Jules left saying he would see me at lunch. Looking around, I wondered if Joseph had appropriated any of the things the Andrés lent me. I found two books marked for return to the Catholic Mission's Library (Hoelstaert's collection of Mongo folk sayings and the pamphlet *La Philosophie Bantoue*). They still sat on the sideboard. I could not, however, find *Epitaphe pour un Ennemi* about which Thérèse raved so often that I finally asked to borrow it. Maybe she took it.

In the kitchen Joseph had cleared out the refrigerator. Looking at its empty shelves I remembered wolfing down the crepes he prepared the last day. He was proud of his initiative and I complimented him on it.

Then I sent him out to wash the car so that I could pack without arousing his curiosity, this before I knew we were leaving that day.

Joseph had made off with the water filter. That was a surprise. Thérèse's brown teapot out of which I had my morning Kivu tea remained on the shelf. Beside it lay the tiny *passe-thé* to strain out the tea leaves. I was relieved to see these André possessions, especially after watching Thérèse in Leo serve tea boiled in a saucepan and passed through a spaghetti strainer. The two lamps I balked at letting Sally pack stood on the alcove floor. A year's supply of toilet paper sat on the alcove bed.

Before lunch I made two visits. At the UN headquarters across the street technicians, mainly World Health doctors called in from the bush, played ping-pong in the lounge. Rishi and Samy slouched in the little PX—this was the first time I'd ever seen it—leaning on its counters for all the world like a couple of *duka wallahs,* Indian shopkeepers. They seemed the same as always, unconcerned by The Situation, even by the threat to Boende. Rishi did wonder how he would evacuate the last of the UN trucks since rumors floated around claiming that Otraco had stopped accepting cargo. As for himself, Samy and the doctors? They would wait for radio instructions from Léo. How reassuring—almost amusingly so—to see this calm!

At the cultural center Jules' words "Taken down the sign" hardly described what had happened. Judging from the state of the wall above the entry, the letters of the sign were ripped off in a panic. The facade of the center looked a mess. With a little patience and control the boys could have unscrewed the individual letters. Instead they yanked them out. Chunks of plaster had been torn away from the wall. Now it looked bullet-spattered. The paint was gashed and scarred.

Before going inside I took a long look at the damage, assuming a consciously disgusted expression for the employees watching from inside. That was show. My real reaction was one of resignation to the seeming inevitability of this sort of thing. Surely a negative approach, criticizing the locals even before greeting them, but I was unhappy with what I saw.

Even when in full operation, this little center was largely a symbol. Without officer supervision, that was *all* it was. A symbol of America, of America's link with Africa, of American encouragement of and involvement in the Congolese striving for stability, development, nationhood, and broadened contacts with the world. If we had simply closed the center and left, I thought, looking at the wall, it would still symbolize those things. The untouched sign might have said to the rebels: "America is still here. You have to contend with it even if its people have gone."

But not now. This hasty, fear-driven denuding of the facade said all the wrong things. To Congolese it first declared: "The Americans are afraid;" and second: "The rebels must be strong if the Americans are so afraid;" and third: "The Americans have deserted you. That proves they were never really interested in you." What else would a Congolese think when he looked at the wall?

I went inside to greet the guys. Even before I appeared outside they knew I was in town, as Africans seemed always to know such things. Ahenga, N'Djoku, Edouard and several library clients watched me enter. Raphael sat tensely in studied idleness at the check-out desk. We shook hands all around, but without friendship. After my performance before the facade, we managed only the greetings. I started my routine of displeasure, asking, "Where are the letters?"

The others sat without speaking as Edouard led me to them, stacked in a heap in that junkhouse storeroom across from the radio shack. There was nothing that could be done with them now. Screws writhed in them. One letter was broken. The plastic dowlings that held them out from the wall had been lost.

"Je n'aime pas ca," I said, returning to the library.

"What did you want us to do?" Ahenga challenged.

Looking at him, I hardly recognized this man to whom I refused to give a job because his obsequiousness made my flesh creep. Now he confronted me. His expression, contorted with hate, said plainly that I was the enemy. He believed, I suddenly realized, what the wall now proclaimed: that we had run out on our people. "The day after you left," he cried excitedly, "they threatened us. They said, 'When the rebels come, you will be the first ones we kill.'"

The others corroborated this, all talking at once. I believed them. We had known all along that dissident elements were operating in Coq. The day after we evacuated, Radio Stan congratulated Coq for "ridding itself of the Americans." That meant organized sympathizers were operating in town with communications equipment.

But there was no point in pursuing this business of the letters. Had there been any point, I wondered, in showing my displeasure? After all, I sympathized with their reaction. Still there seemed an obligation, as long as we worked with these people, to insist on disciplined reactions. So that some day they would unscrew the letters instead of ripping them off.

None of it mattered much now that rebels had taken Boende.

Still, I realized, the basic fault lay with us. Madison and I should have discussed what, in case we evacuated, we would do about the locals. Surely they had higher priority than saving expensive books. As he was hurrying us to leave, Tom should never have suggested to the guys that we might try to evacuate them. His fear naturally communicated itself to them. They began to anticipate a trip to Léo. They exaggerated their personal danger and our responsibility for putting them into it. In the first three days we were gone, they sent two telegrams.

I told Edouard to watch the library and invited the others into the office. There I tried to calm their fears. I reminded them that we had never asked them in any way to endanger themselves by staying at the center. If danger really required removing the letters, then that was more danger than we wanted them to face. They had no loyalty to the United States beyond doing their jobs. That did not include physical danger.

I suggested they answer threats by saying: "I'm working for the Americans because they pay me. If you pay me, I'll work for you." They saw their Léo trip vanishing. However, they were reassured by the prospect of my being around to make decisions for them. I would also be the focus of anti-American feeling.

After our meeting I did a look-around the center to see what changes had been made. There had been an increase in outward symbols of authority: a confusion of ill-lettered announcements blocked the windows of the door. N'Djoku had resumed morning film showings and had transferred the projector to the theater itself. In view of the 3:00 PM curfew on all commercial establishments, the boys had in a happy wedding of convenience with wisdom begun closing the center at 2:30. Edouard had moved his family from the *boyerie* to the communes. The air-conditioner was now operating on high, and I was about to freeze. Ahenga had taken the director's chair and N'Djoku mine. While I went over the property inventory, Ahenga sat at his desk and busily read—or at least stared at—a brochure on American aid to the Congo. I regarded him with affection; at least he was trying.

I realized that this was what it must have been like at independence in 1960. Congolese found themselves sitting in the Belgians' chairs—without the slightest idea of what to do.

Before meeting Jules at the river house for lunch, I returned home. I took my suitcase upstairs. In my bedroom last Thursday's mess lay untouched. Again the feeling of stepping back into an historical still life. Armoire doors hung open. A fistful of spare keys lay spread out across the dressing table. The little toilet *cabinet* seemed quite empty without the picture of *Notre Dame de la Toilette*, the quiet Memling madonna cut from an advertising supplement in *La Libre Belgique*. She had watched with dignity over that tiny cell. I missed her now, but she could not have been left behind.

I straightened up a bit, pulled the sheets from my suitcase, and made the bed. The armoire's unnatural state of nakedness tempted me to settle in: its empty shelves, unused hangers, abandoned plastic bags. But was there any real reason to unpack?

From the bedroom window I looked out at the town. How could one guess what was going to happen? Coq never gave hints of its mood. Its face never changed. On the surface it was always only what it seemed: a swamp town, a tiny toe-hold of man-things at the edge of the jungle. It broiled in the sun. At its center, along the river, lay an unfocused scattering of corrugated roofs and whitewashed walls: the European houses. Behind them stretched palm-thatch roofs and mud-and-wattle walls: the close-packed *cité* huts.

Below me, across the unrealized concept of a central square, drifted the figure of a woman. She had wrapped herself in swirls of cloth and carried a carton of bread loaves on her head. She wandered across the emptiness, soundlessly, hardly seeming to move. Motion did not seem part of life here. Man was too insignificant in terms of the unchanging landscape: the water, the jungle and the sky. Nor was noise. The tangle of vegetation seemed to absorb all sound.

All morning I had been trying to gauge the feeling of the town, but I was not able to. This eternal inactivity, this insignificance of man, and the tenuousness of his hold here: these made it impossible to believe that danger was coming. Yet in the week I had been gone something had changed. Something had happened. A week ago Congolese sentiment was confused, unformed. It was looking for signals, seeking a direction. I felt now—without being able to say why—that it had found its alignment. It had moved to the side of the rebels.

What part, I wondered, did our evacuation play in this? It was undoubtedly one of the hand-lines used to read the future.

Nothing had changed on the surface, but this change of sentiment had created a new atmosphere. Rebel sympathizers could surface now. They could threaten our employees at the center and other Congolese with reprisals. They could bribe or threaten or undermine what was left of the shaky will of the Army. They could organize, enlist, and train cadres.

It was an atmosphere in which that local combustion which we had so long talked about and feared, which had so long been a question mark in our planning, might actually take place. If it did, it would bring danger—possibly death—to non-rebel sympathizers. And if it turned racist or anti-American, to me as well.

I decided not to unpack my bag.

Having put in a good morning's work, Jules was pleased at lunch. With himself. With the presence of company. With having shown Teriot and Herman that he was working while they were worrying. "What's Fret going to drink?" he asked as I came in. "*Un petit whiskey?*"

"*Un petit gin-tonic Michejda,*" I answered. It was my usual request, a code phrase devised by the now-departed Dr Michejda who was uncomfortable having someone ask for a soft drink in his house.

Jules poured "*un petit whiskey*" and set it before me. Then he brought my usual Pepsi-Cola and with a playful smile took the little whiskey for himself. He raised it to me. "*A votre santé, Fret.*"

"*A la vôtre.*"

Jules, who loved his tranquility, settled into his chair. *Ah, bon!* He had been savoring this independent bush life he could now permit himself to lead. Thérèse and the children were safe. They had been away so short a time that their absence was still a luxury. But Loka, the only servant, who cleaned, laundered, served lunch, and disappeared in the afternoon leaving dinner on the stove, had not proved much of a companion. Jules was even more talkative than usual.

Among other things he told me about this good life—how, for instance, he passed the previous evening: in bed at 7:00, a little reading of history till he was sleepy at around 8:00, then peaceful slumber till something woke him in the small hours of the morning. He had turned on the radio and listened to a French language reading of a Shakespeare play. As Jules related it, his voice was hushed in imitation of the early morning stillness, his eyes alive, hands gesturing—*"Toujours la réaction vive,"* Thérèse said—there was nothing quite so fine as to lie in the darkness of the African night, the silver Congo sliding by outside, listening to recitations of Shakespeare.

Loka served lunch and we went to the table. "Your place has been changed," Jules noted. I took Thérèse's usual place facing the windows. We talked of the river. And of the dredge that scooped sand from the river shallows for the bricks that Jules and Pierre Bogaerts manufactured.

On the sideboard at the end of the table several of Thérèse's paintings sat. They included the river scene she painted the day we boated out to the sandbar, a large watercolor of a tree at sunset, and the small oil of the river road passing through eucalyptus trees near the Cégéac garage. "The progress Thérèse has made is really amazing," I commented.

"Yes," agreed Jules in a kind of mutter, a grunt shrugging through some mental preoccupation.

"The tree, for instance. I like the colors. And there's a wonderful freedom. . . ."

Jules regarded the watercolor. Watching him, I smiled to myself, wondering what he saw beyond the outline of the tree.

"Ah, Fret," he said, suddenly animated, "I must thank you for the film." I had given him several rolls of Kodachrome before leaving the week before. "I passed all one very long evening photographing these paintings." He grinned. "As a surprise for Thérèse."

The very long evening was obviously fun for him, being with Thérèse while being without her, the camera challenging the technical side of his mind. He recounted it in a rush of words and gestures. His green soup got cold, but no matter. He must show me the camera *now.* He re-enacted the entire scene: where he placed the paintings, how he lit them, how he set and timed the shutter, even how and where he stood to press the trigger.

It amused me that we were talking about different things. I was thinking of Thérèse's progress in painting. Jules was speaking of photography, of making a record for the record's sake. He looked up from the camera. "I wanted to have a record," he said. I realized he was preserving something cherished in a Thérèse I would never know.

Loka cleared away the soup bowls and set a fish and rice casserole before us. We served ourselves. As we ate, we talked of Léo and the confusion of life there. At one point we touched on the news, but quickly veered away from it. We had, however, admitted its presence. As a result, a heaviness crept over the rest of lunch. Underneath the surface ebullience—which he tried to maintain—Jules was very concerned. Finally he said: "You know, Fret, if things turn out badly, there is a place for you in the *canot.*"

I said, "What would I have done in the Congo without you Andrés to get me out of trouble?" We laughed. How many times had I asked myself that question?

Later, Jules mentioned once more how good it was to have work and gates to work behind. He told me once more about 1960. "While the others were sitting in bars and running from house to house," he said, "I worked and stayed out of sight. Few people knew I was here."

We fell silent for a time. Jules followed my eyes out onto the river. It was sunny at the river house that afternoon with darkening clouds across the river. An Indian file of hyacinth clumps moved by, then a huge mass of them, almost a floating island.

Finally Jules asked: "Could I send out some of Thérèse's paintings when the plane that brought you goes back to Léo?"

"Of course," I agreed. The plane should be returning soon from Boende and would go on almost immediately to Léo. "We can address the package to Madison."

Jules hurried off to choose and wrap the paintings. I returned to the center where it was less than forty-five minutes before the 2:30 closing hour. The boys and I reviewed the disposition of the expensive items of equipment. Ahenga, Raphael and N'Djoku had each taken one of the newly-arrived air-conditioners to their homes for "safe-keeping." I told them that the air-conditioners must be back the next day. If things grew worse, we would try to send them out via Otraco.

On the way to the airport, I stopped by the Madisons' house to check on things and to search for what Sally described in a note of instructions as "an intimate item." (After a year of down-to-earth living in the Congo, this seemed a strange way to describe what Tom explained was a bra.) As usual Louis greeted me, all smiles. He hurried over the gravel on bare feet to unlock the gate, as if my honk had catapulted him out of the kitchen door. *"Oui, Monsieur,"* he grinned, *"tout va bien."* The house was clean and in good order. But, alas! I could not find the intimate item. Probably Louis's woman was now strutting around the market showing it off.

At the airport the same men who watched our arrival this morning once again waited for Bugsmasher. And for news. More than anything they seemed like a group of management people in a suburban factory enjoying the sun and the last minutes of lunch hour. The bell had not yet rung for the afternoon shift. It would not—neither for them nor for me—until something more was known of Boende.

I, too, gave myself to the sun. I closed my eyes and felt its warmth on my body. What a relief to escape from Léo: from that atmosphere of parasites, from the confusion of that office, from seeming everyone's responsibility and no one's friend.

I gazed out across the runway and saw at the beginning of the jungle the tall *bokungu* tree that gave me my first real impression of the Equateur. As I looked, the assembled Lions chuckled at some joke. Although not one of them, it felt right being back in Coq. If I belonged anywhere in the Congo, it was here. Where I had a job and perhaps a contribution to make. I would swim later that afternoon, work my muscles into the pleasure of feeling tired again.

Fifteen minutes passed. Where was Bugsmasher? Jules arrived with his packet of paintings.

The joking slackened as the men looked more and more frequently at their watches. The plane was now half an hour overdue. It seemed less and less likely that the news from Boende would be good.

One of the Lions checked with the control tower. He returned with one of the tower operators, a Congolese. "This fellow," announced the Lion, "says he heard the Boende tower talking to Ikela."

"To Ikela?" The group crowded around the Congolese. Ikela, east of Boende, was in rebel hands.

"What did you hear?"

"The Boende tower said: 'Ikela, Ikela, there's an unknown airplane flying over Boende. Can you identify it?'"

"How long ago was that?"

The Congolese glanced at his watch, "Almost an hour ago."

"What did Ikela say?"

"Ikela didn't know anything about the plane. So the two towers talked about it." The Congolese shrugged.

"Boende has fallen," someone declared.

The embassy political officer and I stepped aside to huddle together. The civilian authorities in town, he told me, talked of nothing but reinforcements of arms and men, even when a shipment of arms had arrived only the previous day for the defense of Ingende. He was concerned about the quality of leadership left in Engulu's absence. Rumors that could not be checked claimed that rebels had regular contacts with a key minister.

More than anything the officer was concerned about Major Kwima. He had recognized Kwima as a member of some influence in the MNC-L, the Lumumbist party providing political leadership for the rebellion from Brazzaville. Thus, besides the question of the major's competence, there was now reason to question his loyalty. This, I realized, was what Tom and I had suspected without ever putting our fingers on it. General Mobutu had been cautioned several times, the political officer said, to replace Kwima before the danger grew too great to the province. He had promised to act. Promises, promises.

The shrill whirr of the warning siren screamed from the tower. As one body, the waiting men started out toward the terrace on the runway side of the building. The fire truck headed toward the runway. We scanned the sky, saw a dot appear in it, watched it grow into a plane, and set down on the tarmac.

DeWalsch and Kohlbrand dismounted in a state of excitement. Kwima appeared spent. "We got our tails shot at over Boende," reported Kohlbrand, laughing as one does at the end of a roller coaster ride. He crouched to search for bullet holes in the plane's belly. "Good thing those monkeys don't know how to shoot."

Satisfied with the condition of his plane, he gave the political officer and me a systematic briefing. The rebels had crossed the river. Boende was definitely in their hands. He could only guess as to whether or not there had been a battle. He suspected not. He had been surprised to see the number of men wearing ANC uniforms. They might have been taken from soldiers captured or killed or picked up where fleeing ANC soldiers shed them. Or the men wearing them might be turncoats from Stanleyville.

"Or from Boende."

He nodded. "Quite possible."

"What about Kwima?" asked the political officer.

We looked over at him briefing some of his officers a little distance from us on the tarmac. He seemed sober, exhausted by the excitement.

"He laughed like a maniac the entire time we were over the town."

"Why?"

"I don't know. Fear maybe. Immaturity. Maybe he just got a kick out of watching from a low-flying plane. He kept laughing and shouting: 'Look at them run! Look at them run!'"

"Think maybe he was glad to see Boende fall?"

"That had occurred to me, too."

Kohlbrand readied the plane to leave. I stuck Jules' package into the tiny luggage compartment and asked the political officer to have it delivered to Tom Madison. Kohlbrand inspected me and joshed, "Well, Fred old boy, have a big time here!"

It did seem weird to return expecting to stay on the very day Boende fell. I laughed with him. "Don't get too far away now."

"Just give us a call when you need us."

"How shall I do that? Send a note down the river in a bottle?"

"That might be the fastest way!" We shook hands all around. Kohlbrand & Co. climbed into the cockpit, smiling, waving. No sweat, I told myself as the plane taxied onto the runway. But I felt a little uneasy as I watched it take-off and fly out of sight.

Back in town I worked for a while at the center trying, now that the workday was over, to get some idea of what needed to be done. Later I went out to the pool. The old *colon* Lermusiaux sat alone on a bench watching his two mulatto daughters swim. We waved and he asked me some questions about news from Stanleyville that I could not answer. I swam my usual twenty laps. As always the backstroke laps were the most enjoyable, providing a view of the sky and the magnificent clouds of Africa.

Having returned home, I was about to nap for half an hour when a car stopped in front of the house. A loud banging sounded at the door. Glancing through the windows downstairs, I saw that the fall of Boende had produced its expected result. Herman was at the door. I knew why he had come. Teriot stood behind him, obscured in the shadows.

"Entrez, entrez, je vous en prie."

Herman shuffled in. *"Bonsoir, M Oontaire."* The anti-American pout he wore in my presence was more than usually pronounced. The perfunctory handshake. Herman surveyed the room as if the homes of Americans smelled bad, too. Teriot followed at a distance.

"Asseyez-vous, je vous en prie. I'm sorry, but there's nothing I can offer you to drink."

They sat down, Herman leaning forward, his elbows anchored to his knees, his face much more drawn with worry than when I had seen him just that morning. Teriot settled back in his chair, crossed a calf over the opposite knee and put his hand over his mouth.

"What news?" I asked.

Herman leaned even more forward as if bracing himself and pursed his lips. "Mâitre Teriot and I have talked to a number of Europeans this afternoon." He looked to his colleague for agreement. But if Teriot had come to lend his support, he did it only through his presence. He gave Herman nothing else, not even a nod.

I looked from one man to the other. An interesting relationship. They had never particularly struck me as friends. Was the reluctant Teriot an unhappy brother's keeper to Herman? I thought not. He seemed not quite merely Herman's chauffeur. Yet, as he made clear by remaining silent, neither did he wish to be considered the sharer of his opinions. Teriot would not—probably could not, I felt—demean himself to ask for the evacuation plane Herman would soon request. Yet he evidently wanted it made available. Why else had he come to help Herman do what he could not do alone? I recalled Thérèse disapproving of Teriot. She claimed that when his wife and children were in Belgium, he took an African mistress.

I studied them again. It was not pleasant to see a man as frightened as Herman. But better that than to see a man like Teriot too proud to be frightened. Too proud to appear concerned in front of other men even in so dangerous a situation as this one. Too proud to ask for a plane, but not too proud to help a frightened man do it.

Herman continued. "Everyone feels that things look very bad now that Boende has fallen."

I nodded, but gave no more encouragement than that.

"All the men agree that the women and children must be taken out."

I wondered about this. Teriot stared from his corner, his hand still over his mouth. He had not moved and did not look ready to evacuate his wife and children.

I asked, "Is someone going to defend the ferry crossing at Ingende?"

"The gendarmerie."

"Can they hold it?"

"They're Congolese. Have they held anywhere else? You see how well they held the crossing at Boende."

"Will Marcus be leading them?"

"Yes. But he is only one man."

"The gendarmerie captain, the Congolese, looks like a good man to me," I said. I played down my personal concern because I was wary of the request that was coming. There was real danger in asking too soon, in calling for C-130s before people were genuinely scared and thus actually ready to board them. I doubted that such a readiness had matured yet, no matter how many Belgians nodded their heads when Herman visited them and voiced his fears.

Herman shifted his weight with frustration. "Nobody can defend Ingende without arms."

"I thought arms arrived yesterday for its defense."

"They were delivered to the ANC."

"And the ANC won't give them to the gendarmerie?"

Teriot spoke for the first time. "The ANC won't fight at Ingende and it won't give arms to the people who will."

We grunted a laugh, Teriot and I. Herman sat with the pout on his face. *"Ca, c'est vraiment le Congo, n'est-ce pas?"*

Yes, that was definitely the Congo. And if that news were true—as seemed highly probable—things were worse than I suspected. But I was still wary of crying wolf.

"There's nothing between Coq and Ingende," Herman continued. "And the gendarmerie can't hold the ferry while it remains in Coq." We were silent for a moment. "The women and children must be gotten out," he said. Teriot and I nodded. "Could you ask your embassy for one of the big planes to come and take them out?"

"When? Tomorrow? The day after?" I looked at Teriot.

"The rebels could be here tomorrow," grumbled Herman.

"How many are there: women and children?"

"Two hundred."

Teriot nodded in agreement.

"How many Europeans all together?"

"Maybe five hundred."

"How many men will want to go out?"

Herman shrugged and wore a speculative expression. "Probably most of the Belgian Technical Assistance." He named several men. Teriot questioned one of them. *"Oui, oui,* he told me he intended to go," Herman replied hastily. Then after a pause: "Me—I don't know—I will probably go, too."

"I'll send a message," I promised. When I walked them to the door, Herman looked relieved and Teriot noncommittal. "I'm here without a transmitter, you know." Poor Herman. "I'll go through the UN. We've sent messages that way before."

A strange approximation of English squawked out of the KWM-2 receiver when I arrived across the street at the UN. Herman was certain to be disappointed at the message I carried in my hand. It was more a sitrep than anything else. More than requesting planes, it informed the embassy that a growing number of foreign nationals were getting ready to evacuate, that the military situation was worsening, that C-130s might be needed the next day or the day after.

However, the squawking was in vain. The office was empty. I threw a hip over the desk corner and waited, glad that it was not my job to decipher messages through a blur of static and accents.

When he returned, Mr Rishi and I greeted each other in shouts. He gestured against the noise. We laughed, sharing a mutual confusion about radio. His total lack of concern about The Situation amazed me. "If Rishi is so calm," I kept asking myself, "why am I so excited? Am I panicky? Or is he misinformed?" He agreed to send the message.

When I arrived at the river house, I did not at first detect Jules' depression.

He came smiling along the terrace to greet me, the dog Météor at his heels. As he often did in the evenings, he was wearing a clean pair of white shorts, white knee socks and a short-sleeved white shirt. The cut of the *colon* shorts always struck me as odd. There were huge leg openings—for air circulation?—that hung only to the middle of the thigh. That night they emphasized Jules' slightness, his fragility. His legs were thin, as breakable as kindling. The shirt, hanging from his shoulders, covered too little muscle and bone; there was not a scrap of fat on him. I wondered once again how much larger he'd have been if the war had not deprived him of growth as it deprived him of adequate food and sufficient coal in the winter.

As we shook hands and went inside, I felt a reserve. I saw the worry in his eyes. His reserve made me wonder momentarily if our whole friendship would have to start again from scratch. He was nervous. He moved in the room without needing to, almost pacing.

By contrast, nervous was something I was not and had no reason to be. My calm pointed to a crucial difference between us. Jules might lose everything; I could lose almost nothing. The United States government stood behind me with special responsibilities toward me as one of its representatives. It would use considerable of its tremendous resources to keep me from harm. But who stood behind Jules? A tiny nation with citizens trapped in pockets all over the Congo.

Jules paced and fondled Météor. "What to drink?" he asked.

I shrugged.

"I have some champagne." Jules lit up. "We must have it!"

I laughed at the suddenly ebullient Jules. He laughed, too, delighted at the way this magnificent idea had crashed through his gloom. The glee did not surprise me. After months of indecision, a decision was finally forcing itself upon him. After months of waiting, there would be action.

"Ah, champagne!" he continued. "That stuff gives me bounce. I have *two* bottles. I'll put them on ice."

But before he did that he must tell me, of course, how the bottles came into his possession. A French UN expert needed a *frigo* repaired. Naturally he approached the only electrician in town. Jules promised the repairs. But when one was the only electrician in town with much work to do, a promise occasionally slipped one's mind. (Jules might acknowledge this—as the glint in his eye almost seemed to now—but it would be disastrously impolitic ever to suggest it.) To jog his memory, the Frenchman presented him two bottles of champagne, a very good reminder, indeed.

"This champagne is for us, Fret. Right now! We need to bounce." He stood in the room, uncertain of me. "Will you have some?"

But what was the purpose of vices if one did not succumb to them when he most needed to spurn them? Mine was asceticism. I submitted to it and declined the champagne. I was the product of long training in saying no. As soon as I saw the disappointment in Jules' eyes I wanted to kick myself for that training, for my vice. "You jerk!" I thought to myself. "Have the champagne!" But the good Jules accepted in me what he could not understand and I could not control. He poured a little whiskey for himself and showed me where there was fruit juice in the *frigo*.

It had been a long time since either of us had cooked for another person. We guffawed from time to time at our efforts to prepare what Loka left for us. In spite of this laughter, however, the atmosphere returned to what we had been feeling all day: uncertainty, discouragement, dejection.

While eating, we talked of the *canot* and specific preparations for making an escape on the river. How much food could we take? How much gas and oil? Where would we go? After our Sunday caught in the swamp channel in that windy rainstorm, we understood the importance of shelter. What could we rig up? What would be the last moment, if the rebels actually came, that we could slip away? Would Congolese living and working on this strip of riverbank reveal the location of boats they knew about? For certainly they knew about them. How could we avoid getting cut off by rebels between where we worked in town and the boat dock on the outskirts of it?

Mulling all this my mind drifted from practicalities. It showed me a series of images: An inky black night. Pierre Bogaerts and Jules and I slipped the *canot* into the river. We pushed off. We jumped aboard and slid into the current. Rebels shot at us. We ducked, maneuvered, and made good our escape.

One summer—was I thirteen then or fourteen?—we were camping up in the backlands of Yosemite. I was one of seven guys, out of perhaps thirty, who decided to hike from near Tuolomne Meadows down to Mirror Lake. I had a wonderfully clear foreknowledge that we would get lost. The trail was badly marked. It crossed broad stretches of rock. When at last it disappeared, we climbed down into the streambed and followed it. Eventually we came to a thirty-foot drop and had to turn back. This delighted me.

We hiked back to a pool we'd passed that was drying up and full of trapped trout. We fished in it naked, using our tee shirts as seines, and caught seventy-five fish. Toward dusk we started back to where we began. We arrived there after dark. We built a fire and slept in the happiness of teenaged fatigue until we were fetched at midnight. The hike was perhaps the crowning experience of my boyhood. Soon afterward I went off to boarding school. There, because of that hike, if I was not yet a man, I was at least something more than a boy.

I went to college on the banks of the Mississippi. Sometimes at night, stretched out on limestone bluffs, I would watch the stars and think of Huckleberry Finn, lying on the raft, drifting down the river. In the spring of my sophomore year I hatched a plan to build a raft out of empty, sealed oil drums with a plank floor and float down to New Orleans in June. Alas! I was never able to sell the idea to my friends.

The boy still existed in the man. As I listened to Jules and in my mind saw us push off into the night, I joined up with Huckleberry Finn. Part of me delighted at the prospect of this adventure. It would be the New Orleans trip realized at last.

I looked at Jules and wondered what he was thinking. Our motivations were so complex. As an adolescent he ran messages for the underground. Did the prospect of adventure excite him, too? I thought of Boudart, now back in Belgium, who always wished he had lived in the Wild West. Wouldn't he love to be in on this? And yet I said, "A trip like that could be rugged." It seemed wise to make appropriate noises. We regarded each other as companions would in an adventure film. But it was hard to see ourselves—mere mortals— as tight-lipped adventurers.

"It might be fun, too," said Jules. We had to laugh and shrug agreement.

The laughter stopped. Reality intruded.

"If my government sends in planes," I said, "they will insist I leave."

"Have you called for planes?"

"Not yet." I told him of the visit of Herman and Teriot. And about the message I had sent through the UN.

"This begins to seem more and more like 1960," Jules said. He sank back into his depression. "The running from house to house has started again."

"But this time it's more dangerous than it was in '60," I offered.

Jules stared, thinking. His flesh seemed suddenly to sag. The work and the tension of the last four years, the hoping and the disappointment, had carved their lines. "This should be such a lovely corner of the world," he finally said. He glanced around at the house. "It was so tranquil here before. A little paradise where one could work and make something for himself and give something to this country."

Jules stared at his hands. The lines seemed to deepen in his face. It hurt me to watch. And yet in a way I was glad to see it. Despair was Jules' friend now. He must not let himself get caught as the people did in Stan. Hope was the enemy now. It would betray him into staying, into holding on, holding on, holding on.

"Don't you agree it's more dangerous now, Jules, than it was in '60?"

"Oui, oui." He nodded. "There is no question of staying this time." We had finished dinner and moved from the table. There was some coffee. I poured. Jules paced. "Pierre Bogaerts and I tried to persuade his mother of that this afternoon," Jules said.

"She stayed through all of it last time, didn't she?"

He nodded.

I knew which women stayed. They had become almost legendary: Mme Bogaerts, who was not a widow then; Mme Schambourg, the baker's wife; Mme Devos who left with her husband four or five months earlier when they sold their garage. "And Mme Bogaerts doesn't want to leave," I said.

"She refuses. Categorically." Jules paced back and forth in front of where I was sitting. "That's a real *kaas-kup,* that one. A real cheese-head."

I smiled. I hadn't heard that expression since I was in Brussels. "I thought that was the Dutch."

"No, no. True cheese-heads are Flemish. There is nothing so stubborn as a *flamande* when she has made up her mind." He stopped pacing for a moment. "The Walloons are *têtes de caillou,* stone heads." He smiled. "I'm one of those."

"She can't really intend to stay."

"She stayed in '60. There's the Belgian mentality. The commercial mentality. It can't bear not to protect all its little riches."

"Can't her son persuade her?"

Jules shrugged. "It's a household where one does not interfere with the other."

"That's fine, but—"

"I said to her: 'Madame Bogaerts, you have a responsibility to leave. To your society. If you don't, you ask men to risk their lives to save you.'" He resumed pacing, quite nervously now. "That's the way the soci—"

Jules stopped short. His words got choked inside him. He surveyed the room, stumbled a bit in turning to see it all. Then he crouched, his hands before him, poised and open as if to grapple with an enemy. He flailed his arms.

"Everything!" His voice burst through the knot of frustration in his throat. "Everything!" he cried. "I'll burn everything!" He looked around the room. "A little kerosene." He stumbled toward the furniture spreading kerosene in jerky movements from the imagined can in his fist. "Matches!" A swooping gesture as he struck a match, thumb and forefinger fused together. His hand burst open and the match flew toward fuel-soaked furniture. "Whoosh! Whoosh!" He fired the furniture. "Why let the blacks have it? Why should all my work go to those blacks?"

Abruptly he stopped. He stared about him and at me. And staggered into the kitchen.

I was alone with my coffee in the sudden silence.

Again I sensed Jules' fragility, his strength held under tension too long. I felt the Congo was killing him inside.

Glancing about the room, I found myself moved by his idea of fire, by its—grandeur. Grandeur! To burn it all! That would be the act of a man. Almost Grecian. A cousin to Oedipus ripping his eyes from his skull. Thank God Jules wasn't whimpering. Thank God he was roaring! I liked the idea of Prometheus shouting at the gods. Burn everything! Clean the Congo's wounds, cauterize them, then rest and heal, and somewhere find the strength to start again.

I wandered outside and rested a foot on the terrace wall. Here there was only silence. And beyond the light at the edge of the garden only emptiness, darkness. And the Congo. The river. But not the daytime river. Not that familiar phenomenon which Thérèse could reduce to brushstrokes, which my eyes could measure and my mind perceive. Not that well-known gray-brown surface carrying its sewage of plants ever wearily on. No, not the daytime river. Not in this silence. Now it was something more.

In the blackness that night river's presence swirled around me. Its movement now was instinct. It had independent force like emotion. It reached out to something inside me. A shiver slid along my back. Africa grabbed hold of me. I shivered again. I heard the beating of its heart. Africa's dark blood flowed past me full of pounding rhythms, full of smooth-gliding crocodiles, full of man-eating fish, full of the secrets of dawas and magic. It might be conceivable to escape on the daylight river. But on the night river? Would I be willing to trust my destiny to it?

The door clattered. Jules came out into the night.

I shivered again. Then the strong presence of the river diminished. Jules stood beside me. Together we looked at the sky.

"The rebels won't get here tomorrow," he said.

"No."

"Maybe not even the next day." We faced the river. "Tomorrow I start loading the barges. With everything I have: clothes, books, furniture. What I can take of the electrical equipment." He stopped a moment, released a sigh. "I have enough light bulbs to keep Coq lit for three years."

For a moment we said nothing.

"I'll weld the barges shut," Jules said, "so no Congolese can open them. I'll mark them for Bell Telephone Company in Lêo and set them adrift. They'll be waiting when I get onto the river. I'll collect them and steer them down with me."

"How long will it take?"

"Two months, maybe three." We listened to the night. "But when I get down there, we won't have lost everything."

"And the rest?"

"Burn it." His look was hard. "Why should I leave it for them?"

Together we surveyed the house.

"It will help me navigate if I have to get out on the river at night. There'll be soldiers along the banks. They'll shoot at anything. To escape I'll have to travel out behind the islands. I'll see it burning out there."

We watched the river again. Just within the thrust of the light at the garden edge a pirogue drifted by. Two fishermen stood in it. One crouched working nets over its edge. The other bent forward, slipped his paddle silently into the dark water, and pulled against it. Mêteor growled in his throat over near the kitchen. Jules greeted the fishermen in Lingala. They answered the greeting with one of their own.

We glanced at the night sky. There were no stars now. Rain would come tonight or tomorrow morning.

"Fret. . . ." Jules smiled. "This experience is good for your *formation*. But me. . . ."

I laughed. *"Deja formé, huh?"*

"Already formed. Since several years."

It was time for the curfew and mosquitoes had begun to pick us. We walked toward the cars.

"Jules. . . ." We shook hands. *"Merci beaucoup."*

"Dormez bien, Fret."

"You get some good rest, too."

He smiled skeptically, as if I were pulling his leg. He waved and watched me to the gate.

Ten minutes later I was in bed, the odor of insecticide fading in the darkness. I listened to the night. Nothing stirred except the air carrying the coming rain. All was quiet. I would sleep better here than I had in Lêo. In the flooded corner of the square that had reverted to marsh, frogs sensed the rain. They grunted hoarse love calls. All was quiet now except this. And my own apprehension of what that dark river was bringing toward us.

FIFTEEN

DAWN WOKE ME. LIGHT SHIMMERED IN THE ROOM. There was a moment of struggle to hold onto my slumber, a moment of savored semi-consciousness. Then my elbow pushed my torso toward wakefulness. It lifted me off the bed and above the brink of the windowsill. The sun, just above the trees on the eastern horizon, was like a white disc standing on its edge. The morning was as crisp as chilled payaya. No sound. Nothing stirred on the square. It was before 6:00. I lay back down.

When I woke again, shaved and dressed, the square had begun its morning life. A cluster of Congolese loitered on the terrace that jointly served Schambourg's bakery and the coffee shop next door. Women drifted toward me carrying on their heads cardboard cartons filled at the bakery, bread for the *cité* markets. Clerks moved toward their jobs, some of them on bicycles. They pedaled slowly, conversing with friends who trudged along on foot. ANC guards on the porches of the UN Headquarters and the Conseil Monetaire had mostly wakened at last. As usual they sat spread-legged and half-asleep on metal folding chairs, their rifles lying on the cement beside them.

A picture I had seen dozens of mornings.

Judging from the streets, rain had not come during the night, after all. The dawn had been sunny, but now dark clouds crowded the sky. Rain might well come before noon.

As I walked to Schambourg's bakery, Lermusiaux passed me in his black Oldsmobile, taking his daughters the three blocks to school. We waved to one another. The town fool, as he often did this time of morning, stood in the Conseil Monetaire driveway, dressed only in khaki shorts with a red necktie knotted and pulled tight against his skin. He executed close order drill, roaring orders to himself, falling over his feet, and amusing the clerks who snickered and sometimes stamped their feet in enjoyment.

In the bakery a Katangese soldier who claimed he had no food was begging bread from M Schambourg. Leaning on his rifle, he gazed imploringly into the baker's eyes.

"You're no different from anyone else," Schambourg told him. His tone suggested the importuning had been going on for some time. "If you want to buy bread, I'll sell it to you. But I won't give you any."

"But, *patron*, I'm hungry."

"*Monsieur?*" said the baker, addressing me.

As usual I bought three *couques,* small Flemish sweet rolls, and handed Schambourg ninety francs. He shook his head, commenting silently on the Katangese. Before I left the shop, his begging began again.

Back at the house I sat in the living room among the remainders of last Thursday's hurry and had an unsatisfactory breakfast. Schambourg's *couques,* often delicious, were too dry this morning. Soda was the only water now that all the coffee and tea had been evacuated as well as the boiling pans, now that Joseph had taken the filter. I opened a can of fruit juice from the food stocks remaining in the *magasin* and quaffed it as one would a beer. I missed Joseph's omelet and the Kivu tea. Outside I heard Jules talking to his men.

When I went out to the courtyard and we shook hands, he asked, "Did you sleep well?"

"Yes, thanks. And you?"

He nodded. We regarded each other closely during this ritual, ready to sense any change that had taken place since we saw each other last night. But we seemed the same as before.

"What news?"

Jules shook his head—nothing!—and we went our separate ways. "I'll see you at lunch," he called.

The first order of business at the center was to send equipment out by Otraco. As I drove N'Djoku over to the port where he would get shipping papers processed, he told me, "*Patron,* I am not happy." He knew—they all knew—that I would leave once more if I had to. He did not want to be left behind again.

Back at the center, Ahenga and Raphael sought me out in the office with the same plea. Once again we went over the ground covered yesterday: that they were not Americans, that they had no loyalty to the United States, etc, etc. The director, they reminded me, had said that there might be places for them in the USIS operation in Léopoldville. Could I make inquiries for them? I agreed to try to get some message to Madison so that a decision could be made in Léo.

N'Djoku returned to report that Otraco had taken the expected move. It would no longer accept large cargo of any kind. I could stop preoccupying myself with the equipment. I had felt critical of Madison for preoccupying himself with it. Now I understood that it represented something to do.

What to do now? From all indications, though I had gotten none yet this morning, the situation was continuing to fall apart. It seemed ever more certain that circumstances would force me to leave again, perhaps in a matter of hours. There was little to be done in the center. I told the guys to remain at their work in the library and with the films.

When I arrived at UN Headquarters, a new feeling buzzed in the air. Lacking other gathering places, the European community had focused on this one as its information center. Belgians talked outside, awaiting news of developments. As I passed through the game room, shadowy in the early morning light, I had the impression of other figures sitting by the magazine tables, looking up with interest at every newcomer who, like me, hurried past the ping pong table to the office.

The radio was on in the empty office, humming contentedly to it-self. Rishi was nowhere to be found. I glanced around for him in the halls and other offices. The secretary appeared. I had never been able to decide whether she was Portuguese or an English-speaker from the Indian subcontinent. I addressed her in French. She didn't know where Rishi was either. Back in his office, I thumbed through papers on his desk searching for some acknowledgment from the embassy in Léo of my last night's message. I found nothing.

As I left the UN, a car sped into the drive, its door flew open, and almost before it stopped DeWalsch seemed to be walking from it toward the group of Belgians. They opened their circle. He moved into its center.

"Van Nitsen," he announced. Then he expelled a short, brutal mouth noise and drew his finger across his throat.

"Dead?"

"Executed by rebels."

"When?"

"Yesterday."

Van Nitsen was the manager of the Hevea rubber plantation just outside of Boende. As such, he was the dean of the European community in and around that town. He would have been the first person targeted when the conquering rebels wished to introduce a reign of terror against the whites. He was a personal friend of most of these men.

"Where did you hear this?"

"Radio Stan."

But was it reliable? What kind of source was Radio Stan? We didn't know. Such an announcement would be just the thing to break the European morale in Coq—or in Boende itself if by some chance it was still holding out. Could the rebels really have killed Van Nitsen? Many Congolese enjoyed threatening a white man, from government clerks and soldiers on guard to thugs and bandits. But to kill one? For that a Congolese had to overcome tremendous psychological blocks. Had the rebellion pushed Congolese beyond that psychological barrier? If so. . . .

We did not even want to think of the cruel death Van Nitsen might have met. And what had happened to the Europeans and Americans in Stan?

"Radio Stan said Boende was taken yesterday morning," DeWalsch reported. "It congratulated the rebels on their victory. Then it announced that in the afternoon Van Nitsen had been executed at the edge of the river."

There was a moment of silence.

DeWalsch continued: "And it announced that Coq would fall soon."

Before returning across the street to the house, I looked around at the group. This news had hit these men hard. At last the question—go or stay—had been posed in a very direct way.

Writing letters was the task I set myself to back at the house. I had plans to meet a young woman in less than two weeks in Munich. It would be Oktoberfest. According to a letter picked up only an hour before we evacuated last Thursday, she had succeeded in getting me hotel accommodations. Reading through my answer—which told her only that I didn't know what the hell was happening—I realized that this activity was a kind of waiting. I did not really believe these letters would be sent. But as we entered the lull before the storm, they gave me a sense of virtue and orderly accomplishment. And what could be better than that?

Outside the usual town noises continued: cars passing; Congolese women yakking in shrill voices as they walked past; work sounds from Jules' men in the courtyard; occasional barking; a car door slamming; more cars than usual coming and going from UN Headquarters. The sky had grown black with clouds. Without noticing any of these things, none of them unusual, I wrote another friend, a Wall Street securities analyst, whom I hoped to see in Europe.

Before finishing this note, an urgent pounding came at one of the windows in the courtyard door. It was Jules for anyone else would come to the front door. He burst through the door in the manner of *la réaction vive:* eyes alert, head poised forward (as if he were sniffing), his stride measuring more than two-thirds his height.

"Did you hear that?" he asked.

"What?"

"Just a minute ago there was—"

Jules cocked his head as the sound repeated itself, a metallic rat-ta-tat-tat like those heard after midnight that evening I played cards at the Madisons'.

Shooting? Machine gun fire? We looked at each other with these questions in our eyes. Our ears strained for repetitions. They did not come. It could be any number of things. As usual the Congo was stretching our sense of credulity. Could there actually be machine guns firing in a town where I was living?

Suddenly it was as if Jules' visit had ended the lull of waiting. Hardly had he disappeared into the courtyard before Rishi knocked at the front door. Hardly had he confirmed that no answer had been received to my message of last night than Teriot and Herman were at the door. They asked if I had received news from Léopoldville.

I had not.

Teriot took a cigarette from his breast pocket and asked if I had a match.

Let's see. . . . The only matches I could think of were those stuck away with the candle in the medicine cabinet where I would know how to find them during an electricity failure. I excused myself and ran upstairs to fetch them. While my body took the steps two at a stride, my mind detached itself for a sidelong look at myself. It was ironically amused to watch me doing for Teriot what it felt certain he would not do for me.

I was piqued with him for sending me off on an errand when the need for taking decisions hung momentously in the air. I was amused, too, at my preoccupation with being a host. I had already excused myself for having nothing in the house to offer them. I smiled, in fact, at my being absorbed by everything—hosting, letters, a trip to Europe—except The Situation.

I got the matches—there were about five left—returned below and helped Teriot set himself afire. We turned our attention to The Situation. Herman asked again that I request rescue planes from the embassy. We reviewed things as they seemed to be developing.

The two *maîtres* insisted that, as the threat to Coq grew, ANC officers were losing confidence. They were disputing among themselves what should be done. The ANC would certainly not relinquish the arms shipped in to reinforce the gendarmerie's defense of Ingende. It appeared that the gendarmerie had abandoned any idea of making a stand at the ferry crossing there.

Discussing the military picture Major Kwima's probable incompetence and the questionable loyalty were not mentioned.

There was the ever-worrisome possibility of a local explosion. That it would come, that the rebels would be welcomed, none of us doubted. The question was when it would come in relation to the rebels' arrival.

There was the problem of trying to escape in the face of these uncertainties. Land escape was impossible since the only road out was the one on which the rebels would enter. As the events of 1960 showed, we could not count on getting out by the river, especially not now that the local control of Otraco rested firmly in Congolese hands. The road to the airport could be easily cut.

"And in any case," noted Herman, "the Europeans are having great difficulty boarding Air Congo flights."

"But why is that?" I asked.

"The Congolese authorities are taking over the planes," Herman said. "What was left of the provincial government went out on the plane this morning." If the Belgian Embassy decided to evacuate its citizens, it would use Air Congo planes, Air Congo being an affiliate of Sabena, the Belgian National Airline. There would be no point in the Belgian Embassy sending them if its citizens could not get aboard.

Then there was the report of Van Nitsen's execution in Boende.

Everyone understood what that meant in terms of the direction the rebellion had taken. It indicated a direction even if the report itself was false.

Now Herman reiterated what he told me last night: "The women and children must be evacuated." Teriot leaned forward, elbows on his knees, the cigarette still burning between his fingers,

"What about the men?"

A look passed between the two lawyers. Again Herman spoke: "Most of them are ready to go, too." Teriot nodded in agreement.

"When?" I asked.

"Today," said Herman. "Now. People are going to the airport right now to wait for planes."

"For what planes?"

"For any planes. Air Congo. American planes. Anything."

If I had been waiting for some demonstrated willingness by the Europeans to leave, their flocking to the airport would seem to meet that requirement.

"Okay," I said. "I'll write a message immediately."

Taking a pad of paper, I moved to the dining table and started to print in large block letters: FOR 250 LÉOPOLDVILLE AMERICAN EMBASSY. This was the embassy's telex address. Without our KWM-2 transmitter, I had no direct contact with Léo except via UN radio or the telex at the post office.

I didn't really trust the UN radio. There was no assurance that last night's message got through. In any case the message had to be transferred twice: from Coq to Léo, from UN Léo to the embassy. Judging from my own transmission experience with the KWM-2 and from the fact that UN people were talking in second or third languages where the mutual comprehension must often fall below fifty percent, the possibility of transmission errors seemed enormous. As did the possibility of a snafu in getting the message from UN Léo to the embassy. (What if this rescue plea got into the hands of someone who didn't know what to do with it? Horrible thought!)

The post office telex, on the other hand, was a commo channel I had occasionally used for one-way messages, even in preference to our own transmitter. It served as a kind of telephonic typewriter. The post office technician dialed the address and connected with a telex inside the embassy. In principle two telex machines could converse with one another (via typed messages). In practice, however, the post office would get no more answer from the embassy than an acknowledgement of receipt. But that would be all I needed to verify the message reached the embassy.

There were only two problems with the post office telex. First of all, it was an open channel, in these circumstances even more open than the radio. While its messages could not be intercepted as could those sent by radio, any official could look through the outgoing messages, of which copies were kept. That presented a danger. If the wrong people saw the message, they might set off a panic or the local combustion we all feared. Fortunately, diplomatic usage tended to understate and my message would be in English. Both would act as fairly effective codes in this underdeveloped, francophone region.

The second problem was that the telex, like everything else, didn't always work. We would just have to take our chances with that.

The message briefly outlined developments. As I printed it, I felt on the fleeting edge of dizziness, at the border of a trance. The words flowed easily: EUROPEAN POPULATION READY TO EVACUATE TOWN NOW MORALE OF MILITARY LOW WRANGLING AMONG OFFICERS APPARENTLY NO DEFENSE CAPABILITY.

For a moment I let myself feel swept up in history, participating in it a little. But only for a moment.

Herman and Teriot conversed in low tones.

"How many people?" I asked them.

"Four hundred fifty? Five hundred?" The number of evacuees Herman gave me was the figure most people offered as the total local European population.

I finished the message: CAN YOU SEND C-130 AIRCRAFT TO EVACUATE 300 PERSONS TODAY TODAY RESPOND VIA UN RADIO. I signed the message: HUNTER.

The capacity of a C-130 Hercules, each refugee carrying one suitcase, lay between 125 to 135 people. The embassy would probably send three planes into Coq. They could evacuate around 400 refugees. The Belgian Embassy, too, would undoubtedly try to do something. If other C-130s were needed, they could probably be sent.

Finished, I read through the message. It struck me as understated.

No need to follow too closely the traditions of the profession! I stuck in at the top: URGENT URGENT URGENT and imagined the embassy commo clerk doing a backflip when he saw it coming in on the machine.

"All right," I told the two men, the message in my hand, "I'm asking for the kind of planes that came in here last week. I'll send it right away."

Herman smiled with relief. Once more I saw that expression of doglike appreciation, that we-can-really-count-on-you-Americans look. He had worn it last Friday when he saw me at the Andrés and signaled "thumbs up." But the smile transmitted to me less gratitude than a reminder of last Thursday afternoon when he called to me in the airport waiting room and his glare said: "*Vous américains, vous rats!* You think you can sneak out on us!"

Teriot smiled, too. If not yet ready to leave himself, he would be glad to have his wife and children safe. "When will you have an answer?" he asked.

"I don't know. It will have to come through the UN."

"And the planes will come today?"

"That's what I've requested."

"When you get an answer," said Teriot, "let us know. We'll spread the news."

We shook hands and they went to the door, leaving less burdened than when they arrived. I was glad of that. Before leaving myself I found Jules in the courtyard and told him what I was doing. Since he had left the house, we had heard no more rat-ta-tats. Probably it had been machinery of some kind at Otraco.

When I returned to the UN HQ, the sky had grown very black. The storm would break in a matter of minutes. Already men standing in the growing circle of Belgians, Teriot among them, were wearing raincoats. There seemed almost as many cars as on those bygone evenings when the club showed an exceptional film. Expecting rain, the clusters of men had moved to the covered walkway on the terrace.

Figures milled around in the game room, now quite dark, no one having bothered to turn on a light. I found Rishi, showed him the message, and told him I was hoping for a reply through his channel.

Outside Rishi's office I ran into Marcus dressed in a black gendarmerie uniform. He was carrying a lightweight sub-machine gun, the stock only a curved aluminum pipe. Seeing him, I was immediately struck with a sense that this was one of the men who wasn't going to get out. He would get stuck leading a gendarmerie outfit that would not fight, that would eventually bug out and leave him. No matter how untrained and ill-armed the rebels were, Marcus and his sub-machine gun could not hold them off alone.

When he offered his hand and greeted me in English, however, he didn't seem to share my estimate of his fate. He said an officer from the Belgian Embassy, a young count, had arrived on the early plane to report on the situation.

Marcus corroborated Herman's report that the defense of Ingende had been abandoned. He said, in fact, that thirty-five mercenaries would be flown in specifically to hold the airport. The 1960 strategy all over again: hold the airports and evacuate the Europeans. What about the town itself? Had it been written off? Would the mercenaries stay? There had been talk about them, but so far as I knew they hadn't yet seen much action. Would action actually come? So much had been requested that had not been received.

These questions raced in my head, only half-formed. Things were beginning to happen too fast to thoroughly process them. The question about the mercenaries was: Would they actually arrive?

As I talked with Marcus, a newcomer appeared from the admin offices. He passed quickly through, followed by DeWalsch. He was a young man with a young man's mustache, very Belgian-looking, wearing a tie, coat, and a raincoat. These more than anything else marked him as the Belgian Embassy's man, the young count. I gave him the once-over; after all, one needed to know what the other big embassy was fielding this year.

Just then the storm broke with a roar of thunder and the quickening splatter of rain. I wanted to get to the post office before the worst of it fell. I excused myself from Marcus and headed into the heavy tropical downpour. With rain pelting down, the streets were absolutely deserted.

At Air Congo, though, across the street from the post office, I had never seen so many people, Europeans and Congolese both, pressed against each other in the ticket office. All of them trying to buy a way out of town.

In the telex room, upstairs just beyond the urine stench in the stairwell, a gloom pervaded: dark light entering from the small, high window, the gray banks of Siemens equipment, black typewriters. It was quite cold. The temperature always dropped sharply during a rain and in here the air-conditioner was still running.

As I entered, my friend the technician looked up, smiled, greeted me with a few words, indicated a chair, and returned to his work. He was wearing wool trousers, a tie and a sleeveless pullover sweater as he had learned to do during his training in Hamburg, about which he had told me. From the noise he produced striking typewriter keys, one expected metal castings to clink out somewhere. The banks of equipment clicked and flashed.

"It's working all right today, huh?" I asked when the noise of his typing stopped.

"Yes, fine. You have a message? I'll do it in a minute."

He continued to work. Then he rose, went to the door and, promising to return immediately, disappeared. I waited, sitting at first, glancing through an old copy of a Léo-published magazine. Then I got up and moved around, read the messages on his machine.

"Tu es là, mon cher ami?" my operator had written to his counterpart in Léo.

"Je suis là. Comment ça va, ami?"

Finally I went out and looked through offices for the operator. He found me, having seen me looking for him. We went back to the telex room. He prepared the tape that would actually send the message, fed it into the teletypewriter, and started it. The keys begin to print. The same impulses that formed these words formed identical words in the embassy commo room.

I watched the message go.

When it was finished, the operator sat down at the keyboard and asked: *"M'avez-vous reçu?"*

The keyboard printed almost immediately: *"Bien reçu."*

About half an hour after I returned to the house, Rishi knocked at the door.

"Come on in."

"Not just now, thanks." He handed me a sheet of paper. "Here's a telex for you."

He watched as I stood in the doorway to read it. It said:

coquilhatville-

most urgent.

tab 618 rishi from saunders. please transmit urgently following message to Fred Hunter, us consulate coquilhatville. quote c-130 scheduled arrive coquilhatville 1300 zulu today will evacuate up to 130 persons with one bag each. also understand two air congo DC3's left this morning for coquilhatville carrying fresh troops and should be available for evacuation. you instructed to return by next aircraft.

signed godley unquote

As I expected, I had been ordered to leave.

"What time is it now?" I asked Rishi.

"About 10:45."

The plane would land in Coq in a little over three hours, at 2:00 o'clock. Since the Congo spanned two time zones, messages usually indicated zulu hours, which was Greenwich mean time, an hour ahead of Coq and Léo.

I wondered what Rishi was planning to do. Beside him and Sami, only a few doctors were left, called in from the bush several weeks earlier. These latter felt an obligation to the Hippocratic oath. Earlier this morning, though, I had heard a Belgian doctor, a pre-independence hand, saying to a UN colleague: "That's fine, but are you going to stay around and let these savages chop you up the way they did Van Nitsen?"

"You going to send your people out?" I asked Rishi.

"I guess we'll wait for instructions from Léo."

Gee, he was always so calm! I admired that, but wondered about the wisdom of leaving his staff's fate to people in Léo who didn't know what was going on in Coq.

After Rishi left, I went into the courtyard where Jules' men worked. The storm had stopped; the sun was out again. As I looked for Jules, I realized that I was a little disappointed with the order to leave. Did I still yearn to be Huck Finn on the Congo? Was there—God forbid!—some part of me that thought it might be interesting to get caught? (My counterpart in Stan had told me in the safety and boredom of writing endless photo captions in Léo: "Getting caught would have been tough, but what a helluvan experience!"

He escaped on the last plane out. I wondered if he regretted catching it.) There was certainly a part of me that was horrified by the idea of capture. Given the rebel hatred of Americans, I'd be the Van Nitsen of Coq.

Considering this ambivalence, this relief mixed with disappointment, I saw in myself the same thing that motivated Herman. I valued Jules' opinion of me just as Herman valued the Lions' opinions of him. I did not want Jules to think I was running away. As I showed him the message and its instructions to me, I wished he could read English better. Suddenly I felt that my desire to justify my leaving to Jules was adolescent. But then again maybe it was not.

I zipped past Teriot's house. He was an orchid fancier and plant boxes hung from the trees. Recognizing my car, he and Herman emerged from the house. They promised to spread news of the plane.

Next out to the Madisons'. When I honked, Louis, all smiles as usual, ran out to unlock the gate. I paid him and the other two boys.

To the Mission. Dr Mullen was there, discouraged with the futility of trying to get out on an Air Congo plane. I told him to be at the airport at 2:00, even offered to come by for him. He had already made arrangements to get to the airport and was going now to hide the DCCM's new Landrover at Bolenge.

Tall, smiling Maurice was at Ron Sallade's old desk in the treasurer's office. *"Oui, tout va bien,"* he said. I asked for mail that had arrived for the missionaries since last week. Laughing, he showed me a pouch full of it. No question of trying to lug that along.

Up in Gary Farmer's old office, I visited Jean Bokeleale, the new Secretary of the Church, upon whom its entire direction now depended. He opposed the missionaries' withdrawal last week as an abandonment. He greeted me more coolly than he ever had before. He looked at his desk blotter as I told him that I was going out again that afternoon and that I wanted to leave my car for the mission's use. "I will leave it at the airport," I told him. "You can pick it up there."

"May Jesus be with you," he said.

Going back to the car, I felt puzzled. Something had changed on this mission ground that had so long seemed a haven of friendship to me. Something more than the mere departure of my compatriot missionaries.

The back screen door which I had heard so often slam over at the Farmers/Taylors' slammed again. I glanced across the road at the house, surprised that it should have been reoccupied so quickly. Watching women move in and out of the house, I was still trying to decide what caused Bokeleale's coolness. His sense that I was one of those who abandoned him? His own fear? Or was it just his business manner? Did I unconsciously want a big fuss made over my presentation of the car? Or did he perhaps resent my reappearance?

Now one of the mission's VW's drove up. Three Bolenge Congolese waved to me from it. When we greeted each other, their faces were wreathed in grins.

On my way back to the house it suddenly hit me. *"Les blancs partent!"* "The *mindeli* are leaving!" And the Congolese were delighted to see us go. Delighted! It was like independence all over again! Once more they would get our cars and houses, our furniture and mattressed beds, our cutlery, plates, glasses, radios, soft chairs, clothes, everything that was left. And they wouldn't have to work or do what they didn't want to or take orders. They were delighted. Delighted! Most of them would welcome the rebels with open arms.

Back at the house I received another caller, a Belgian whose name I did not know, though I recognized his plain face, chubby figure, and slightly pigeon-toed walk. I recalled that he borrowed books occasionally from the library. I had seen him around town, knew that he worked at Otraco and rode a bike (which meant that he had missed out on the financial gain that was supposed to attract all *colons*). I had not talked to him since the morning months ago when he stopped me to ask if we had the National Geographic in the library. I liked him for reading that, for having a collection of issues that he'd sent home to Belgium. He had made a friend of me because, unlike so many Belgians, he had always smiled and waved when we passed on the street.

After the preliminaries he said: "I've heard American planes are coming this afternoon."

I assured him they were and told him the time.

"I'll have my wife out there," he said. "And I'll go, too, if there's room."

He looked a little sheepish and dropped his eyes to his slightly in-turned toes. "I stayed through all of it in 1960," he told me. "And nothing ever happened to me. But this time. . . . This time I'm scared."

"You're not the only one," I assured him. Indeed, he spoke for people all over town now packing their one suitcase. He smiled, relieved to have gotten it off his chest. "I'll see you at the airport."

I tried to pare myself down to one suitcase. Couldn't leave the typewriter. It had seen me through every day of this Coq experience, though I didn't quite know how I'd get it on board. Upstairs I decided to leave the cash box, put the money in my wallet and the papers in the suitcase. In the bottom of the cash box, where I had put them to discourage petty theft, three ball-point pens rolled around.

A while back I had given each clerk a pen, telling him he'd have to replace its loss from his own pocket. About six weeks later N'Djoku lost his and began to pester me regularly for a replacement. (*"Patron?"* the prodigal returning, hesitant voice, big downcast repentant eyes. I would burst out laughing, so would he and he'd wait another week before trying again.) Remembering this game, I stuck the pens in my pocket to give to the guys.

When I loaded the car, Jules and Pierre Bogaerts were talking together in front of the driveway gate. I joined them, heard their speculations about the boat and the river and listened to their estimates of the safe time left in Coq. These varied from late this afternoon to sometime tomorrow. We joked a little—there was still enough safe time for that—and Jules mentioned he was about to return to the river house for lunch. I said I'd follow immediately after dropping by the center.

Contrary to my instructions, the boys had gone to lunch, leaving only Tata Edouard. More likely, they had closed for the day, figuring on the basis of rumors that I had already gone. Inside the center I looked around at what were only empty rooms ten months ago. Outside stood the old *tata*, pensioned but still man enough to produce yearly kids. That first day I was here alone, sitting on the floor, he came in with his two tiny daughters, naked except for a little cloth and the charms. They had unnerved me with stares.

When I went back outside, he shuffled from his empty quarters. *"Tu pars?"* At first the familiar *"tu"* had disconcerted me.

"Oui, Edouard, I'm leaving." I gave him the pens for the clerks and realized immediately that little joke gifts built on allusions were not right for the occasion.

"Qui va me payer? Je demande qui va me payer?" Abruptly he was quite angry, almost spitting the food he munched, waving his arms about his head. "I ask who's going to pay me."

"You'll be paid," I told him.

"Qui? Qui va me payer?"

I had a sudden feeling we were in the moment before the storm where it was dark, the wind had begun to blow, we were shouting at each other, and events were pulling us apart. Was this how things were going to end with Edouard?

"Qui va me payer?" It was what every Congolese wanted to know.

"You'll be paid. Have I ever failed to pay you?"

"Mais qui? Qui? Tu pars!"

"You'll be paid." I got into the car.

Grumbling, frowning, he walked back to the empty *boyerie.* I hurried off.

Passing Boudart's house on the river road, where his partner DeLinte was now living, I saw Jules' white BMW parked in the drive. Jules himself was talking on the lawn with DeLinte and a man I failed to recognize. Their expressions were tense, their stances poised as if to take action. When I paused, still in the car, the man I did not recognize approached. He was tall, nervous, and distracted. In a quick instant he gave a bird-like impression of being frightened and completely confused by events, as if he were flying in circles.

"M Oontaire?" he addressed me. "Are you coming with us in the boat?" I looked confused, too. "The Sédec boat."

So that was what DeLinte and Jules were discussing. And this man was Clochette, manager of the local Sédec store who had been instructed by his superior from Léo to give me a place in the boat.

"We are preparing the boat now," Clochette chattered on. "We are about to go down to stock it now. Are you with us?"

I thanked him and told him I would leave on the plane. He hurried back to the group. I drove on to André's house at the river.

When Jules pulled in beside my car at the house, he was irritated. "DeLinte wanted me to let him put the Sédec boat into this pier!" he grumbled. "He would have this beach the center of attention for everyone watching the shore."

Hardly had we entered the house when a car sped into the *chantier*. It threw up a mist of dust skidding to a stop. We rushed outside. It was Clochette.

"Your plane just came in," he announced.

Already? It was not due for an hour.

"Did you see it?"

"Someone told me it was in." He paused a moment, then: "Major Kwima won't let anyone board it."

"What?"

"Major Kwima refuses to permit anyone to board it."

"Why?"

"I don't know. They didn't tell me."

As usual the town was deserted under the noon sun. Jules and I raced through it to DeWalsch's house where he and the Belgian attaché were. Rishi and Sami from the UN arrived just before us. DeWalsch and the attaché received us at lunch, their mouths full. They were just as alarmed as we were when they heard the news.

It was quickly decided that someone must talk to Kwima. We limited the delegation to a carload of people. We would take only one car so as not to frighten Kwima with our numbers and excite his stubbornness. But a carload of European men would not much affect Kwima.

There had been a steady stream of cars on the airport road since early morning. What we were really doing, I believe, was limiting ourselves in order to control ourselves. We were resisting the strong pull toward panic, trying to remain well on the sane side of it. The delegation comprised Rishi who represented the UN's principles and prestige, DeWalsch, dean of the local Belgians (who alone among us spoke Lingala), the Belgian attaché and me as a representative of the US government that sent the plane.

Rishi offered his car, an official one that would pass—easily, we hoped—through military barricades. I handed my key purse over to Jules so he could take the car. We looked at each other, wondering when we would see each other again. *"A tantôt,"* I said. "See you in a little while."

"A tantôt."

Moving out through the African *cités* Rishi drove calmly and was forced to drive slowly. Large trucks that hired out to do drayage, old wrecks kept working by expediency, ingenuity, and need, clogged the pavement, chugging forward. They were loaded high above their cabs with European furniture: lounge chairs, armoires, floor lamps, tables. So the looting had begun.

Approaching the airport on the long spur of road the paralleled the runway, we saw the looming bulk of the C-130, parked seemingly isolated on the boarding area tarmac. The US paratroop guard stood before it, facing the crowds milling around the airport building. In battle dress, rooted at parade rest on the pavement, the guard appeared very military and capable after the sloppiness of the ANC.

The airport parking lot was a jumble of cars. I had never seen so many there and so many ill-parked, as if abandoned. Figures filed through the mass of automobiles. Many of them struggled with suitcases. Since they had been limited to one, they had taken the largest they could find and packed it with more weight and bulk than it should hold.

I noticed a teenaged girl, three coats over one arm, the other pulled stiff, almost unsocketed by the weight of her suitcase. She arched her back to lift it, teetered forward on unproven high heels and shook her head in frustration. The sun caught the swinging, stringy locks of her hair.

Inside the terminal the waiting room was dark with people. I caught a glimpse of Major Kwima. Outside surrounded by Belgians, ANC officers, and what was left of the provincial government, he was vehemently shaking his head.

I broke free from our little delegation to go out on the tarmac to make contact with the flight crew. Two ANC soldiers manned a barricade. A long file of Congolese with suitcases, woven baskets, and belongings wrapped in cloths stood before it. *"Tu ne peux pas passer,"* one of the soldiers told me. "You cannot pass."

"Mais c'est mon avion," I explained. "But it's my plane."

He regarded me dubiously. But he knew I was *"l'américain."* He allowed me through.

"Say, what the hell's going on here?" asked one of the officers as I introduced myself.

The question was so appropriate that I grinned and tried to explain. He was wondering—so were the paratroopers; I could see it in their faces—if they would have to fight to get off the ground.

"You speak French?" he asked.

"More or less."

"You're gonna hafta load 'em then, if they ever get out here."

A few Congolese were already on the tarmac. Somehow they, too, had gotten past the barricade. A paratrooper nervously watched them edging forward, a little like in "Simon Says," the child's game where players tried to advance without being seen. The trooper shouted in English. He retreated a step or two, cursing under his breath, and tried to motion the advancers away from the still propellers.

"You must stay back. If you please. If you please." My sing-song French and flapping arms got them to retreat a little. "Everything will be organized in just a few minutes." I didn't like once again being the man who seemed to save white Europeans and turn away black Congolese. But, face it, I was going to be that guy.

At the loading ramp at the rear of the plane I greeted the other officers. The DCCM's Dr Mullen was among them. Inside the plane were some Flemish priests, refugees from Lisala and Basankusu. At the very back of the plane huddled two Portugese families who seemed superstitious, death-absorbed and very frightened indeed.

I returned to the huddle around Kwima. DeWalsch was trying to explain why women and children must be allowed to leave. Kwima shook his head. "We must avoid a panic," he kept insisting. "If any Europeans leave, there will be a panic." It was an argument that made little sense. Even Kwima seemed to realize that. Nevertheless, he continued adamantly to shake his head. "No European will leave."

The words fell on my ears with the weight of a sentence. I felt a kind of shuddering hollowness inside me all the way to my bowels. Trapped in Coq, with the rebels already on the road to take it, with the looting already started, and the ANC betraying us. All the fears that had visited my sleep the night before I left Léo hit me again. I thought of those poor guys trapped in Stan. Nobody had heard anything of them for weeks. And of my mother whom I told I was going to Europe. She thought I was in Paris.

Now a Congolese I had worked with in the government, the provincial public relations director, stepped forward, holding a paper.

I could see that it was a telex message. More fear jumped onto what I already felt. Almost immediately, however, I saw that the message was too long to be mine. And it was in French. It began: *"La situation à Coq est catastrophique."* The rest of the message (I was told later; there was no time then to read it) outlined why things had deteriorated and what actions needed to be taken. It specifically mentioned Major Kwima's incompetence and fears that he intended to betray the entire European population.

"Who sent this telex?" demanded the Congolese who held it. "He's the man we must find." He pointed to a name at the end of the message, that of the young Belgian attaché who had signed the telex.

Most of the Europeans in the group looked at the young diplomat. While maintaining a surface calm, he stuttered and could not control the trembling of his hands. All in all, it was a commendable performance, but I could hardly believe what he had done. He had sent an alarm message, questioning a key man's loyalty, over an open, public commo channel. And he had sent it in French, the country's first language, when he could so easily have used either Flemish or English. Incredible!

The attaché tried to divert the discussion away from the telex back to the need to evacuate the women and children. Kwima stood against the wire fence that divided the waiting area from the grass that led to the tarmac. Never had he looked so small inside his uniform. Nor so scared. As everyone else stared at the young attaché, Kwima stared across the field, shaking his head.

Rebel money might have passed into Kwima's pockets. That was what the Europeans feared. He might have made agreements with rebel elements already in town. But at this moment it was hard to believe that he would betray us into their hands.

Suddenly able to act with independence, Kwima could not break with the dependence that had shaped his life. (That was how I read the situation, perhaps sentimentally, perhaps naively.) Always in the past *les blancs* took decisions. Always *les blancs* found the solutions. *Les blancs* were the fathers and *les noirs* the learning children. Kwima may have hated the system; he might still hate whites. Perhaps he was right: that if we left there would be a panic—at least inside him where he was trying vainly to find some courage.

The Europeans sensed that Kwima was unable to decide on a course of action. That meant he could be palavered, cajoled, flattered at least into letting the women and children go. And finally this was what happened. Kwima relented. The women and children of Europeans might board the plane, but all the men had to stay

Did he expect these men to fight the rebels as they entered? I sensed that they would not allow themselves to become embroiled in this. Or did Kwima hope to turn them over to the rebels as hostages?

Suddenly once again there was the naked emotion of goodbyes. The tears. The passionate embraces. Men crouching beside their children. The contradictory desires, on one hand, never to leave these loved ones and, on the other, to get the emotion done with and the refugees loaded and the plane gone.

The women and children began to file out toward the plane.

I remained in the crowd of men around Kwima, uncertain what to do. I felt a strong pull to stay. I knew how the Belgian men felt: that they would sacrifice their own sense of themselves if they left. That they would have to live for some time with the feeling that they were cowards, the sense that Tom Madison was now dealing with in Léo.

But why should I stay? There was no useful work that I could accomplish. There was little I could do for Jules and last night's communion with the river on the Andrés' terrace had made me realize how foolhardy and arduous that adventure would be. Jules estimated two months on the river! What would we eat? How would we survive the heat, the sun, the glare? My instructions ordered me to return with this plane. I would do myself no good in Léo if I ignored those instructions. In any case I was needed to help load the plane.

When Kwima moved off, I nudged Jules, next to whom I stood, and offered my hand. He nodded to me. We shook hands. I melted into the file of refugees and hurried along it to the plane.

The file of refugees stood at the plane's rear loading ramp. Crewmen had strung straps of webbing in lines across the width of the cargo bay. They signaled to the women and children to climb inside the plane and take designated positions on the cargo floor. Finally the plane was loaded to capacity. I told those whom we could not accommodate that another plane was on its way. I hoped this was true.

Finally everyone was set in the cargo bay. Apprehension caused a quiet to descend. I jumped aboard. The crew raised the cargo ramp.

Goodbye, Coquilhatville!

198 A YEAR AT THE EDGE OF THE JUNGLE

The motors started. We heard their sound, felt their vibration. The crew guarding the plane hopped on. The huge machine began its crawl across the tarmac. In the dim running lights the passengers listened intently. Wide-eyed, they saw in each other our various emotions: fear, uncertainty, and a relief that brought forth tears.

The plane inched onto the runway. The motors roared. The plane shook. We glanced at one another. Suddenly the plane hurtled down the runway. Then: whoosh! An enormous surge of power! The plane lifted. It tilted us all. We started sliding backwards on the cargo bay and reached for the straps of webbing, understanding now why they were there.

And we were in the air.

Léo was another world altogether.

At the embassy the chill of air-conditioners. My shivering corpuscles swam in thin blood. Officers frowned into telephones: coats, beautifully knotted ties. Political Section secretaries (scarlet lips, pancaked cheeks, titillating tits) swung girdled asses inside tailored skirts. Like Ad Agency Career Girls in New York. They wondered at the bush bumpkin sitting cold and wide-eyed in short-sleeved shirt, cotton trousers and gooseflesh. Was he really officer corps?

A short meeting with the ambassador. This huge, friendly man stood behind his desk in rolled shirtsleeves, wrinkled trousers. His hair was mussed. Political Section officers, coated, unmussed, danced attendance in the great space of his office. He regarded me over the top of reading glasses with lenses shaped like quarter moons.

"That was a short trip," he observed.

Very quickly we reviewed how things had deteriorated.

"What about our locals up there?" he asked.

I reported what I had told them about loyalties to the United States.

"Good," he said. "Let's hope you're right."

That was the end of the interview. He looked around at his POL Section officers and said, "Well, we're out of that place."

As I left the office, I had the sinking feeling that the people in Coq— and what I had tried to build there—had been wiped away.

A long session in the POL Section office with the good Paul Bergman. He felt the US government usually tried to do too much. We composed a telegram to the Department of State. As we were sitting in his office, the Press Attaché came in, then USIS chief John Mowinkel. He greeted me with his big Norwegian smile and sparkling eyes.

When Bergman stepped out of the room, Mowinkel asked: "Did you take the first plane out?"

I told him that I did.

"Good. That'll make the Old Man happy." He lowered his voice a little. "There's been cable traffic going back and forth about you. The Department questioned his judgment in sending you back there and told him to get you out."

SIXTEEN

At last out alone in the Léopoldville night. I passed by the *pied-à-terre*. Therese and Martine were out somewhere. I went over to the Hotel Memling lobby where there was light and scribbled on the open spaces of a Sabena timetable a note to Therese about Jules. I returned to the apartment to slip the note under the door. Leaving, I met Thérèse and Martine on the street, coming back from dinner.

In the apartment Thérèse read my note about Jules. That avoided the necessity of discussing his safety before Martine. Thérèse got me a Pepsi from the *frigo* and told me a little of what she had learned. A second C-130, only partially loaded, came down from Coq. On it, among others, were Mme Bogaerts, whose son had at last persuaded her to leave, and M DeWalsch. The ANC finally arrested DeWalsch and the Belgian attaché, realizing they had sent the message. The telephone rang. Someone asked about Jules. Hanging up, Thérèse re-read the note. Finishing it again, she stared woefully at the wall.

"You said DeWalsch came on the second plane," I said to give her a nudge.

"Oh, yes," she answered. She pulled her thoughts back to that story. She gave me one of her ironic smiles. According to what she had heard, the attaché and DeWalsch were taken to ANC headquarters. At a propitious moment DeWalsch, who had no diplomatic immunity, snuck out, went to the airfield, and boarded a plane. Word had come that the attaché was released.

"I hope he's out on the river right now," Thérèse said, assuming that Jules would have made his escape in the boat with Pierre Bogaerts. "Do you think he could be?"

"I'm sure he's safe. He can take care of himself."

Martine whimpered with boredom. Thérèse read the note yet again. I excused myself.

We did not know then that mercenaries flew into Coq late in the day. They rushed immediately to the ferry crossing at Ingende and blunted the rebel advance. Rebels never arrived in Coq. Jules and the other men stayed in town. They never needed to escape on the river.

Unaware of that I had dinner alone. I felt exhausted and thought briefly about my year at the edge of the jungle. *Bon pour votre formation*, Jules had noted. I did not know then how much that year would form the man I became. At that moment I thought mainly about getting myself to Europe and leaving Africa behind.

AFTERWORD

WHEN I RETURNED TO THE CONGO IN OCTOBER, the Coquilhatville center had limped along for a couple of months without the services of an American officer. Tom Madison did not return there. Instead he worked out of the Léopoldville office where his experience could be put to more productive use. He soon went on a combination of home and annual leave that kept him out of the Congo until March.

Ambassador Godley and PAO Mowinkel expected to send me back to Coquilhatville. While rebels no longer threatened the town, the rebellion produced a state of collapse throughout the Equateur. In the towns they captured the rebels systematically executed educated Congolese.

As a result, they effectively ended what remained of the Belgian colonial era. The Boende planter Van Nitsen had, in fact, been killed. Many *ex-colons* were abandoning the region. Down in Léo to straighten out affairs with suppliers, Thérèse confirmed that the Andrés would leave Coq as soon as they could liquidate their stocks of equipment. Maître Herman had been looking for work in the capital. The Schambourgs who had consistently contended "rebels need bread" had decided to close the bakery and leave. Boudart wrote the Michejdas in Cotonou —who in turn informed the Andrés—that DeLinte & Boudart would also liquidate and withdraw.

DCCM missionaries were very worried about the future of their work. Missionaries, both Protestant and Catholic, had labored selflessly, facing hardships, for seventy years, lighting and keeping alive a spark of Christianity in the jungle. The rebels had snuffed out their spark of enlightenment with firing squads, leaving the future of their churches in question.

My returning to Coq would mean restarting the cultural center in what was becoming a completely African town. I did not look forward to serving another eight months there alone.

However, the State Department was feeling the bite of popular and Congressional criticism about Americans, both missionaries and consular officials, still caught in Stanleyville. As long as rebels remained west of Boende, the Department nixed the idea of a solitary American officer in Coq.

Then Boende was retaken, renewing the prospect of reviving a US presence there.

I wrote my family: *When I think about returning to Coq, I wonder if I can stand the isolation. What I can only express as girl-hunger (and it's not only physical) continues to plague me. Sometimes in Coq I feel like a priest or a monk. I just don't know if I can put up with another eight months of this isolation.*

That was late October. From Léo in late November I reported:

Back from four days in Coq yesterday. My time there was uneventful. Jules has agreed to act as our financial agent during our absence. He will also sell my car. (It had not gone to the DCCM, after all.) *I stayed at the house, but took my meals with Thérèse and Jules. How incredibly generous and hospitable they are!*

Thérèse even prepared a moambe *as a kind of celebration. I've never seen them happier together. I think the marriage may have found a new sense of direction in their having decided at last to leave, in their having found again something to aim at together after these hard years of drifting along wondering if they could take it. They laugh together a great deal. Jules seemed relaxed and didn't raise his voice to Thérèse; he even touched her affectionately now and again. They called each other* chou *a great deal. I'd never heard that before. Nice to be in that atmosphere.*

The letter also reported: *When I went into the office, John Mowinkel told me I'm now Acting Branch PAO in Bukavu. He suggested that I take a plane up tomorrow morning. (Sometimes you feel like a package. They just slap a new label on you and send you off to the next place.)*

What a beautiful situation, Bukavu! I was delighted to finish my Congo tour where I'd started it. Once again, as before, I was serving temporarily as the post's top USIS man. The town lay in Africa's Rift Valley, riding the backbone of the continent. It stretched across five peninsulas that reached like fingers into Lake Kivu. Mountains receded, ridge after blue ridge, toward the horizon. Bukavu's climate was mild, the nights crisp. Foodstuffs were plentiful. Every morning women walked down from the hills surrounding the town, carrying baskets of small strawberries to market.

The rebellion had rocked the town. There were ragtag rebel units still operating in the hinterland. It was considered a hardship post. That meant I would still qualify for the twenty-five percent differential in pay. It was isolated in the sense that it existed in a remote part of Africa, but in Bukavu there was nothing like the isolation of Coquilhatville.

Bukavu had an American consulate and the personnel—from State, USIS, CIA and various military services—associated with it. Most of us assigned there lived in the consul's residence, a mansion from the Belgian era built on a bluff with a splendid view of Lake Kivu. The consul engaged a cook who fed us well and almost every evening there was a cocktail hour when we assembled for drinks in the living room of the residence, talked about the day and the country while listening to the consul's collection of Italian love songs. We monitored the antics of the pet bush baby that could jump twenty feet, sometimes landing unexpectedly on your shoulder. It had a fondness for licking the tops of open whiskey bottles and falling tipsily asleep in a bed of curtains that stretched to the floor.

The love songs made us dream of or reminisce about women. Although American women were prohibited from serving in Bukavu, we were not deprived of feminine company. Bukavu had a social life, an active *Cercle Sportif*, an excellent restaurant. There were a fair number of Europeans still in the town. Belgian female secretaries served at the consulate and at the USIS cultural center. The two American Army personnel assigned to the town—a lieutenant colonel and his translator/driver—both managed to find "friends." So did the consul's commo man.

With a more or less trained staff, USIS Bukavu accomplished purposeful work. My American associate, an officer with immaculate French, put out a daily news bulletin taken from Voice of America broadcasts. It was mimeographed for several hundred local subscribers and used daily by Radio Bukavu. He was also a member of the local Table Ronde, the Bukavu equivalent of Coq's Lions Club, where he made solid friendships.

And what a trio of African local employees! Paul Wemboyendja. Deogratias Mpunyu. Jean Rusenyagugu. What a set of sounds to roll your tongue around!

Jean Rusenyagugu was our janitor-factotum, had been when I was first there. He spoke to me in smiles, in chuckles and laughter. That was because French was our common language, and neither of us spoke it well.

Soon after I first arrived, he studied me with his broom. *"Vous êtes marié, Monsieur?"* he asked.

No, I said, I was not married.

Jean was stunned. He scrutinized me. How could I not be married? Was I not an adult? Was not marriage a symbol of adulthood? How could foreigners be so strange?

Months later, about to leave Bukavu, I bought as a souvenir a large cowhide drum, three feet tall and almost as wide. When Jean saw it, he smiled with delight. "A wedding drum!" he exulted. "You are going home to get married!" He must have thought that my parents had finally found me a bride. (The wedding drum stands today in my office.)

When I asked to take a photo of Jean, he cast his dust cloth aside and ran off. He reappeared with a book in his hand, a book he could not read. He posed for me in the sunny parking lot, stiff of stance, but grinning, nonetheless. He held the book before him, tenderly and proudly, and I took his picture.

Déogratias Mpunyu, librarian-driver, was a long sliver of a man, easily 6' 8". He was a Tutsi, a refugee from Rwanda, just across Lake Kivu where Tutsi rule, stretching back into unremembered time, had recently been overthrown.

Literate, educated, adept in French and even attempting English, Déo seemed an ideal librarian. But the passion of his life was to drive. He longed to escape the library, fold his long frame behind the steering wheel of the center's truck and drive it around town, honking and waving and shouting at friends. Young ladies with bundles on their heads would stop and turn their bodies to watch him pass.

Reports came that Déo brought little more than jubilation to his driving. He had no license—not too surprising in the strife-torn Congo—and he was vague about how he had learned to drive. I grew concerned that claims of damages might be brought against the center, for why were Americans in the Congo if they were not rich and ripe for suing? It became clear that I myself must be the licensing authority.

I proposed a test drive. Déo laughed gaily. Anything to get behind the wheel! But I detected some uncertainty, too. As we started out, I hoped very much that Déo really did know how to drive.

Perhaps his legs and arms were too long. Perhaps his head sat so high on his long Tutsi neck that his eyes had no proper field of vision. Perhaps I unnerved him. Whatever the cause, at the end of the first block, Déo drove into a traffic sign. It was wood; it splintered in half.

The Congo experience of that era offered a chain of expectations painfully blasted by events. Déo was a child of his time. He graciously accepted the consequences of his accident and contented himself in the library.

Paul Wemboyendja, projectionist, film truck operator, was tallish, stocky, charming. A man of broad acquaintanceship. A connoisseur *par excellence* of women. A suave wheeler-dealer. He had served as a delegate to the Congo's first constituent assembly. My USIS colleagues considered him a real find for the center. I had gotten to know him— we had done film shows and traveled together—during my first stint in Bukavu.

My first morning there—I was two weeks in Africa—Paul had entered my office with distressing news. His wife's mother had died. Could he have time off to attend her funeral in Usumbura, the nearby capital of Burundi?

Of course I was being tested. But I did not even know yet what I was supposed to accomplish as temporary center director. So why play martinet? I let Paul go. If he liked to travel, that was fine with me. If I had any goal in Bukavu, it was to see some country.

I never figured out exactly how many wives Paul had—serially or simultaneously—or how many mothers-in-law he could claim. There were certainly girlfriends *beaucoup*.

But Paul and I did see country. We showed films in the Bukavu communes of Bagira and Kadutu. We gave showings in Goma, Congo, and Gisenyi, Rwanda, twin towns across the border from one another at the north end of Lake Kivu. On that trip Paul and I returned to Bukavu via Kagera National Park in Rwanda. I waxed poetic about the sleekness and grace of gazelles. Paul said: *"Beaucoup steaks, Monsieur."*

I thought: "How aesthetically deprived this African."

And he must have thought: "How foolish this American."

I considered Paul almost as much a friend as a center staffer. He and

I sometimes had dinner together at the splendid Bodega.

A weekend before I left Bukavu when I was first there, he and I and the consulate's commo man zipped up to the Congo's Parc Albert. Although permission to go there was denied me, I was determined to encounter East African wildlife before heading to the Equateur. On our first game run we saw elephants, buffaloes and gazelles that took my breath away. However, at dusk we managed to get immovably stuck in mud near a hippo wallow. Rather than spend the night in our vehicle, we hot-footed it away from hippos to Vitshumbi, a fishing village on the shore of Lake Edouard.

Once there, Paul led us to the porch of the director's house where a group of people sat having *apéritifs*: a Belgian of middle age and a family of East Indians, his wife's people. The Belgian stood squinting at us as we came out of the darkness. The two groups stared at one another.

Then Paul laughed. "*Ah! C'est toi!*" he exclaimed. The Belgian studied him, then grinned and stuck out his hand. "*Tu habite ici, eh?*" Paul asked, using the familiar form. "You live here, do you?"

"*Qu'est ce que tu fais ici?*" the Belgian asked, responding in the familiar form. "What are you doing here?" He and Paul shook hands.

A man of wide acquaintanceship, indeed! Paul had ferried the Belgian across Lake Kivu when he needed to escape anti-Belgian operatives in Bukavu just after independence. The Belgian gladly lent us a truck. With it we extricated ourselves from the mud and I was spared the disgrace of being sent back to Washington, having lost a film truck in Parc Albert. What a friend Paul Wemboyendja was!

I served out my two-year Congo tour in Bukavu. I set up a schedule of rotating film shows in the environs of the town and even up to Goma. Tom Madison replaced me as Bukavu's BPAO. It was a good post for him and Sally: a small, but sophisticated town with a US consulate, a cool climate, a beautiful setting, and interesting European residents. Before I left, Tom told me he would have to curtail the film shows. Some things never change.

On my return to Washington I learned that I had been reassigned to Karachi, Pakistan. I liked USIS work. It gave me a feeling of involvement with my times and offered me contact with peoples of varied backgrounds and ideas. The Karachi post sounded interesting. However, Brussels, three posts in the Congo, then Pakistan. Did that look like a career path?

I was uncertain about what to do next. Would my being young and unmarried mean that post-shifting in Pakistan might send me to another Coquilhatville, a place there where more senior, married officers refused to serve? Although I enjoyed living overseas, loved basking in diverse cultures, did it make sense to do that unmarried? There was also my confusion about living two years in Africa, but feeling I understood almost nothing about the place, the upheavals, the Congo's still unsettled circumstances.

Returning to California on home leave, I found the affluence and convenience of American life disorienting. As a way of coming to terms with my experiences in the Congo, I did some writing about them. I saw that I needed more perspective. There was much I did not understand. So I resigned from USIS and enrolled in the UCLA master's program in African Studies.

While a graduate student, I met a young woman on the steps of the church I attended. The daughter of a Foreign Service couple, she had spent portions of her girlhood in India, Greece, and South Africa. She had just finished an advanced degree in Library Science. I told her she should join USIS. It offered fabulous overseas travel opportunities for trained librarians. She wondered why I should encourage her to join an outfit from which I had just resigned. Eighteen months later we were married.

For several years after leaving the Congo, I kept in touch with Thérèse and Jules André. They pulled out of Coquilhatville and lived for a time in Kinshasa, the former Léopoldville. But it's Donanne's recollection that when they sent the lovely Belgian lace tablecloth as a wedding gift, they had returned to Belgium and were living in Namur.

During graduate school I hung out at the UCLA Theater Arts Department. Two plays of mine were performed there. One of them was *A Marriage of Convenience* which I'd labored over while stationed in Coquilhatville. Once I received my degree in African Studies, I began to do journeyman television writing.